MW00803675

STANDARD CATALOG OF®

BROWNING

FIREARMS

©2008 Krause Publications Inc.,
a susidary of F+W Media Inc.

Published by

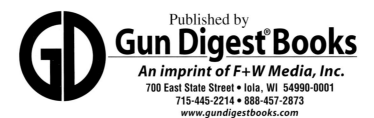

Gun Digest® Books

An imprint of F+W Media, Inc.
700 East State Street • Iola, WI 54990-0001
715-445-2214 • 888-457-2873
www.gundigestbooks.com

Our toll-free number to place an order or obtain
a free catalog is (800) 258-0929.

All rights reserved. No portion of this publication may be reproduced or
transmitted in any form or by any means, electronic or mechanical, including photocopy, recording, or any information storage and retrieval system,
without permission in writing from the publisher, except by a reviewer
who may quote brief passages in a critical article or review to be printed
in a magazine or newspaper, or electronically transmitted on radio, televi-
sion, or the Internet.

Library of Congress Control Number: 200897701

ISBN-13: 978-0-89689-731-1
ISBN-10: 0-89689-731-1

Designed by Elizabeth Krogwold
Edited by Dan Shideler

Printed in China

STANDARD CATALOG OF®

BROWNING
FIREARMS

BY JOSEPH M. CORNELL
CMA, ASA, ISA

Other Gun Digest & Krause Titles

STANDARD CATALOG OF COLT FIREARMS

STANDARD CATALOG OF WINCHESTER FIREARMS

STANDARD CATALOG OF REMINGTON FIREARMS

STANDARD CATALOG OF MILITARY FIREARMS

STANDARD CATALOG OF SMITH & WESSON

STANDARD CATALOG OF FIREARMS

STANDARD CATALOG OF LUGER

GUN DIGEST

GUNS ILLUSTRATED

THE COMPLETE GUN OWNER

FIREARMS, FAKES AND REPRODUCTIONS

ANTIQUE FIREARMS ASSEMBLY/DISASSEMBLY

GUN DIGEST HANDBOOK OF COLLECTIBLE AMERICAN GUNS

THE GUN DIGEST BOOK OF RUGER PISTOLS AND REVOLVERS

OLD GUN SIGHTS & RIFLE SCOPES IDENTIFICATION & PRICE GUIDE

FLAYDERMAN'S GUIDE TO ANTIQUE
AMERICAN FIREARMS AND THEIR VALUES

DEDICATION

*To my mother, Ava Vey Madden Cornell,
who dedicated her life, her will and her all to
my father and to her family; and to my father,
F. R. Cornell, who was a true man of honor.*

CONTENTS

ACKNOWLEDGEMENTS

The author is indebted to Browning North America and to Rock Island Auction of Moline, Illinois, for their cooperation in preparing this work. Any errors contained herein are mine, not theirs.

Browning® and all registered and trademarked names are property of their respective owners.

ABOUT THIS BOOK

John Moses Browning cast a huge shadow over the firearm's industry for well over as century, and in respect, still does. He is credited with having secured over 128 firearm patents, more than any other firearm designer. John Browning sold Winchester the rights to 44 guns, 34 of which were never produced. In addition to all these firearms, he produced guns for Colt, Stevens, Remington, and Fabrique Nationale of Belgium, among others, and many of his basic designs have been produced by innumerable manufacturers around the world.

He designed sporting weapons, self-defense weapons, target weapons, and military weapons. Many of his designs are among the most collected firearms today, and many, during their day, had profound effects on the world; Hermann Goering, head of Germany's *Luftwaffe* in World War II, said in a secret memo discovered after the war that if Germany had had the .50-caliber Browning machine gun, the Battle of Britain would have turned out differently. Browning was a very prolific, equal-opportunity weapons designer. Today, weapons he designed decades ago are still in use, and in demand, by all types of gun aficionados. The company that bears his name is known for selling some of the finest weapons being produced in the world today. Certain weapons bearing the Browning name, because of John Browning's legacy, or because of the quality inherently found in these guns, are very collectible and eagerly sought-after.

We are not writing this book about John Browning himself, but, rather about the company that bears his name. We shall also discuss Browning-designed weapons that bear the Fabrique Nationale (FN) name. We are including FN-manufactured weapons because many of these are considered to be weapons made for, and marketed by, Browning Arms Company, or are specifically collected by Browning collectors: the FN-made Auto-5, the Superposed shotguns, the .22 semi-automatic rifles, etc. Many of the weapons manufactured by FN and those manufactured by Browning Arms Company are considered by some collectors to have been made by the same company, and to a very large degree, they are correct. The business relationship between Browning Arms Company and FN, and their mutual fates, continues to be interwoven to this day, as many high-grade, custom-order weapons currently available through Browning Arms Company are manufactured in Belgian by Fabrique Nationale.

However, having said all that, we are not going to include in this book John Browning-designed weapons that bear the names, for example, of Winchester, Remington, Colt, Stevens, etc. Information for values on these weapons can be found in other fine Krause books including *Standard Catalog of® Firearms, Standard Catalog of® Winchester Firearms* (which was written by the author of this book), *Standard Catalog of® Colt Firearms, Standard Catalog of® Military Firearms, etc.*

There are specific differences, within certain models manufactured by Browning that collectors recognize and differentiate between, e.g., weapons made in Belgium vs. weapons made in Japan. Beginning in 1965, Browning Arms Company began negotiating with Miroku of Japan for the manufacture of certain Browning weapons to take place at the Miroku factories. For collectors, whether the weapons carrying the Browning name are made at Miroku factories or other Japanese factories doesn't seem to matter. These weapons, as a class, are called "Japanese Brownings." For collectors, however, there is a great deal of difference in value between Japanese-made Brownings and those Brownings manufactured at Fabrique Nationale. In the collector market of today, FN-manufactured Brownings are worth considerably more than Japanese-manufactured Brownings. This doesn't mean that Japanese-manufactured Brownings are of lesser quality than FN-manufactured Brownings, but for whatever reason, the market stigmatizes Japanese-manufactured guns and discriminates against them in terms of pricing. This all relates to their desirability and/or their collectibility. Consequently, you'll find, in this book, information about all weapons distributed by Browning Arms Company, irrespective of their place of manufacture.

Because of the high prices commanded by FN-manufactured Brownings and older John Browning-designed Winchesters, Browning has reintroduced many of these older guns for today's market. These guns are manufactured in Japan and are marketed toward consumers hungry for older, collectible Brownings or Winchesters. However, the market values for contemporary-manufactured weapons are much different from values for the older original Browning-designed weapons. Some of these, as examples, are the Winchester model 42,

the Winchester model 1886, the Winchester Model 12, etc. These guns were reintroduced for nostalgic purposes and to commemorate famous John Browning-designed weapons – and because Browning Arms recognizes that there is an evergreen market for such arms. For the most part, these later Japanese-manufactured weapons were manufactured in two grades, the high-grade model and the field grade model. Field grade models are very similar to the standard Winchester-issued model of the past, while the high-grade models are engraved and often contain gold figures. While this complicates things, we will deal with the value issues regarding these reintroduced models at the appropriate place in this book. Interestingly enough, some of these reintroduced models have become what I referred to as semi-collectible, which means that people buy them with no intention of shooting them, but rather as an investment based on anticipated increases in value. As a matter of fact, some of them – for example, some models of the recently-produced Model 1886 – are already worth more than they were when they were originally manufactured. This sort of appreciation has led to the accumulation of this model, and other reintroduced models, for the purposes of investment, or as semi-collectibles.

We hope you'll find the information we provide in this book to be interesting, thought-provoking, and profitable. As it used to be said, "There's gold in them there hills"; we can also say, "There's money in them there guns." Investment is always a question of information, and that is what we try to provide to our readers in this book.

INTRODUCTION

JOHN MOSES BROWNING
1855-1926

*T*his book continues to represent our continuing commitment to follow the tradition set by Krause Publications, as reflected in the *Standard Catalog of® Firearms* and the *Standard Catalog of® Winchester Firearms*, the latter of which was also written by this author. It is our intention and desire to produce the very best informational book available to help all interested in firearm research, pricing information, and identification. In our quest to be the very best book possible regarding Browning firearms information, we are going to do some things that are entirely unique to this volume. For example, we are going to provide a "Collectibility Factor," which will help our readers to get a unique fix on the author's opinion as to which Brownings are highly collectible. Hopefully, this will help our readers gain a unique perspective regarding the collectibility of certain Browning firearms and the possibility for an upward movement of the cost of a particular model of Browning firearm.

This book is not about John Moses Browning, but about his guns and the company that bears his name. In this book, we will provide specific as well as general information about John Browning and Browning firearms. We recognize that information is power, and it is our never-ending desire and goal to supply our readers with as much quality, accurate information – and therefore power – as is reasonably possible. We are unique in that we provide the maximum number of pictures of Browning firearms, which helps our readership identify, more quickly and more accurately than any other publication, the firearm they are researching. This is a reflection of our desire to be indispensable and the very best in-

Photo Courtesy Browning.

formational publication on Browning firearms. We do this because we understand that while a picture may not be worth 1000 words, pictures can and do provide information to our readership that would otherwise not be obtainable in a book. Pictures provide valuable information that the written word is ill-suited to accomplish.

We wish this book to be recognized by our readership as an excellent investment, as it provides real knowledge and therefore real power – power that has real practical value as our readers pursue their interest in Browning firearms and their involvement in the firearm marketplace. In short, we endeavor to be the best source of pricing information, identification of firearms, and research available today. We recognize the size of our daunting task, and we recognize that we are undertaking a huge assignment, and while we recognize that perfection is impossible, it is our intention to do our very best.

While our readership expects up-to-date and the relevant pricing information, we visualize ourselves as also being able to provide our readers with valuable information relative to identifying various Browning firearms and their variations. We wish to become the "go-to book" when it comes to supplying information about Browning firearms. Browning has made many models, and while manufacturing these models, the Company has made many changes to the various models during the time they were being manufactured. These variations provided much of the basis for collector interest in Browning firearms. Certainly, one of our main objectives is to help collectors identify these variations as they exist within the various models, and in addition, we strive to deal with these variations in a way that will provide the collector with the maximum amount of information as to how to identify these dissimilarities within each model, and how these variations cause dramatic differences in prices. It is our goal to give our readership and advantage in the highly sophisticated and competitive atmosphere that surrounds the collecting of Browning firearms.

It's important for us to take a moment and discuss a few of the factors that influence cost/value:

Condition: For many models of Browning firearms, condition is everything and is often times more important than any other single factor.

Rarity: Rarity often has huge effects on value -- but also, in some cases, rarity can have a little overall effect on price. The reason for this is that, all condition factors being equal, a rare, one-of-a-kind Browning currently-manufactured shotgun will not be, relatively speaking, as valuable or as desirable as a rare discontinued early model Browning Superposed shotgun.

Collector Interest: Some models of Browning firearms have relatively low collector interest, while other models have very high collector interest. The more collector interest a firearm has, the more desirable that firearm is in the marketplace. There are many reasons for variations in the desirability of different models of Browning firearms, e.g., history, mystique, interesting variations within the model, the variety, period of manufacture, cinematic exposure, obscurity, celebrity association, "sex appeal," reputation in the firearms industry and among other firearm collectors, etc.

Availability: Some models and their variations, while manufactured in large numbers, appear, for one reason or another, to lack availability in the marketplace or in certain market places. (For instance, because there is an overall lack of bird hunting in Alaska, there is a lack of availability for certain Browning shotguns there.) In order to have mass collector appeal, large numbers of a particular model or variation must be available in the marketplace so that many people can become interested in it.

Factory or Aftermarket Enhancements: Other than condition, nothing causes more interest in the marketplace and in the Browning firearm collector's circle than factory special-order enhancements. Special factory enhancements, such as unique engraving by a famous artist, can also have a dramatic effect on the value of a particular firearm. This includes all factory work done by Browning, and to a lesser degree certain types of work done by recognized artisans whose work is recognized as being the very best.

Provenance: Ownership by famous individuals, or in association with a historical event, that can be proven to the market's satisfaction can vastly increase the value of any firearm.

It's very important for the readers of this book to understand that there is a huge difference between price and value. This book is a price guide and provides very little information pertaining to "value." This book reflects prices realized for firearms in given conditions. It does not offer appraisal information, nor should it be considered a substitute for a professionally prepared appraisal. Legally and professionally speaking, value is quite different from price. An appraiser finds for as many as 13 separate values, depending upon the situation and relevant circumstances. As an example, replacement value is used for many insurance matters. Fair Market Value is used in situations such as divorces, the IRS, and/or were courts are involved. Fair Market Value is a hypothetical value that does not exist in the real world, but has a definition that was developed by the IRS for its purposes. This value, and its definition, has been adopted by almost all courts and legal proceedings, and because it is not found in the real world, there is much debate about not only its use but also its determination. As you can see, this can all become quite complicated. To further exacerbate the problem, none of the values, described above, have anything to say about what an item is actually worth in the relevant marketplace, or about how an item should be priced in the marketplace, or about what collectors should expect to pay for an item in the relevant marketplace used by the collector.

In addition, within various market places there are various levels, e.g., wholesale, retail, and several in between. All of these various market levels have different price levels at which Browning firearms change hands. For our purposes, none of these are relevant except retail. All pricing done in this book is based upon the author's opinion as to what a particular firearm might be expected to be priced, at retail, in the relevant market.

A certified, accredited appraiser, with appropriate professional designations as granted by the three different national and international appraisal organizations that grant such designations, is expected to provide the apposite value – in other words, as suitable or relevant value – of the item being appraised. This is not a simple thing to do, and the process is much more objective than the average user of appraisal reports might think. Pricing is much more subjective. Because the market for firearms is very fluid, pricing information supplied in any price guide can be somewhat obsolete by the date of publication. We are what we say we are: we are a price guide, and by that we mean that it is our intention to provide our opinion as to pricing trends within the firearm marketplace. We are in the firearm's market on an almost every day basis, and we will do our very best to offer to you, our readers, our very best thoughts and opinions as to the proper pricing strategies. Our pricing recommendations come from a variety of sources: gun shows, retail gun stores, individual collectors, auction houses, interviews with important dealers, and personal research/participation in the firearm's marketplace. It is our intention to keep this book is simple as possible and to cause as little confusion as possible, and to help our readers sort out pricing dilemmas as they appear within the Browning firearms market.

Manufacturers often offer pricing recommendations in terms of MSRP, but as we all know, these are only recommendations and dealers are often willing to deviate from the manufacturer's recommended price depending on what they think the local market will sustain. Some gun dealers ask (and get) even more than MSRP on extremely desirable models (Sturm-Ruger's Gold Label side-by-side shotgun, for example); while on other, less desirable models, they are willing to negotiate substantially below MSRP. It's all about developing a feel for the marketplace and developing a strategy for balancing the maximization of profits while taking into account the need for cash flow and inventory turnaround.

The firearms marketplace has several different levels. In this book, we will try to provide our opinion as to what price a willing buyer and a willing seller would agree upon to transact and consummate a sale between the parties. (In determining certain types of values, especially in cases dealing with the IRS, auction values are not considered highly reliable and are not highly regarded.) Because of this, in our pursuit to establish and provide the best possible pricing information, we use auction results very sparingly, and only then with the application of our experience, training, education, collaboration with others, and market knowledge.

We hope that you, our readers, will find value in our pursuit of excellence in providing you with the very best possible information. We suggest that you check out other Krause publications, as they are almost countless, in your pursuit of valuable information regarding all kinds of different collectibles.

We hope to see you in the marketplace. We are all gun lovers, and I appreciate input from everyone. If you would like to contact me you may call me at 303-455-1717, or if you would like to read more about me, as an appraiser, please go to www.weappraiseguns.com.

It is our goal to give our readership an advantage in the highly sophisticated and competitive atmosphere that surrounds the collecting of Browning firearms.

COLLECTING
BROWNING FIREARMS

This is where it all began. Ogden, Utah, 1880. Courtesy Browning.

TIMELINE OF JOHN M. BROWNING AND BROWNING ARMS COMPANY

(Information Courtesy of Browning)

JAN. 23, 1855

Birth of John Moses Browning in Ogden, Utah.

OCT. 1869

John assembles a slide rifle out of spare parts.

SPRING, 1878

John Browning begins work on his first single shot rifle.

APRIL 10, 1879

John Moses Browning marries Rachel Teresa Child.

MAY 12, 1879

The application for patent on the single shot rifle is filed.

OCT. 7, 1879

U.S. Patent No. 220,271 is granted to the single shot rifle.

1880

With the aid of his brothers, John Browning establishes his arms factory in Ogden.

John Browning's personal workbench in Ogden. Courtesy Browning.

MAR. 20, 1882

Patent application is filed on bolt-action repeating rifle with a tubular magazine.

JULY 25, 1882

U.S. Patent No. 261,667 is granted to the bolt action repeater.

SEPT. 13, 1882

Patent filed on lever action, exposed hammer, tubular magazine rifle.

SPRING, 1883

Mr. T. G. Bennett, Vice-President and General Manager of Winchester Repeating Arms Company, comes to Ogden, Utah Territory, and forms an alli-

ance that is to last nineteen years and is to change the course of firearms development. As part of the transaction, the Single Shot is sold to Winchester, and Mr. Bennett is assured of first rights on a new repeater. The Single Shot becomes the Winchester Model 1885.

MAY 26, 1884

Patent filed on lever action repeating rifle that employs sliding vertical locks.

OCTOBER, 1884

Patent No. 306,577 is granted on the new repeater and John, together with his brother Matt, travel to New Haven, Connecticut, to deliver to T. G. Bennett what is to become the famous Winchester Model 1886.

FEB. 16, 1886

Patent No. 336,287 is granted on a lever action repeating shotgun. Known as the Winchester Model 1887, it is the first successful repeating shotgun.

MAR. 28, 1887

John leaves for Georgia to spend two years as a Mormon missionary.

DEC. 13, 1887

Patent is filed on a 22 caliber pump action repeating rifle. It has been called "the most popular 22 caliber pump action rifle ever made." Patent No. 385,238 was granted on June 26, 1888. First marketed as the Winchester Model 1890.

FALL, 1889

Begins development of the first models that were designed to employ the expanding gases behind the bullet to operate the action.

JAN. 6, 1890

John files his first patent dealing with gas operation.

JUNE 30, 1890

Patent application is filed on a pump action repeating shotgun later marketed as the Winchester Model 1893. A later, improved take-down version was known as the Winchester Model 1897.

AUG. 3, 1891

Patents filed on two separate automatic gas operated guns.

NOV. 7, 1892

Files first patents on the Colt Model 1895 Automatic Machine Gun. Earned the name "Browning Peacemaker" during the Spanish-American War. Also known as the "Potato Digger."

JAN. 19, 1894

Files patent on what would become the Winchester Model 1894, the first repeating action sporting rifle to handle smokeless powder cartridges. This rifle is ascribed by many to be the most popular high powered rifle ever built.

A bearded John Browning (second from left) compares shooting scores with his Ogden buddies. Courtesy Browning.

NOV. 19, 1894

Patent is filed on a lever action repeating rifle with a non-detachable box magazine designed for jacketed sharp-nosed bullets. Marketed as the Winchester Model 1895.

SEPT. 14, 1895

Files patent application on first semi-automatic pistol.

OCT. 31, 1896

Three basic pistol patents are filed that concern blowback action, a locked recoil system with a turning lock, and a locked recoil system with a pivoting lock.

JULY 17, 1897

A contract between Browning and Fabrique Nationale is signed which authorizes the Belgium firm to manufacture a blowback operated, 32-caliber semi-automatic pistol for all markets outside the United States. Production commences in 1899.

FEB. 17, 1899

Application for patent is filed on a single shot 22-caliber plinking rifle known as the Winchester Model 1900.

FEB., 1900

Colt places a Browning designed 38-caliber recoil operated semi-automatic pistol on the market. It was the first semi-automatic pistol in the United States.

FEB. 8, 1900

The first of four patents is filed on the revolutionary autoloading shotgun. It would be manufactured by Fabrique Nationale in 1903 and by Remington Arms Company in 1905.

OCT. 6, 1900

The first successful autoloading high-power rifle receives Patent No. 659,786. U.S. manufacturing and sales rights are granted to Remington Arms Company, and the rifle first appears in 1906 as the Model 8.

JULY 16, 1901

Browning submits a blowback operated 32-caliber semi-automatic pistol to Colt, who immediately accepts it. The marketing agreement stipulates that the pistol will be priced low enough to compete with the revolvers of the period.

JAN., 1902

In a disagreement about the public acceptability of the autoloading shotgun, John Browning severs his nineteen-year relationship with T.G. Bennett of Winchester.

JAN. 8, 1902

An appointment is made to show the new shotgun to Mr. Marcellus Hartley of Remington. This meeting is cancelled due to Mr. Hartley's untimely death that afternoon.

FEB., 1902

With his autoloading shotgun securely tucked under his arm, John Browning embarks on his first ocean voyage. He offers the new shotgun to Fabrique Nationale.

MAR. 24, 1902

A contract is signed granting FN exclusive world rights to manufacture and sell the autoloading shotgun.

JULY 10, 1903

Patent application is filed on a pump action shotgun that would become the Stevens Model 520.

SUMMER, 1903

At the request of FN, Browning develops a 9mm military semi-automatic pistol.

1904

In the face of restrictive tariffs, FN agrees to cede to Remington the rights to manufacture and sell the autoloading shotgun in the United States. It appears as the Remington Model 11.

JUNE 21,1909

The application for a patent on a 25-caliber semi-automatic pistol was filed. It is manufactured and sold by both FN and Colt. It is part of the Browning Arms Company line from 1955 to 1969.

FEB. 17, 1910

Patents were filed on a 45-caliber semi-automatic pistol. It serves as the official United States military sidearm for almost 75 years.

NOV. 26, 1913

Files patent on a pump shotgun that would be marketed as the Remington Model 17. It is John M. Browning's last repeater-type shotgun.

JAN. 6, 1914

Patents are granted and production begins on a semi-automatic 22-caliber rifle. Reming-

ton also produces this rifle as the Model 24.

FEB. 27, 1917

First public demonstration of the Browning 30-caliber Heavy Machine Gun at Congress Heights, Washington, D.C.

JULY, 1917

Begins work on the 50-caliber Water Cooled Machine Gun. Completed too late for World War I, this weapon plays a prominent role in World War II and Korea.

AUG. 1, 1917

Application for patent filed on the Browning Automatic Rifle. The B.A.R. first saw combat in 1918.

JULY 26, 1919

Patent application filed on a 22 pump action rifle that would be produced exclusively by Fabrique Nationale.

EARLY 1921

John M. Browning begins work on his first 37mm Aircraft Cannon.

OCT. 15, 1923

The first of two patents are filed on the Superposed Over/ Under shotgun.

JUNE 28, 1923

Patent application was filed on a 9mm short-recoil, locked-breech, exposed-hammer semi-automatic pistol. This was John M. Browning's last pistol development.

John Browning and one of his water-cololed machineguns. Courtesy Browning.

NOV. 26, 1926

John Moses Browning dies of heart failure at liege, Belgium.

SEPT., 1927

J.M. & M.S. Browning Company is incorporated in Utah with the Browning Arms Company as a subsidiary.

1928

The Superposed shotgun is introduced into the Browning Arms Company line.

1930

St. Louis distribution center and sales organization is established. Ogden remains the headquarters, directing all activities.

1936

Auto-5 "Sweet Sixteen" is introduced.

1940-42

After the German occupation puts a stop to Belgian production, Remington makes an American-made Auto-5 for Browning. This is their Model 11, but included the magazine cut-off, which was not a part of the Model 11. U.S. entry into the war ended this production.

1945-49

Remington resumes making the American-made Auto-5 for Browning until discontinuing production of the Model 11 to introduce their new 11-49 autoloader.

1946

FN resumes Auto-5 production.

JUNE, 1948

Light 12 Auto-5 is introduced; 12 gauge Superposed is re-introduced to the American market.

1949

New 20 gauge Superposed introduced.

1951

J.M. & M.S. Browning Company liquidated, and Browning Arms Company becomes an importer with wholesale functions.

1954

25-caliber. 380 caliber and 9mm pistols introduced into line.

1955

Double Automatic 12 gauge shotgun introduced.

JAN. 1, 1955

A newly created Browning Industries assumes the import functions previously held by J.M. & M.S. Browning Company. Browning Arms Company becomes the parent company.

1956

22-caliber semi-automatic rifle introduced

1958

Browning Arms of Canada created, 70% Browning owned, 30% FN owned. Also a 20 gauge model of the Auto-5 added to the line. 3" Auto-5 Magnum 12 introduced.

1960

FN Mauser Bolt Action rifle added to the line. Trombone 22 introduced to Canada.

1962-63

Acquires Silaflex and Gordon Plastics, makers of bows, rods and vaulting poles.

1962

22-caliber pistols added: Challenger, Nomad and Medalist. Archery equipment, fishing rods, ski poles and vaulting poles are added to the catalog.

1964

Browning Corporate Headquarters relocates to Route 1, Morgan, Utah.

1965

T-Bolt 22 rifle introduced. A line of leather goods including belts, holsters and flexible gun cases also becomes available.

1965

Browning begins negotiations with Miroku Firearms in Japan. Enters the sailboat business with the acquisition of Newport Boats of California and Virginia. Assets liquidated in 1976.

1966

Archery accessories added to the line.

1967

BAR semi-automatic sporting high powered rifle is introduced. 3" Auto-5 Mag. 20 gauge introduced.

1968

St. Louis sales operation relocated to Morgan, Utah. Warehouse/parts and service moved to Arnold, Missouri. Barth Leather Company and Caldwell Lace Company (Auburn, Kentucky) acquired. Hunting clothing introduced. Introduced BT-99 single barrel trap shotgun.

1969

Acquired Harwill, Inc., manufacturers of Fiberglass outboard and inboard motorboats as well as small aluminum boats and canoes. Liquidated in 1974. BL-22 Lever Action 22 rifle and knives added to the line.

1970

Medalist 22 target pistol added.

1971

New 380 pistol and BLR Lever Action high-power rifle added to the line.

1972

B-SS 12 gauge side-by-side shotgun added.

1973

New guns introduced: 12 gauge Citori over/under shotgun, 12 gauge Liege over/under shotgun, B-SS in 20 gauge, B-78 single shot rifle in round or octagon barrel options.

1974

Browning line was enlarged with the B-2000 automatic shot-

gun in 12 gauge, the Citori 20 gauge and the Citori Trap & Skeet models.

1975

Citori 20 gauge Skeet introduced. B-2000 in 20 gauge added to the line.

1976

Further additions: Challenger II 22 pistol, BT-99 Competition, B-78 in 45-70 and 7mm, and BLR 358, Citori became available with extra barrels, Auto-S 16 gauge discontinued, Auto-5 production went to Japan latter part of 1976.

1977

Superposed discontinued (Grade I, Diana, Midas), Presentation Superposed introduced. BAR 22 and BPR 22 introduced, BPS pump shotgun introduced (12 gauge only), Jonathan Browning Mountain Rifle introduced, BBR bolt action rifle introduced, B-2000 Trap & Skeet introduced with high post rib, BDA pistol introduced in 45, 9mm and 38 Super. Also, 90% of Browning Arms Company outstanding stock was purchased by FN and Miroku.

1978

Browning enters the company's Centennial year. To commemorate this event, five limited Centennial editions were prepared. The included a Superposed Continental over/under rifle combination, a Centennial edition of the Jonathan Brown-

ing Mountain Rifle, a replica of the Winchester Model 1892 called the Centennial Browning 92, a chromed version of the 9mm Hi-Power, and a special set of folding knives.

1979

B-92 in 44 Magnum introduced.

1980

Grade II BAR 22 introduced, 9mm nickel and Waterfowl Superposed, (Mallard Issue) introduced. Citori Sideplate and the B-80 gas operated shotgun introduced.

1981

Model 81 BLR lever rifle and Citori all gauge skeet set offered.

1982

Waterfowl Superposed (Pintail issue), BBR Lightning Bolt, 9mm silver/chrome pistol and Ltd. BAR (Big Game) introduced. Model '81 BLR changed (it features new flush magazine, flat sides), new B-80 Superlight, B-92 in 357 Magnum and Challenger III pistol added.

1983

Standard Invector chokes offered. Black Duck Waterfowl Superposed, Citori Grade VI and Grade I introduced. Sidelock (B-SS) introduced. Challenger III Sporter with 6-3¾" barrel added to the line.

1984

Gold Classic A-5 introduced. Model 1895 in 30-06 caliber,

Citori Upland Special and Sidelock 20 gauge introduced. BPS Upland Special offered.

1985

A-Bolt centerfire introduced. Model 1885, Gold Classic 9mm, Pigeon, Pointer, Diana, Midas Superposed and the Grade III Citori was introduced. Buck Mark pistol, made in USA offered. New finishes offered in the 9mm pistols.

1986

Model 1886, Ltd. Edition, A-Bolt 22, Gold Classic over/under and BPS pump Youth & Ladies offered.

1987

Sweet Sixteen Auto-5 and Citori 16 gauge introduced. Model 71 offered in 348 Win. A-500 shotgun introduced and 3 barrel Skeet Citori set. BPS Stalker and Stainless Stalker A-Bolt introduced. A-Bolt Camo Stalker offered. Grade VI Semi-Auto 22. Buck Mark Plus, Silhouette and Varmint models added.

1988

Custom Gun Shop reinstated in Belgium featuring the B-125 and B-25 Superposed. B-80 "Plus" offered for a short time. Model 12 20 gauge in Grade I and High Grade offered. A-Bolt Composite Stalker, A-Bolt 22 Gold Medallion, Micro-Medallion and Composite Stalker introduced. Lightning model Citori, and new calibers in 280

and 338 BAR included. Clothing Division created.

1989

Citori Sporting Clays introduced, fixed chokes, 2 3/4" only. BT-99 Plus and Recoilless introduced, but the latter gun not released. 3 1/2" Magnum BPS introduced. A-Bolt 284 caliber introduced. Model 65 introduced in 218 Bee, limited edition. A-Bolt 22 Mag. Offered. Ambidextrous safety appears on all 9mm models.

1990

Model 12 in 28 gauge, and the A500-G gas operated shotgun available. Gran Lightning Citori and BT-99 Plus introduced with back-bored barrels. 10 gauge and 3 1/2" 12 gauge BPS added. The Model 53 in 32-20 caliber rifle, limited edition offered. Giat Industries, owner of Browning USA, acquires U.S. Repeating Arms Co., licensee for Winchester rifles and shotguns.

1991

BPS shotgun with new engraving. New models include Youth/Ladies, Upland Special, Buck Special, Stalker and 20 gauge Hunting. BDM (Double Mode) pistol and 9mm Hi-Power Practical introduced. New Buck Mark pistols include Standard Nickel, 5.5 Gold, 5.5 Field and Unlimited Match. Browning Fishing division licensed to Zebco of Tulsa, OK.

1992

Citori Plus Combo, Auto-5 12 gauge Stalker, Model 42 410 bore Grade I, BPS Game gun, Model 1886 Carbine Grade V, Model 1886 Carbine Grade I, 9mm Hi-Power Silver/Chrome, Buck Mark Micro Standard Nickel, Buck Mark Micro Plus and Buck Mark Micro Standard added to the line.

1993

Citori G.T.I. 325 and Citori Plus Pigeon Grade, BT-99 Plus, Signature BT-99, Signature BT-99 Plus and BT-99 Stainless, BSA 10 gauge, Gold Autoloading shotgun offered. The Recoilless Trap again advanced. BSA 10 gauge Stalker, BPS 10 gauge Waterfowl model, BAR Mark II Safari with open sights, BAR Mark II no sights and A-Bolt Euro bolt models introduced.

1994

BOSS (Ballistic Optimizing Shooting System) introduced. A-Bolt II Hunter, A-Bolt II Medallion and Euro Bolt, A-Bolt II Stainless Stalker, Composite Stalker and Varmint added. Citori Golden Clays Target, Golden Clays G.T.I., Pigeon Grade Special Sporting, Golden Clays and Citori Skeet. BPS 20 gauge. Gold Semi-Auto shotgun introduced in 12 and 20 gauge. 40 S&W caliber Hi-Power offered.

1995

Citori 425 Sporting Clays, WSSF Sporting Clays Ultra

Sporter, Special Trap and Special Skeet introduced. BT-99 Max, BT-100 and BT-100 Thumbhole stock offered. A-Bolt shotgun Stalker with rifled choked tube and A-Bolt shotgun Hunter with rifled barrel introduced. Fire protection offered on safes. Giat board nominates Jacques Loppion as Giat Industries chairman and CEO.

1996

New introductions include A-Bolt II Stalker in Varmint and Eclipse models, BLR Lightning with fold-down hammer, M-1885 BPCR in 45-70 and 40-65 calibers, Citori 802ES Light Sporting Clays, Gold 12 gauge, Gold Sporting Clays, Buck Mark Plus Nickel, Micro Plus Nickel, Bullseye with rosewood grips, Bullseye with rubber grips.

1997

BPR (Browning Pump Rifle) in long and short action. Seven calibers in long action 270, 30-06, 7mm Rem. Mag., 300 Win. Mag. Short action in 243 and 308. A-Bolt II M-1000 Eclipse in 300 Win. Mag., M-1885 Traditional Hunter in 30-30, 38-55 and 45-70 calibers and BAR Mk II Lightweight rifle offered. BDM offered in Silver/Chrome and Practical, 9mm BPM-D (Browning Pistol Mode Decocker) double action pistol with all steel slide and frame, 9mm BRM-DAO (Browning Revolver Mode Double Action Only).

1998

Gold 3 1/2" Hunter, Gold 3 1/2" Stalker, BPS Cantilever game guns, Citori White Lightning, Citori Sporting Hunter offered. M-1885 Low-Wall Traditional Hunter with 24" half round, half octagon barrel in 22 Hornet, 223 Rem. and 243 calibers, M-1885 BPCR Creedmoor in 45-90 caliber, has windage front sight and Vernier rear sight. The famous Auto-5 shotgun, invented in 1903, and one of John M. Browning's greatest inventions lives out its life. After much concern and thought, it is discontinued from the line.

1999

Gold shotgun offered in Waterfowl Mossy Oak Shadow Grass, Turkey/Waterfowl in Mossy Oak Break-Up, Deer in Mossy Oak Break-Up, Classic Stalker, Turkey/Waterfowl Stalker, Deer Stalker, Classic Hunter, Turkey/Waterfowl Hunter, Classic High Grade, Classic 20 gauge, Golden Clays and Ladies/Youth Sporting Clays. BPS 12 gauge Waterfowl in Mossy Oak Shadow Grass. Citori shotgun offered in Superlight Feather, Lightning Feather, Satin Hunter and XT models. BT-100 Satin. BAR Classic Mark II Safari. The Acera straight pull rifle from FN debuts. A-Bolt II offered in Classic series, Micro Hunter, and White Gold Medallion. Buck Mark pistol offered in two new models, Challenge and Micro Challenge.

2000

Auto-5 Final Tribute offered. Gold Waterfowl Mossy Oak Break-Up, BPS 10 gauge Turkey/Waterfowl, BPS 12 gauge Waterfowl Mossy Oak Break-Up introduced. Citori 20 gauge Lightning Feather, Citori Lightning Feather Combo, Citori White Lightning Special, and Citori Privilege available. Citori B.G. VI Lightning, Citori B.G. III Lightning, Citori Ultra XS Skeet, Citori Feather XS in 12, 20, 28 and .410 bore introduced. Mr. Don Gobel, president of Browning since 1980 retires. Provided a total of 34 years in the Hunting and Shooting industry. Mr. Charles Guevremont, formerly with Browning Canada takes the reins as the new president.

2001

Browning licenses its Archery production to PSE, AZ. Archery production ceases after 38 years. Browning licenses its footwear division to H.H. Brown Shoe Co. (Browning introduced hunting boots in 1968.) In partnership with Winchester Ammunition, Browning develops the new 300 Winchester Short Magnum (WSM) cartridge. It was voted "Ammunition of the Year" by the 2001 Shooting Industry Academy of Excellence. The Gold Fusion Autoloader and four new models of the Gold shotgun, a new BPS Micro 20 ga., special National

Wild Turkey Federation guns are introduced. The BT-99 Trap gun returns and new Citori's offered in a 20 ga. XS skeet and 20 ga. Privilege.

2002

The Browning/Winchester 300 WSM cartridge becomes a family with the addition of the new 270 WSM and 7mm WSM. The 270 WSM was awarded "Ammunition of the Year" by the Shooting Industry Academy of Excellence. These calibers offered in the A-Bolt and BAR rifles. Citori 525, with the most features ever, introduced in many styles/models. Citori XS Pro-Comp, Esprit, and Gold Classic high grade offered. Dura-Touch stock finish and new Buck Mark Classic target rifle with heavy barrel offered. A new conservation series of safes offered. A smaller compact model safe introduced. Browning prepares to celebrate its 125th year anniversary in 2003.

2003

Browning celebrates 125 years of innovation in firearms and outdoor sporting products. Many products are introduced to commemorate the event. Browning and Winchester take the short magnum concept to the next level with the introduction of the 223 and 243 Super Short Magnums. This not only includes these new calibers, but a new class of bolt-action rifle - the super-short action. Super-short

action A-Bolts are chambered for 223 WSSM and 243 WSSM. An ABolt in White Gold for the RMEF is offered in 7mm Rem. Mag. only. Many BAR rifles are offered in the new WSM calibers. The BLR comes out in a new straightgrip style stock. A Classic Carbon Fiber Buck Mark 22 rifle is introduced, and the Citori 525 is offered in 28 gauge and .410 Bore.

A Golden Clays BT-99 with adjustable comb makes its debut, and the NWTF Gold Autoloader turkey shotgun is offered.

2004

The Cynergy over/under shotgun, promising a new revision in shotgunning history is introduced. The Citori Lightning, Gran Lightning and the White Lightning with new engraving are offered. The Citori XS Special and a BT -99 Micro are new. The Gold Evolve autoloading shotgun with new, innovative ergonomic styling is introduced. The 25 WSSM short-action caliber, (.290" bullet diameter), perhaps the ultimate whitetail deer cartridge is new for 2004. Handsome European styling, including new alloy receivers, hammer-forged barrels, shims to adjust the stock and lightweight profiles characterized the new BAR ShortTrac and LongTrac rifles. An A-bolt rifle with a titanium receiver, called the Mountain Ti, is introduced. It weighs only 5lbs. 80z. The A-Bolt Eclipse

is now available in the popular WSM calibers, no BOSS. In the BL-22 rifle lineup, a new Classic Series Grade II with a 24" octagon barrel is available. Decals for vehicles are new.

2005

Browning celebrates John Browning's 150th birthday. Citori's new models for 2007 include the 525 Feather, 525 Field Grade III, GTS High Grade and Grade I, Citori XS Special with low and high post rib and Grand Prix Sporter. The Silver and Gold Autoloading shotguns introduce a new Mossy Oak@ Duck Blind"IM camo. Extra barrels for the Silver shotgun are available. The BPS Pump shotgun comes out in Mossy Oak@ Duck Blind"IM and the BPS Rifled Deer in Mossy Oak New Break-Up is offered. A new BPS Trap and Micro Trap gun is announced. The BAR ShortTrac and LongTrac are offered in Mossy Oak New Break-Up and both models are available in left-hand with the standard satin finished stock and blued receiver and barrel. A new A-Bolt Special Hunter and RMEF A-Bolt White Gold are new for 2007. The T -Bolt, introduced last year is offered in a new Target/Varmint model with a heavy target barrel and Monte Carlo stock. Models of Buck Mark pistols have new Ultragrip DX ambidextrous wood, laminate and composite grips with ergonomic finger grooves.

2006

The Cynergy, with its ingenious design inside and out, now includes the traditionally stocked Classic Series.The Gold Superlights utilize the new Active Valve System for reliability with any factory load. Totally new for 2006 is the gas-operated Silver shotgun; a perfect match between value and performance, representing ruggedness, fast handling, balanced to perfection. A revolutionary old-timer returns: The Browning T-Bolt is back, with an innovative Double Helix rotary magazine. Also, the Buck Mark pistol adds a new Lite model, saving weight with alloy-sleeved barrels and the soft UltraGrip RX adds shooting comfort. The new ShortTrac and LongTrac Stalker have a non-glare composite finish, alloy receivers and gripping panels on the rugged composite stock. Nine calibers are offered. New A-Bolt rifles include the NRA Wildlife Conservation Collection, a new M-1000 Eclipse with a matte-blued or stainless steel finish. A new BL-22 NRA Grade I and Buck Mark FLD are added.

2007

The timeless BLR lever action centerfire rifle is offered in two takedown models, one with a pistol grip and one with a scout scope mount in all WSM calibers. Cynergy over and under shotgun introduces new models; the Feather, Feather Composite, Euro Sporting/Adjustable, Euro Sporting Composite, Classic Field Grade II, Grade VI, Classic Field, Classic Sporting and Classic Trap. Citori's new models for 2007 include the 525 Feather, 525 Field Grade III, GTS High Grade and Grade I, Citori XS Special with low and high post rib and Grand Prix Sporter. The Silver and Gold Autoloading shotguns introduce a new Mossy Oak® Duck Blind™ camo. Extra barrels for the Silver shotgun are available. The BPS Pump shotgun comes out in Mossy Oak® Duck Blind™ and the BPS Rifled Deer in Mossy Oak New Break-Up is offered. A new BPS Trap and Micro Trap gun is announced. The BAR ShortTrac and Long-Trac are offered in Mossy Oak New Break-Up and both models are available in left-hand with the standard satin finished stock and blued receiver and barrel. A new A-Bolt Special Hunter and RMEF A-Bolt White Gold are new for 2007. The T-Bolt, introduced last year is offered in a new Target/Varmint model with a heavy target barrel and Monte Carlo stock. Models of Buck Mark pistols have new Ultragrip DX ambidextrous wood, laminate and composite grips with ergonomic finger grooves.

For more information on Browning's mosost recent developments, visit www.browning.com

WHEN IS AN APPRAISAL NOT AN APPRAISAL?

The values presented in this book are a result of my experience as a professional firearms appraiser. As such, I live in the world of used and collectible firearms, especially Brownings, and make my living by appraising guns and gun collections.

As an accredited, certified, and designated personal property appraiser I am often asked by individuals, attorneys, judges, courts, insurance companies, the IRS, museums, and other users of appraisal reports, "What constitutes a credible appraisal report?" I feel it is important for me to help my readership and fellow gun collectors in as many areas as possible. For that reason, I am taking this opportunity to talk about appraisals, because at some point, either during their life, or after they pass away and leave an estate, most firearm collectors will need, for a variety of reasons, a written appraisal report concerning their firearms. To trust an appraisal to an unqualified individual can cause many problems – and it can cost you a lot of money, too.

What constitutes a credible appraisal report? Good question. I am offering the following information mostly because I am asked this question continually by owners of firearms and firearm collections who are looking for an appraisal report that is credible and will stand up to scrutiny by courts, judges, lawyers, insurance companies, and museums – all of whom are users of appraisal reports.

I can tell you one thing for sure: judges in particular do not take kindly to people who are acting in a certain capacity without the prerequisite training, experience, and education. It has been held that a person who holds himself out as an attorney, or a doctor, but who lacks the prerequisite training and education to actually be an attorney or a doctor, is committing fraud. And so it is with individuals who call themselves appraisers but lack the prerequisite education and training to actually be an appraiser. The savings and loan debacle of a few years ago and our current nationwide fiscal crisis in the homebuilding industry can be traced to faulty appraisals, at least to some degree.

One of the things that I encounter most often in my practice as an appraiser are documents titled "Appraisal." Unfortunately, most of these documents are not what they purport to be – they are, in fact, not appraisals. Fairly recently, in order to crack down on charlatans calling themselves appraisers, the IRS introduced a set of regulations that pertain to appraisal reports and those who prepare appraisal reports. To paraphrase, the IRS has said that appraisers must have certain credentials and meet certain standards of experience, education and training in order to write appraisal reports that are acceptable to the IRS, and that appraisal reports must also meet certain industry accepted standards (or USPAP, the Uniform Standards of Professional Appraisal Practice). So far as these regulations are concerned, they make clear that local used car salesmen do not qualify as appraisers for automobiles and that local gun store owners, or gun collectors, do not qualify as firearm appraisers. (For more information, please visit my web site at www.weappraiseguns.com).

If you wish to consult with me relative to an appraisal, or for that matter, anything else contained in this book, please do not hesitate to contact me at 303-455-1717.

WHAT CONSTITUTES A CREDIBLE APPRAISAL REPORT?

I once observed an office of distinguished attorneys become very confused over a very simple inventory list which lacked detail and which bore the label at the top "Appraisal." The part of the document which was causing so much difficulty was a column labeled Fair Market Value. The only thing placed in the column underneath this label was a bunch of numbers with dollar signs in front

-- nothing else. When asked about this document, I explained that hanging a sign around a horse with the word "tractor" on it did not make the horse a tractor, even if someone had painted the horse green. In the very same way, the inventory list that was causing so much consternation amongst the attorneys was not an appraisal just because someone had hung the word "appraisal" on it.

Black's Law Dictionary defines an appraisal as "a valuation or an estimation of value of property by disinterested persons of suitable qualifications" and "the process of ascertaining a value of an asset or liability that involves expert opinion rather than explicit market transactions." Using this as our operating definition, we can see that appraising is not an avocation. Rather, it is a recognized profession and meets all the accepted requirements as such. Familiarity with the pertinent market, according to our definition, is not sufficient. Credible appraisals come from appraisers, who appraise in accordance with recognized standards and who have the appropriate expertise. Capable appraisers who are either accredited or certified provide reports that are consistent, understandable, logical and within the expectations of the industry and the judiciary. Appraisal reports are all about requisite uniformity, ethical observance, adherence to accepted principles, and communication.

Without the requisite training, education and experience, a sporting goods store owner is not qualified to appraise firearms, just as nurses are not qualified to practice medicine in the same way that physicians are so qualified and a used car salesman is not qualified to appraise cars and an antique dealer is not qualified to appraise antiques.

Writing a credible appraisal requires an appraiser to identify the appraisal problem, understand the process necessary to solve the problem, properly execute the pertinent research and analysis, and prepare a report that meets industry standards. Reports that do not demonstrate that the appraiser fully comprehends these essentials and in which the proof of this understanding is not abundantly apparent and properly evidenced, are not credible in the eyes of the judiciary and will not pass peer review

In 1989, The Congress of the United States, in order to codify and standardize the appraisal and the appraisal process, established The Appraisal Foundation as the source of appraisal standards and appraiser qualifications. The Appraisal Foundation first published and copyrighted, in 1987, the Uniform Standards of Professional Appraisal Practice (USPAP), which is the generally accepted and recognized standard of appraisal practice in the United States. Appraisals that meet industry standards are not simple, formless, unfounded "proclamations" of value. To the contrary, appraisals, which conform to USPAP, have many elements, which are compulsory and obligatory. USPAP is a means to measure an appraiser's competency and an appraisal report's compliance with recognized professional methodology, procedures and standards.

The Appraisal Standard Board, ASB, of The Appraisal Foundation annually develops, publishes, interprets, and amends the Uniform Standards of Professional Appraisal Practice on behalf of appraisers and users of appraisal services. In 2003, the ASB will publish its 12th edition of USPAP. Competent appraisal practice requires an explication of what is being appraised, why it is being appraised, and how it is being appraised. USPAP provides specific, legally accepted definitions, rules and methodology under which appraisal reports are to be prepared.

What does all this mean to readers of this book? It means simply that as a professional appraiser, I have arrived at the values contained in this book without thought of personal gain, or to enhance the value of a particular collection, or to influence the market for Browning firearms. Values are always subject to geography, economic conditions and currency fluctuations, of course; but to the extent it is possible to present an accurate, unbiased estimate of the value of Browning firearms, I have endeavored to do just that in these pages.

DEVELOPING A COLLECTOR'S PHILOSOPHY

If one is going to be a collector of guns, or even an accumulator of weapons, I think it's important that the individual develop a philosophy so that his acquisitions make sense and fit into some type of organized and well-thought-out philosophy. Personally, I have been both a collector and an accumulator, but as I get older I have become more of a collector. This is because if one is going to be an accumulator, one needs to either have a gun room the size of the Smithsonian Museum, or not be very active in acquiring firearms. In addition, most accumulators of weapons are either single or have a heavily-sedated spouse. I found out a long time ago it's much easier to buy firearms than it is to sell them at a price that I believe reflects their worth. It's easy to find bargains, at almost any gun show, if one has an encyclopedic memory, and is more of an accumulator than a collector. Remember, one can always sell all the firearms that one owns at wholesale or below almost as quickly as one can unload them from your vehicle at a gun show. Me, I would much prefer to be very active; I am always on the hunt for something that I want. Right now, I have an interest in purchasing Browning Stainless Steel Stalkers equipped with the BOSS. So for me, collecting allows me to continue to be active, aggressive, and involved, but at the same time allows me to curtail and to control my purchasing.

Because I'm sure that there are at least as many philosophies involved in the collection of Brownings as there are collectors, I am going to discuss, in this section, my philosophy about collecting. I believe that it will be somewhat instructive to the novice, because he or she can take my ideas and, using them, develop his or her own pathway. I also believe that accumulators can use this same philosophy to develop their own hybrid purchasing philosophy. The elements, or central ideas, are approximately the same for both.

The first thing that a collector should do is formulate his own goals, both short-term and long-term. What does he want to accomplish, and what are the governing methodologies that will most likely help achieve his long-term and short-term goals?

MY COLLECTING GOALS

1. I want my collection to be something that I can be proud of owning. In this regard, I guess I'm a purist and certainly an elitist. Over the years, I have seen collections that consist of non-original weapons, weapons of poor condition, weapons that make me wonder, "Why would anyone want to own something like this?" But if originality and condition are not important to you, then you should have the philosophy of buying anything without regard to originality or condition. Personally, I would rather own one exquisite example than a whole gun case of "junk." I realize that's just me, and I hope that such a statement does not offend my readership. On the other hand, I have seen collections that make me salivate and make my knees weak. These are the collections that, for me, increase my blood pressure by at least 30 points.

2. I want my collection to be a good investment and to increase in value. I would think that this would be an almost universal goal for almost every collector; however, based upon what I have observed, I'm not sure.

3. I want to be able to own, someday, a complete collection of whatever it is I'm trying to collect. I like order and simplicity and eventual closure; therefore, I want my collection to follow some logical course; to make sense to observers and more importantly, to myself. Years ago, in the late 1970s, I decided to collect Browning Belgian-made .22-caliber semi-automatic rifles. However, in order to have a complete collection

– and because there are an inexhaustible and innumerable number of prototypes, uncatalogued specimens, one-of-a-kind, special order, and custom shop guns – I limited my collection to only Browning catalogue-listed guns, and those made by FN, and their variations. This worked out very well, and within a few years I had a fairly complete, if self-limited, collection of these beautiful and interesting semi-automatic rifles. (I have a friend who collects high grade FN-manufactured Superposed shotguns, and while there are probably weapons out there in the real world that he should own in order to complete his collection, he has the most complete collection of these beautiful weapons that exists in the United States. After accumulating my collection of Belgian Browning .22 semi-automatic rifles, and his completion of his collection, we have both gone on to collect other things. It's a beautiful and orderly world.)

4. I want to be able to own every Browning that I need in order to complete my collection. This precludes me from collecting many different models of Brownings, e.g., the ultra-high grade and very early models of the Superposed shotgun, etc. Consequently, I choose to collect within an area where, if I see something I need or want, I can afford to buy it. To me, this make sense. Why collect something that you cannot afford to collect? I own some high grade Superposed shotguns in exquisite condition, but I do not collect them; I have accumulated/invested in them. In this regard, I might be inclined to trade one of them, or, more if the situation warranted, for something that I really want to own, if it would help me fill in a collection that I was involved in completing. I am only married to those things I collect – not to what I have accumulated.

Let's talk about the investment aspect of collecting Browning firearms. As the only accredited, certified, designated firearm appraiser in the United States, I am continually, on an everyday basis, involved in the market for Browning firearms, and have been for over 30 years. This gives me a special insight into firearm values, including Brownings, because I see and appraise the best guns in the United States. Because of this involvement, I have developed some exacting theories on what makes the best firearm investment. Allow me, to share some of this with you:

Always buy condition. Never buy junk. This is especially true when collecting Browning weapons. Within any collecting category, those properties that have the highest degree of condition will be among the most desirable, and, without question, the best investments.

Always buy originality. Never buy cobbled-up/refinished weapons; they are not collectible. This is especially true when collecting Browning firearms. Within any collecting category, those properties that are 100% original will be among the most desirable, and, without question, will be the best investments.

Rarity is good, but it pales in importance to condition and originality. If one is concerned about making a good investment, even rare items should have condition and originality.

Exceptional, well documented, and historical weapons with market-acceptable provenance usually make good investments. The exception to this is if the weapon in question lacks condition, and/or originality; the investment potential of such pieces is limited, when compared to other similar pieces with condition and originality.

Look for Brownings that are not undergoing accumulation. As every Browning enthusiast knows, the market more enthusiastically pursues some models of Brownings at different times than others. At one time, Browning Superposed shotguns were among the hottest collectible Brownings in the marketplace. At another time, FN-manufactured Browning Safari rifles were among the most avidly-collected Brownings in United States. At yet another time, FN-manufactured .22-caliber semi-automatic rifles were hot. A few years ago,

early FN manufactured semi-automatic pistols, such as the models 1900, 1903, 1906, etc., were being pursued by a great many Browning collectors. If you entered the market when any of these were at thjeir hotetst, your collection would of course require much more money up front than it would in a slack market.

The opposite of accumulation is distribution. Often times, Brownings that are not under accumulation or distribution may be being "held" by the marketplace. They are neither being accumulated nor distributed, in market related terms. However, there are always models of Brownings that are undergoing distribution; this means that they are being sold in unusual numbers and collector/accumulators are converting them to either cash or in trade. Right now, there are more high-condition Belgium Browning Auto-5s on the market than I have ever seen before. I believe these, or at least some of these models, are undergoing distribution. In the beginning of any period of distribution for any highly desirable Browning, there is a type of market frenzy that takes place. It's very interesting to someone like myself who is so involved, on a daily basis, within such an active marketplace such as we see with Browning firearms. High prices and market frenzy often create large numbers of particular models of Brownings to be released onto the market. I never buy weapons when they are undergoing distribution, at high prices, except at the very end of a distribution cycle, when prices usually decline.

After having said all of this, my collecting philosophy is to buy that which I can afford; to buy only weapons with condition, originality, and rarity; and to buy weapons that I believe will, within a reasonable time, undergo accumulation, which means value appreciation.

If you have a collecting philosophy, and if it is significantly different than mine, I would be most happy to hear from you. In the meantime, good luck collecting.

PITFALLS AND SNAKE PITS

I decided to write this chapter because a gentleman called me this morning, and after listening to him, I realized that he had just lost $16,000 in buying a put-together-gun (a gun assembled from mixed parts and passed off as an original). This is a problem that seems to be reoccurring with more frequency. I have seen similar situations countless number of times. Gun shows have increasingly become snake pits, where unscrupulous dealers find innocent victims upon whom to foist put-together and otherwise fraudulent guns. Auctions can also be the source of many bad buying decisions. Auctions commonly misdescribe items they are selling. I hate to publish this unfortunate fact, but it is absolutely true. The reason for this is that certain weapons have become extremely valuable, and therefore the monetary motivation to commit fraud regarding some of these weapons has become more irresistible. Another factor involved in this phenomenon is that new highly advanced technical skills and methodology, such as advances in welding and re-bluing techniques have increased the ability of certain skilled individuals to kafe weapons that are extremely hard to recognize.

In addition, as a matter of record and with great disgust, I report that several icons in the gun world have been put into prison, fairly recently, for fraudulent practices involving fraud in the inducement (i.e., committing fraud) when it comes to the sale and marketing of certain valuable firearms. I won't mention these individuals by name, but to most of us in the gun world who have been around a long time, the news of these individuals being involved in fraudulent deals and subsequently going to prison caused the earth to shake underneath our feet. It's unbelievable, to me, that these individuals would risk their freedom, their livelihoods, their reputations, and their ability to collect firearms for

the sake of a few dollars. If nothing else, this should be a red light for everyone who is considering buying expensive firearms and who lack the knowledge to know just exactly what it is they are attempting to do. The new world of gun collecting and the disreputable practices that are going on indicates that the buyer must beware and take extraordinary methods in order to avoid being a victim of fraud.

Buying a weapon, especially a very valuable weapon, is a hobby or avocation fraught with danger and financial risk. People take the investment of a rather large sums of money entirely too lightly when it comes to the purchase of valuable firearms. This is an added incentive for me to try to give my readers some ideas on how they might avoid some of the pitfalls involved in collecting firearms. As time goes by, it is my belief that there will be more frauds and more trouble, not fewer frauds and less trouble. The frequency where I am seeing these situations is becoming greater and greater. I would like my readers to read those chapters of this book that deal with establishing, for themselves, a collecting philosophy. I believe this is very important. Developing such a philosophy can help in avoiding very costly mistakes when it comes to purchasing firearms.

In those chapters that deal with establishing a collector philosophy, and in other articles I have written, I always recommend that people only buy weapons that are in 100% original condition, and in excellent plus or better condition only. If one is a willing to buy weapons that are cobbled up, and in less than original condition, and in less than excellent condition, then it probably doesn't matter to these individuals when they buy a weapon that isn't what it's supposed to be. Put-together-guns, by definition, are not what they were intended to be when manufactured. However, one of the things I would like to talk to you about is that, if you want to make money relevant to your in investments in firearms, I can tell you, with absolute confidence and certainty, that the best way to accomplish this is to buy factory original guns that have a lot of condition. These are the weapons that will continue to go up in price, and they are also the weapons that will increase in value, from a percentage point of view, the most. There is no question that this is true. In addition, these are the weapons that are the most fungible -- the easiest to convert to cash.

Now that you know where I sit, let me tell you where I stand. As stated elsewhere, fraud involving put-together weapons within the firearms-collecting world is rampant. There is no question that this is true. It used to be that I could go to the gun shows and never see a weapon that had been "helped." Recently, I made a mental note that it has been years, now, since I have gone to a gun show without seeing a fraudulent weapon being offered for sale. So, let's define the words "fraudulent weapon." To me, this means a weapon that has been changed in order to make it more desirable/valuable. This also means that these weapons have been re-blued, redone, refinished, have their original wood altered or changed, and are being sold as if original. Often times, we will see weapons that had been altered, but no attempt is being made to pass them off as something they are not. This is fine, and is quite common. The problem is when a weapon has been altered and is being sold as an original weapon. These, then, are the weapons we shall refer to as "fraudulent weapons."

When should one be careful about this? The answer is quite simple: always. The more pricey the gun, the rarer the gun, the more desirable the gun, and most importantly, the better condition that the weapon appears to be in, the greater likelihood there is that the weapon has been altered. Because I'm in the firearms market on an almost everyday basis, I can name at least six national dealers who in my opinion make a practice of offering fraudulent weapons to the firearm collecting market. One of the sure signs, in my opinion, that you are looking at a dealer who is offering fraudulent weapons for sale is when you notice that most of the weapons on his tables are rare, very desirable, and in high

condition. For me, this makes the hair on the back of my neck go perpendicular. I love to walk up to these tables and be able to establish, at least in my own mind, that most of the guns on the tables are fraudulent in one way or another. I know of one national dealer whose wares I have observed on many occasions, and I don't think I have ever seen a gun he is trying to sell that isn't a put-together-gun, except in the case where he took in a lesser gun on trade, and for whatever reason, decided to sell at in the same condition as when he acquired it.

Part of the tragedy of this story and this particular dealer is that this dealer sold several guns to a person who has become a friend of mine; and, fortunately for me, this friend has never asked me my opinion about the guns in his collection about which he is so proud. I have thought about it, and I believe it if I were ever to be asked by this friend of mine about his guns, I would try to come up with an answer that would not be a lie, exactly, but would not tell him that most of his guns were bogus. This is a bad position in which to find oneself.

Did you know that factory-appearing boxes, recoil pads, and hanging tags have been counterfeited for years? This is a fact. Many older, very collectible firearms that are in new or mint condition and are being offered for sale along with what appears to be original boxes, along with accompanying documentation, are, in my opinion, fraudulent firearms. Back in the sixties and early seventies, it became fairly easy to purchase red Winchester recoil pads, which looked to be correct but were in fact reproductions. These were then added to Winchesters that had been shortened or had other pads added to them and needed a "genuine" Winchester pad to make them appear to be original. This started a wholesale series of reproduction items whose sole purpose was to make prospective buyers believe that the weapon they want to buy is either original or very rare. Back in those early days, I knew a very distinguished dealer, who shall remain nameless and who has since gone to his reward, who had a Winchester proof die. Back then, there were a lot of Winchester Model 42s and Winchester Model 12s that had Simmons ventilated ribs placed on the barrel. This person used his Winchester die to put the proof mark on the left side of the rib, where it should properly be if the weapon were factory original. This made these altered guns appear original. As you might imagine, the value of a gun so altered increased dramatically. This particular individual thought enough of me to confide in me as to what he was doing. He even went so far as to show me weapons that he had altered, and were then being sold, by him, as factory-original weapons. I was absolutely horrified and shaken.

What this did for me was to make me determined, more than ever, to become an expert in discerning whether or not I was looking at a "righteous" weapon, or a weapon that had been altered. And so 30 or 40 years ago I started to become very interested in the knowledge and the intellectual minutia required to recognize the difference between the righteous weapon and one that had been altered. I began to become a student of original factory finishes,and factory stampings. I studied original weapons and committed what I found to memory so that I could use those memories to analyze weapons that I found in the field. This was very helpful.

I'm still learning. I advise all collectors to do the same.

Before we go any further, I'm going to tell you another story. Back in the late seventies I came across, and purchased, a Bulgarian Luger. This particular weapon was not in very good condition, it had some pitting, and it had been nickeled, but it was a true Bulgarian – at the time, one of only four known. Even though it was extremely rare I had a very difficult time in selling it. I went to a large national show and sold it to one of the largest Luger dealers in the world. He did not pay a lot of money for it, but seemed to be happy to have it even though it was less than original. Two years later, at the same show, I ran into the same dealer and there on his table was my Luger – which had

been completely redone! It looked new. The pitting was gone, the nickel was gone and now it looked almost as if it had just left the factory. I knew that it was my pistol because of the serial number, which was a number that was very easy to remember. The dealer, himself, was not at table but was a being occupied by an assistant. I asked this person about this particular weapon, and was told that the dealer had just acquired it from an estate in Wisconsin. The price had gone from $400 to $7500. I have often wondered in whose collection this pistol now resides. Does crime pay? You tell me.

Some people have more money than common sense, and when it comes to the purchasing of expensive weapons, there are *many* people who have more money than knowledge. These lambs enter into the gun show snake pits with a trusting nature and are just asking to be seriously abused. Buying an expensive gun is no time to leave your common sense at home and allow yourself to be taken advantage of by people, some of whom are the moral and ethical equivalent of snake-oil salesmen. So, let's see if we cannot come up with some ideas on how to avoid these kinds of problems. (Because I believe in only buying factory-original and high-condition weapons, these rules will best be applied to these types of weapons.)

1. If you're going to spend any real amount of money for a weapon, and it can be factory lettered, do not buy it without a factory letter. All dealers, who wish to maximize the price they placed on a weapon, will, as a matter of course, have that weapon lettered. If not, proceed with caution – a lot of caution. You had better know what you're doing when the situation presents itself.

2. If you're going to collect a particular type of weapon manufactured by a particular manufacturer, study what the original finish on both the metal and the wood looks like. Study the radiuses on original weapons so that you can recognize an original when you see it. Study the stamping on original weapons so that you can recognize it when you see it. All classical

manufactures (e.g., Winchester, Colt, Browning) have finishes that are easy to recognize. Study them until you know when you are looking at an original finish and when you are not. DON'T BE IN A HURRY -- TAKE YOUR TIME! STUDY THE GUN CAREFULLY.

3. Know your own limitations. Know what you know, but, more importantly, know what you do not know. You must compensate for what you do not know, and you must figure out how to find out about those things that you do not know about. My father told me that one of the real secrets of success was to know what you know, know what you do not know, use what you know, and always strive to know more. This should be your motto, and if you follow my father's advice you will really help yourself when it comes to making good decisions about which guns to buy and when to walk away.

4. Learn the telltale signs of a gun that has been refinished: wood to metal fit; crisp, clean stamping; sharp, clean, straight radiuses; polishing marks; etc. If you haven't mastered this knowledge, you are probably not ready to be buying expensive firearms. Look for inconsistency of wear and beware of ones that are pristine in some areas but show wear in others. (This must be reconciled in your mind before you purchase that weapon.) Take the time to know what you were doing. THERE IS NOTHING LIKE PRACTICE, PRACTICE, AND PRACTICE.

5. Always get a receipt when you buy a gun, and have the seller describe to you on the receipt the condition of the weapon and whether or not it has been modified in any manner. Also, get the dealer to put in writing that if this weapon has been modified in any way, in the opinion of your expert, he will take the gun back and refund your money. Or, better yet, have the dealer give you a time when, without any question, he will refund your money regardless of reason. Always make the dealer sign the receipt. (He may wish to put at a time limit on the refund, which you will have

to deal with as a business decision.) In addition, if you purchased a weapon that can be lettered but has not been lettered, stipulate on the receipt that if the weapon will not letter, the dealer shall return 100% of your money immediately.

6. I believe it is essential that you learn about the reputations of the dealers with whom you are going to do business. Asked other dealers about the reputation of other dealers.

7. Some of the dealers who travel around from show to show are the ones who are least trustworthy. They also are the dealers who usually have the best guns. They are, however, also the ones with the best connections with those people who are capable of altering guns that are so well done that only an expert can tell for sure (and, even then, not always).

8. One of the problems with auctions is that auctions houses make it very clear that they make no claim as to the authenticity, originality, or the condition of any item they are selling. This is understandable; their job is primarily to introduce buyers and sellers. In fact, most of them will say, "You are the experts; do not rely on anything we say." Therefore, educate yourself before buying high dollar guns at auctions.

9. I am sure that everyone has heard the old adage that if it is too good to be true, it probably isn't. This is particularly true when buying weapons from any knowledgeable person, i.e., any person other than the little old lady who lives across the street. One of the reoccurring themes that I encounter when I am dealing with people who have been taken advantage of is that the price they paid, in and of itself, should have given a clue that something was wrong. Many times dealers will use low prices, compared to what a righteous weapon would bring, to entice collectors who really do not know what they are doing. Often times, a part of the swindle is that the buyer thinks he is getting a real bargain. Cheap pricing is often a good indication that something is wrong. Beware the bargain! REMEMBER, GREED KILLS!

Greed is the human emotion that con men use to trap their suckers, and so it is often the case at gun shows and auctions. A few years ago, I was at a major gun show in the midwest and one of the guns I was specifically looking for was a model 42 Winchester Double Diamond Trap. I saw one on the table of a person who was an associate of one of those individuals who was known for selling fraudulent weapons. I picked it up and noted that it was in brand-new condition. It was just what I was hoping to find. The price for this weapon was at least 50% less than what it should have been. The particular individual who was selling it assured me that it was a righteous gun – even told me the story about the little old gentleman who owned it. Of course, I got excited and bought it. I went outside and looked at it under sunlight, which is always recommended; I immediately reversed direction and went back and got my money back. The gun was a skillful re-do, but it was being sold as original. (Leopards never change their spots.) The seller was not happy, and wanted to argue with me about whether or not it was straight. I vowed I would never make such a mistake again, and so far, I have kept that promise.

Another case in point: a person recently called me who had purchased a Colt single action from a big-time national dealer. This particular revolver had a later barrel put on it – one could tell because of the stamping. If it had been correct, the revolver would have been worth a lot of money, but with the replaced barrel, if was worth about 50% of what the person had paid for it. The dealer would not take the revolver back. Of course.

10. Develop a librray of print reference materials dealing with the object of your collection, and consult it before making a high-dollar purchase. Keep the most valuable reference works with you when you're "on the hunt."

11. If you're unsure about whether or not a weapon is correct and righteous, contact an expert immediately and be willing to pay a small fee for his opinion. (I do this all the time for many of my friends and clients. I have never kept track of it, but I suspect that I have saved people quite a bit of money.)

The above rules encompass just about all you can do. If you follow them, the chances are you'll make many fewer mistakes than if you don't. Do not allow your enthusiasm for purchasing a particular weapon to cloud your judgment or take any shortcuts. Often times, with what we have learned recently, even those experts with the biggest and most laudable reputations can be the most corrupt and crooked. When it comes to your money, you should be careful, slow, but most of all, diligent. Remember that in many cases when you enter a gun show you are entering a snake pit. If you take my advice, as mentioned above, almost assuredly you will make very few mistakes. You may not make a lot of friends, but you will make very few mistakes – which in the long run, will put dollars into your pocket.

THE COLLECTIBILITY FACTOR

In order to meet and advance our committment to provide valuable and useful information to our readers, we present the following information and opinion from an expert source: someone who has been involved with firearms for most of his life. Generally speaking, this information is not available anywhere else in print. We have committed ourselves to supplying "hot," up-to-date expert opinions to inform our readership about Browning firearms they should be looking for in terms of investment, tradeability, and collectibility. These are guns that share what we are going to call the "collectibility factor," guns that might be considered by collectors and investors for consideration when they are deciding what Browning firearms to accumulate or collect.

During my 30-year tenure as a professional firearm appraiser, I have had to coin a few words, a few of which are "collectibility," "semi-collectibility," and "tradeability." You will not find these words defined in any dictionary that I have come across. When I am appraising firearms, I use what the appraisers call "connoisseurship" in establishing the value of the particular item. I must be able to rank the items I am appraising; part of this ranking depends on the ability to attach certain factors such as "collectibility quotients" to the firearm in question. I do this so I can communicate with third party users of my appraisal reports; I must be able to talk to the users about an item's value characteristics. And one of an item's value characteristics might be its collectibility, or its semi-collectibility.

For purposes of this discussion, "collectibility" means the amount of buying/purchasing pressure put on a market to acquire a particular model/variation of a particular item by collectors. "Semi-collectibility" means that some "collectors" are buying this weapon, some of which are of very recent or current manufacture, for possible future increases in value. In this book, in some cases, I shall use the term "collectibility" to include semi-collectibility, but I shall not use the word "semi-collectibility" to include collectibility. These are terms that refer to different pressures put on a market to acquire particular models/variations of a particular item because of other factors such as shootability or technical design. The more collectible an item is, the more desirable it is, and at a certain price, the more salable that item is; therefore that item can be said to have a certain, almost measurable, degree of collectibility. Collectible firearms and semi-collectible firearms are usually not extensively used by their owners. They may be fired from time to time, but they are not used in the field where damage might occur. The reason for this is that collectible and semi-collectible firearms, to a very large extent, sell based on their condition. In addition, weapons with a high collectibility factor tend to increase in price at a far higher rate than weapons with either lower collectibility factors or those that are not considered to be collectible.

The reason why this collectibility is important is because it is a major factor contributing to the continual increase in value of firearms. It's very doubtful that collectors would continue to buy collectible or semi-collectible guns if these weapons had no prospect of increasing in value. This also speaks to how hungry collectors are to collect firearms. The semi-collectible firearm is proof positive that firearm collectors will collect all types of guns, so long as the collector believes that the market perceives them to be collectible or semi-collectible. This collector frenzy, created by the acquisition of collectible or semi-collectible guns, is what drives the secondary firearms market, gun shows, and the fanaticism demonstrated by many firearm collectors. Firearms manufacturers, including Browning, fuel this market by limiting the number of certain firearm models that they manufacture, models which they believe will have special interest to collectors.

An interesting case in point: Fairly recently, Winchester discontinued production of its lever action model 94 rifles. The market immediately reacted by making many of these recently manufactured Winchesters desirable, and they immediately began to undergo accumulation. Before their discontinuance, used Winchester model 94s were not particularly desirable, nor were they easy to sell. Winchester commemorative model 94 rifles, which for years were only semicollectible, also began to show, almost overnight, immediate price increases, as collectors began to buy them in the anticipation of future increases in value. There is no question that the firearms market often reacts to limited production numbers. Firearms that the various manufacturers have trouble selling, while still in production, often become semi-collectible as soon as production of that particular weapon stops.

Collectibility is different from desirability, especially where firearms are concerned, because collectibility deals with the wish of collectors to acquire a particular weapon, which for purposes of our discussion will be distinct from buying pressure that comes from another type/class of buyer, e.g., shooters. The concept of desirability is an all-inclusive term in that it includes buying pressure put on a particular weapon not only because of its collectibility, but also because of other factors such as functionality, shootability and utility. Weapons that have a high degree of collectibility and/or desirability are, as we all know, extremely fungible. This means that some guns are almost as easy to convert to cash as gold. Weapons that are less desirable and/or less collectible are more difficult to sell, and, therefore, are less fungible.

Because of my experience with collectible firearms, and in this case Browning firearms, throughout this book I offer my opinion as to the collectibility of certain models of Browning firearms. I rank the collectibility of these weapons on a sliding scale from #1 to #4. I need for my readers to understand that this is only my opinion and reflects my experience in the marketplace. Certainly, my opinion is going to differ from many others, but that's all right because I recognize that my opinion, in this regard, is subjective, and not the result of any objective testing or scientific evaluation. However, it is my hope that because of my experience, novice collectors, who are also part of my readership, will gain some of value from my opinion, experience and knowledge.

Before I tell you where I stand on the issue of collectibility, first, let me tell you where I sit. I am a great fan of John Moses Browning, and I regard him to have been the greatest firearm innovator in the history of the world. I first became familiar with him as a collector of Winchester firearms, which was my first love. Anyone who enjoys Winchester firearms, especially the early lever actions, has to be, by definition, a great fan of John Moses Browning. I am no different. In fact, I will argue that Winchester firearms could and would never have achieved their place in American history if they had not had a close association with John Moses Browning and had not used his designs to manufacture the most famous and treasured weapons

of the late 19th and early 20th centuries. Any discussion of Winchester firearms is incomplete without recognizing the pivotal role that John Moses Browning played in Winchester's success, familiarity, and fame.

I have a fairly large collection of firearms. Amongst my guns are Winchesters, Colts, Smith & Wessons, Brownings, High Standards and other miscellaneous weapons that I find interesting. However, as a hunter, I shoot only Brownings. While these other manufacturers have manufactured some great weapons, Browning, at least during my lifetime, in my opinion, has made the greatest hunting guns. Many of these weapons were just shooters when I was youn, but are now highly collectible and would rank as having high collectibility factors. This means that the most technically advanced weapons, as far as shooters are concerned, have morphed into highly desirable collectible firearms. As you know, this is not only true of Brownings, but also Winchesters and most other makers. For example, during the latter quarter of the 19th century the most technically advanced rifles were most probably Winchesters designed by John Moses Browning. These guns, which were most sought after during that time by shooters and hunters, are now amongst the most collectible weapons in the world, and would have extremely high collectibility factors.

As an example of how this phenomena can work, I cite the following example. A contemporary weapon can become desireable and collectable somewhat simultaneously. Browning's Stainless Steel Stalker, with BOSS attached, is one example. The BOSS (Ballistic Optimizing Shooting System) is an adjustable device that fits on the end of a rifle barrel and functions not only as recoil reducer, but also can be used to adjust the barrel harmonics, which allows a shooter to make the rifle "like" a particular load, obviating the need to adjust the load to the liking of the gun. From my experience, this is a fantastic technical advancement in rifle accuracy, and I can personally attest to its functionality, utility, and usefulness. However, for whatever reason, the marketplace has not taken a particular interest in this advancement, and sales of Browning Stainless Steel Stalkers with the BOSS have not been to the liking of the company. Consequently, the factory has discontinued offering this device as a feature on several different calibers including .223, .22-250, 7mm-08, and .25-06.

I decided, some time ago, to make a collection of all of these BOSS-equipped rifles, partly because they are now becoming quite rare, and partly because I believe them to be, technically speaking, superior to any thing else available in the marketplace. There is no question in my mind that at some time in the future these rifles are going to become extremely desirable and collectible, not only because they are no longer manufactured and now rare, but also because they are so technically advanced that soon shooters will also find them to be highly desirable as field weapons. In this way, a weapon can advance not only in terms of its desirability, but also in terms of its collectibility.

DEFINITIONS

The Collectibility Factor ratings that I use in this book are as follows:

#1: Firearms that I consider to be most collectible, and which, may or not be contemporaneously desirable.

#2: Firearms that I consider to be highly collectible but are somewhat less sought-after than those weapons carrying the #1 collectibility rating. These weapons have sustained collector interest.

#3: Firearms that are somewhat collectible. These are guns that I consider to be semi-collectible but are moving toward being collectible. These have some sustained collector interest but are less important to collectors than firearms carrying either a #1 or a #2 rating.

#4: Firearms that are in the beginning stages of being collected by some adventuresome, investment-minded collectors, and should be categorized as being semi-collectible.

The following caveats shall apply to the use of this Collectibility Factor:

* The Author believes, unless otherwise noted, that only weapons in excellent or better condition are considered to be collectible.
* The Author believes, unless otherwise noted, that only weapons that are 100% factory original are considered to be collectible.

When talking about Brownings and any collectibility factor that might be attached to them, one must talk about the difference between those weapons made in Japan and those made in Belgium. A few years ago there were no Japanese manufactured Browning weapons that I believe the market accepted as collectible. Today, things have changed. I now believe that some Japanese-manufactured Browning firearms will carry a collectibility quotient of #4, and in the case of weapons such as Browning's high-grade .22 semi-automatic Japanese-manufactured rifles, might even carry a collectibility quotient of #3.

It is my hope that the readers of this book will find the information I'm going to provide herein to be up-to-date and valuable. These readers should note that weapons undergo changes in their collectibility and that the market for firearms is constantly changing. Weapon, which are undergoing rapid accumulation, will most probably at some point undergo distribution. This is why it's important for collectors and firearms lovers to remain current on the information they are using to make buying and selling decisions.

I wish you happy collecting, accumulating, hunting, and shooting, and as always, may all of your firearm purchases, in the long run, make you money.

GRADING SYSTEM

In the opinion of the editor, it is our task to offer the collector and dealer a measurement that most closely reflects a general consensus on condition. The system we present seems to come closest to describing a firearm in universal terms. We strongly recommend that the reader acquaint himself with this grading system before attempting to determine the correct price for a particular firearm's condition. Remember, in most cases condition determines price.

NIB—NEW IN BOX

This category can sometimes be misleading. It means that the firearm is in its original factory carton with all of the appropriate papers. It also means the firearm is new; that it has not been fired and has no wear. This classification brings a substantial premium for both the collector and shooter.

EXCELLENT

Collector quality firearms in this condition are highly desirable. The firearm must be in at least 98 percent condition with respect to blue wear, stock or grip finish, and bore. The firearm must also be in 100 percent original factory condition without refinishing, repair, alterations or additions of any kind. Sights must be factory original as well. This grading classification includes both modern and antique (manufactured prior to 1898) firearms.

VERY GOOD

Firearms in this category are also sought after both by the collector and shooter. Modern firearms must be in working order and retain approximately 92 percent original metal and wood finish. It must be 100 percent factory original, but may have some small repairs, alterations, or non-factory additions. No refinishing is permitted in this category. Antique firearms must have 80 percent original finish with no repairs.

GOOD

Modern firearms in this category may not be considered to be as collectable as the previous grades, but antique firearms are considered desirable. Modern firearms must retain at least 80 per-

cent metal and wood finish, but may display evidence of old refinishing. Small repairs, alterations, or non-factory additions are sometimes encountered in this class. Factory replacement parts are permitted. The overall working condition of the firearm must be good as well as safe. The bore may exhibit wear or some corrosion, especially in antique arms. Antique firearms may be included in this category if their metal and wood finish is at least 50 percent original factory finish.

FAIR

Firearms in this category should be in satisfactory working order and safe to shoot. The overall metal and wood finish on the modern firearm must be at least 30 percent and antique firearms must have at least some original finish or old refinish remaining. Repairs, alterations, nonfactory additions, and recent refinishing would all place a firearm in this classification. However, the modern firearm must be in working condition, while the antique firearm may not function. In either case the firearm must be considered safe to fire if in a working state.

POOR

Neither collectors nor shooters are likely to exhibit much interest in firearms in this condition. Modern firearms are likely to retain little metal or wood finish. Pitting and rust will be seen in firearms in this category. Modern firearms may not be in working order and may not be safe to shoot. Repairs and refinishing would be necessary to restore the firearm to safe working order. Antique firearms will have no finish and will not function. In the case of modern firearms their principal value lies in spare parts. On the other hand, antique firearms in this condition may be used as "wall hangers" or as an example of an extremely rare variation or have some kind of historical significance.

PRICING SAMPLE FORMAT

NIB	EXC.	V.G.	GOOD	FAIR	POOR
550	450	400	350	300	200

PRICING

The prices given in this book reflect RETAIL values. This is important. You will generally not realize full retail value if you trade a gun in on another or sell it to a dealer. In this situation, your trade-in gun will be valued at wholesale, which is generally substantially below retail value.

Unfortunately for shooters and collectors, there is no central clearinghouse for firearms prices. The prices given in this book are designed as a guide, not as a quote. This is an important distinction because prices for firearms vary with the time of the year, with geographical location, and sometimes for no apparent reason. For example, interest in firearms is at its lowest point in the summer. People are not as interested in shooting and collecting at this time of the year as they are in playing golf or taking a vacation. Therefore, prices are depressed slightly and guns that may sell quickly during the hunting season or the winter months may not sell well at all during this time of year. Geographical location also plays an important part in pricing. Political pundits are often heard to say that all politics is local. Well, the same can be said, in many ways, for the price of firearms. For instance, a Browning A-Bolt II in .270 caliber will generally bring a higher price in the Western states than along the Eastern seaboard, and a BPS Upland Special may generate less interest in an area where upland game hunting is not popular.

It is not practical to list prices in this book with regard to time of year or location. What is given is a reasonable price based on sales at gun shows, auction houses, Gun List prices, and information obtained from knowledgeable collectors and dealers. In certain cases there will be no price indicated under a particular condition but rather the notation "N/A"

or the symbol "—." This indicates that there is no known price available for that gun in that condition or the sales for that particular model are so few that a reliable price cannot be given. This will usually be encountered only with very rare guns, with newly introduced firearms, or more likely with antique firearms in those conditions most likely to be encountered. Most antique firearms will be seen in the good, fair and poor categories.

As noted above, throughout this edition you will see certain models identified as "sleepers": models that are undergoing, or are likely to undergo, an upward shift in value. These entries are identified by the icon shown at the right. In today's volatile market, however, nothing is certain, so we can make no guarantees as to the future appreciation of any model.

Note that the prices in this book are a GENERAL GUIDE as to what a willing buyer and willing seller might agree on. So how is the reader to use this book? It can be used as an identification guide and as a source of starting prices for a planned firearms transaction. If you start by valuing a given firearm according to the values shown in this book, you will not be too far off the mark.

In the final analysis, a firearm is worth only what someone is willing to pay for it. New trends arise quickly, and there are many excellent bargains to be found in today's market. With patience and good judgment – and with this book under your arm – you, too, can find them.

FABRIQUE NATIONALE (FN) AND JOHN BROWNING

Fabrique Nationale, FN, was created in 1889. From its beginning, FN was very interested in the design and manufacture of semi-automatic pistols. FN spent some time looking at the model 1893 Borchardt Pistol, but found its design to be too clumsy and difficult to handle and fire. FN was well financed and built a very large, modern and spacious factory and by 1897 was looking around for items to manufacture.

FN felt it needed to free itself from being overly dependent upon manufacturing items under contracts for other manufacturing companies. It wanted to find its own line of merchandise and products to market. In that regard, FN's commercial director at that time was an American named Hart Berg. Mr. Berg decided to this end to travel to the United States to study American factories looking for possible products for FN to manufacture. Berg was even considering manufacturing bicycles, and at the time he met John Browning, he was in fact visiting a factory that manufactured bicycles.

Coincidentally, both Berg and Browning were in Hartford, Connecticut, at the same time. Browning had brought a prototype semi-automatic pistol of his design to show Mr. Berg. The two men recognized almost instantly that they needed each other and that their needs were almost a perfect match. Browning's design was somewhat unusual in that it used low-powered ammunition and consequently did not need a complicated and expensive locking mechanism. In fact, the Browning design was unique in that the breech remained unlocked and was held in place by a very powerful recoil spring. For Mr. Berg, this design was particularly attractive because the design allowed for the manufacture of significantly smaller models of pistols than those currently under manufacture in Europe. Mr. Berg saw this, not only as a great advantage in terms of manufacturing a pistol for the civilian market, but also as an opportunity to get involved with someone as famous as John Browning.

Mr. Berg's excitement and interest in this new design was also great news for John Browning, because Colt, which had seen the design first, showed very little interest in it. Colt was more interested in manufacturing larger-caliber semi-automatic pistols which would be more appropriate for military service. In fact, Colt was unaware, apparently, that there was a very large civilian market for smaller semi-automatic pistols. This oversight by Colt was to prove of great advantage to FN.

FN, however, was aware that there was, at least in Europe, a large civilian demand for semi-automatic pistols. This is probably because Fabrique Nationale officials were right there in Europe, watching the development of not only the Borchardt pistol but the remarkable pistol designed by George Luger. The confluence of all these events allowed FN to establish a relationship with John Browning, which they were to exploit over the next century and beyond. The relationship between FN and Browning was to be extremely advantageous for all parties concerned. (It can be said that Colt had made the same mistake made a few years before by Winchester in that they had misjudged the market for certain weapons designed by John Browning. These mistakes were to haunt both manufacturing companies for well over a hundred years, and, most probably, into the foreseeable future.)

Fabrique Nationale and John Browning signed an agreement on July 7, 1897, which granted Fabrique Nationale the right to sell pistols designed by Browning in most of Continental Europe; however, it excluded Fabrique Nationale from selling Browning-designed pistols of its own manufacture, in the United States, Ireland, Great Britain, and all countries having been assigned to Colt under a previous contract. It did, however, allow Fabrique Nationale to sell, in competition with Colt, Browning-designed pistols in all countries not specifically mentioned in either of the two agreements. Within no time, Fabrique Nationale was on the way to financial prosperity, which could be, in no small part, attributed to their new relationship with John Browning.

The partnership between Fabrique Nationale and John Browning – as well as John Browning's descendents and the Browning Arms Company – was to last for decades and, in fact, is working to the mutual benefit of all parties to this very day. The weapons designed by John Browning certainly contributed to the short-term and long-term success of Fabrique Nationale.

Please refer to the timeline as set forth in another chapter in this book, as it will give the reader the opportunity to see some of the interaction between the two companies, and to see how important and fortunate it truly was for all parties involved.

WHAT IF?

Speculation, often times, is the sustenance of the disenfranchised, disgruntled, angry, and those who love to spend time in a fantasy world. It's for those who wish to conjure up the what-ifs of history and the what-might've-beens. Reality, as said by Philip Dick, is unhappily for many, that which persists when speculation and fantasy disappear. He said, "Reality is that which, when you stop believing in it, doesn't go away."

And so, we have our history of firearms manufactured in United States of America. History, that for the most part, we all except as reality. I for one, am not particularly attracted to revisionism and revisionistic thinking, and those that wallow in the what might've beens. However, in the case of John Moses Browning, I feel compelled to conjecture about some "might have beens."

For American firearms aficionados there are many great names within all the companies, the men that worked for those companies, and independent individuals that come to mind when thinking of 19th century firearm's innovators, e.g., Sharps, Winchester, Spencer, Remington, Colt, Smith and Wesson, etc., and, yes, John M. Browning, etc. Of all of these, it's generally accepted that John M. Browning contributed more to firearm innovation and design than any person in world history, not only of the 19th-century, but of all time. But, as far as manufacturers of the 19th century are concerned, only three names really dominate history: Colt, Smith and Wesson, and, perhaps the greatest of all, Winchester. I realize that there will be some controversy here, and I certainly understand that there are grounds for many arguments about that which I believe; but, for me, the greatest American 19th-century firearms manufacturer was undoubtedly Winchester. I'm not going to spend a lot of time supporting this opinion, mostly because I believe that most rational firearm historians also believe that Winchester was the greatest 19th-century manufacture of American firearms. Certainly, Colt was the next greatest name in 19th-century firearm manufacture.

Jonathan Browning, John M. Browning's father, was involved in gunsmithing as early as 1852, in Ogden Utah. Upon his father's death, John Browning, when he was only 24 years old, opened his own gunshop in 1879. However, he made his own single shot rifle for his brother, Matt, when he was only 14, in 1869, in his father's gun shop. It was during John's first year in his own business, 1879, that he came up with his own design for a completely different and revolutionarily constructed single shot rifle, in addition, during the same year, he converted the shop's old foot operated machinery into machinery powered by steam. Four years later, after having married his sweetheart Rachel Teresa Child in 1879, he sold Winchester the rights to manufacture this single shot rifle for the sum of $8,000. The deal was a success for both Winchester and Browning and commenced Browning's collaboration with Winchester, one that lasted approximately 19 years.

We intend to provide general as well as specific information about John Moses Browning and Browning's firearm models. John Moses Browning will probably live in history, for all time, as the greatest firearm innovator who ever lived. There is no doubt whatsoever in my mind that Winchester would never have achieved its place in history if it had not been fortunate enough to gain access to John Browning's designs and patents. Any company with access to Browning's designs and patents, certainly in my mind, would have dominated the firearm industry during the time that Winchester's lever action rifles dominated the firearm's market in the United States. Of course, this supposition assumes that such a company would have been able to market and manufacture such weapons in the same manner that Winchester did, as well as having the same foresight to understand the potential involved in securing an exclusive relationship with John Browning.

When we attempt to analyze history and ask "if"-based questions, we enter into an arena where answers can never be certain. However, what is certain is that John Moses Browning and his weapons were some of the leading weapons in the world, and certainly among the leading weapons in this country, long before his company began manufacturing his own weapons of his design. (John Browning did manufacture, for a very short time, in Utah, a version of his single shot rifle, which rights he sold to Winchester.) In truth, if Winchester had not turned down a repeating shotgun that Browning had designed, the marriage between Winchester and Browning may never have become undone, and Winchester very well might have become the the world's premier firearm manufacturing company of not only the 19th century, but also the 20th. However one wants to argue this proposition, one thing that cannot be denied is that if Winchester had continued its relationship with Browning, it would have had significantly more dominance, financial success, and prestige in the United States firearms market in the last half of the 20th century that it enjoyed. It is certainly ironic, to say the least, that the current-day Browning Firearm Company has become sufficiently financially powerful to purchase many of the assets of what was once known around the globe as the Winchester Repeating Arms Company.

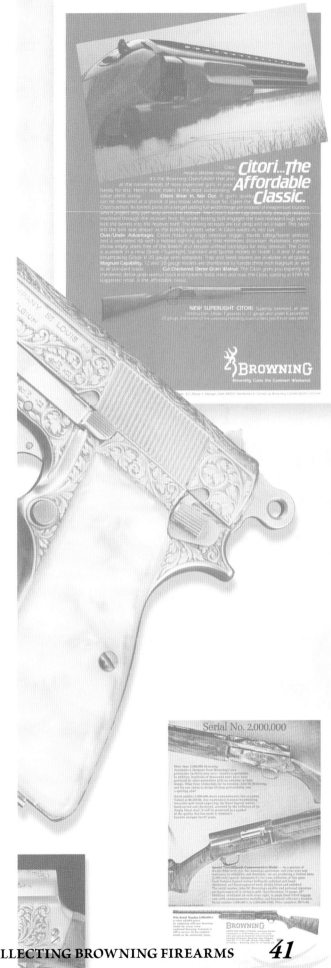

SECTION II

BROWNING RIFLE VALUES

HIGH-POWER BOLT-ACTION RIFLE

*T*his was a high-grade, bolt-action sporting rifle manufactured by FN in Belgium (from 1959 to 1975) or Sako of Finland (from 1961 to 1975). It was built on either a Mauser or a Sako action and chambered for a number of popular calibers from the .222 Remington up to the .458 Winchester Magnum. There were three basic grades that differed in the amount of ornamentation and the quality of materials and workmanship utilized. Certain calibers are considered to be rare and will bring a premium from collectors of this firearm. We recommend securing a qualified appraisal on these rifles if a transaction is contemplated. We furnish general values only.

Early Belgian production Safari Grade High Power Rifle in .30-06 Springfield with box. Courtesy Rock Island Auction.

Belgian Safari Grade High Power Rifle in .30-06 Springfield. Courtesy Rock Island Auction.

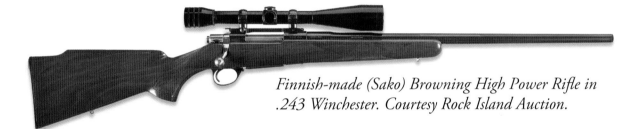

Finnish-made (Sako) Browning High Power Rifle in .243 Winchester. Courtesy Rock Island Auction.

Belgian Browning Safari Grade High Power Rifle in .375 H&H Magnum. Courtesy Rock Island Auction.

NOTE: From 1959 through 1966 FN Mauser actions with long extractors were featured. These Mauser actions will bring a premium depending on caliber. From 1967 on, FN Supreme actions with short extractors were used. Only .30-06 and .270 calibers continued with long extractor Mauser actions.

For buyer and seller alike some rare calibers may be worth as much as 100 percent or more over prices listed for rare calibers such as .284 Win., .257 Roberts, 300 H&H, and .308 Norma Magnum. The High-Power bolt-action rifles seemed to be particularly hard hit by the rust-producing "salt wood" used in cerain older Brownings. Salt-wood Browning High Power Rifles can be recognized by their short extractors; this is why short extractor rifles typically bring less than their long extractor counterparts No factory replacement stocks are known to still be available. Deduct 20-25 percent for short extractor rifles.

This rifle looks and shoots like a one-of-a-kind masterpiece...

Olympian .30/06

yet you can buy it in 16 different calibers!

A Browning Bolt-Action High Power incorporates rare hand craftsmanship with unusual performance...attributes that are seldom combined in today's rifles. In addition, it is regularly produced in a comprehensive series of specifications. Whether you want a Safari, Medallion or Olympian grade, you may choose from 16 proven calibers* — 9 of them hard hitting Magnums.

The quality of a High Power is readily apparent in the rich, figured walnut ...in the tasteful hand engraving...in the careful fit and finish; yet critical attention to detail is more than skin deep. Barrels are forged from specially heat treated billets of chrome vanadium steel and rifling is the ultimate in precision. Actions are strong and reliable and are offered in three lengths appropriate to the caliber. In fact, every facet of a Browning Bolt-Action is designed and crafted to provide its owner with a truly exceptional rifle.

See your Authorized Browning Dealer today and let him show you this one-of-a-kind masterpiece. *You'll like what you see!*

*Calibers available U. S. or Canada:
.222R, .222R Mag., .22/250, .243W, .264W Mag., .270W, .284W, 7mmR Mag., .308W, .308 Norma Mag., .30/06, .300W Mag., .300 H&H Mag., .338W Mag., .375 H&H Mag., .458W Mag.

BROWNING®

Safari .22/250

WRITE FOR FREE
64 PAGE CATALOG

Complete information on all Browning guns and accessories, plus special chapters containing practical shooting information.

Rifles from $199.50
Scopes from $59.50

Browning Arms Co., Dept. 900, P.O. Box 450, St. Louis, Mo. 63166 ZIP

Period advertising for High Power Rifle. Courtesy Browning. Pricing no longer valid.

If you are going to try accumulating these weapons, please proceed with caution. Having said that, for me, these are some of the best bolt action rifles ever manufactured. There is no question that prices have been somewhat suppressed because of the salt-wood scare. At some point, however, I think the market will shake this negative reaction to these fine rifles. Standard rifles, at the present time, rate a Collectibility Factor of #2, while the high-grade rifles would rate a Collectibility Factor of #1.)

SAFARI GRADE

Standard model, standard calibers.

EXC.	V.G.	GOOD	FAIR	POOR
1400	950	650	400	400

NOTE: Add a premium of $200 for Magnum calibers; add a premium of $1000 for .257 Roberts; add a premium of $500 for .308 Norma Magnum; add a premium of $500 for .375 H&H/.338 Winchester Magnum; add an additional premium of 20 percent for Magnum rifles with long extractors.

SHORT ACTION RIFLES
WITH SAKO ACTION

Manufactured in .222 Remington or .222 Remington Magnum. Quite rare.

NOTE: This is a weapon that should be accumulated, especially if new or new in the box.

NIB	EXC.	V.G.	GOOD	FAIR	POOR
1600	1000	700	500	300	150

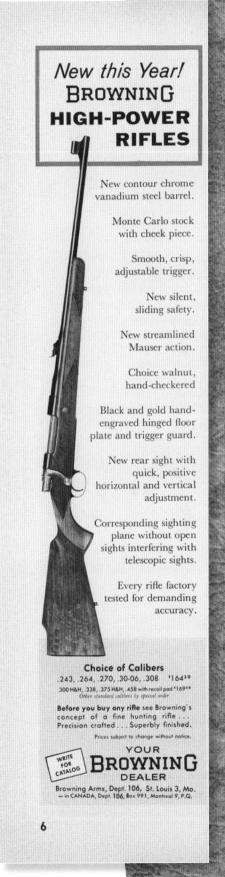

New this Year!
BROWNING
HIGH-POWER
RIFLES

New contour chrome vanadium steel barrel.

Monte Carlo stock with cheek piece.

Smooth, crisp, adjustable trigger.

New silent, sliding safety.

New streamlined Mauser action.

Choice walnut, hand-checkered

Black and gold hand-engraved hinged floor plate and trigger guard.

New rear sight with quick, positive horizontal and vertical adjustment.

Corresponding sighting plane without open sights interfering with telescopic sights.

Every rifle factory tested for demanding accuracy.

Choice of Calibers
.243, .264, .270, .30-06, .308 $164.50
.300 H&H, .338, .375 H&H, .458 with recoil pad $169.95
Other standard calibers by special order

Before you buy any rifle see Browning's concept of a fine hunting rifle . . . Precision crafted . . . Superbly finished.

Prices subject to change without notice.

YOUR
WRITE FOR CATALOG
BROWNING
DEALER
Browning Arms, Dept. 106, St. Louis 3, Mo.
— in CANADA, Dept. 106, Box 991, Montreal 9, P.Q.

6

Period fractional advertising for High Power Rifle (1960). Courtesy Browning. Pricing no longer valid.

MEDALLION HIGH-POWER RIFLE WITH SAKO ACTION

This rifle was manufactured in .22-250 Remington, .243 Winchester, .284 Winchester, and .308 Winchester.

NIB	EXC.	V.G.	GOOD	FAIR	POOR
1500	1000	700	500	300	150

NOTE: Add a premium of 100 percent for .284 Winchester caliber (only 162 rifles manufactured)

MEDALLION GRADE

Scroll engraved, standard calibers.

NIB	EXC.	V.G.	GOOD	FAIR	POOR
2650	1500	1100	750	400	–

OLYMPIAN GRADE

Extensive game scene engraving, standard calibers.

Medallion High Power Rifle in .243 Winchester. Courtesy Rock Island Auction.

Trigger guard detail. Courtesy Rock Island Auction.

Floorplate detail. Courtesy Rock Island Auction.

Factory L. Lambert-engraved Olympian Belgian High Power Rifle in .270 Winchester. Courtesy Rock Island Auction.

Right receiver detail. Courtesy Rock Island Auction.

Left receiver detail. Courtesy Rock Island Auction.

Factory R. Dewil-engraved Olympian Belgian High Power Rifle in .243 Winchester. Courtesy Rock Island Auction.

Detail of left receiver. Courtesy Rock Island Auction.

Detail of right receiver. Courtesy Rock Island Auction

Detail of floorplate. Courtesy Rock Island Auction

Detail of trigger guard. Courtesy Rock Island Auction

Floorplate detail.
Courtesy Rock
Island Auction

Trigger guard
detail. Courtesy
Rock Island
Auction.

I. Baertem factory-
engraved Olympian
High Power Rifle
in .243 Winchester.
Courtesy Rock
Island Auction.

Detail left receiver. Courtesy Rock Island Auction.

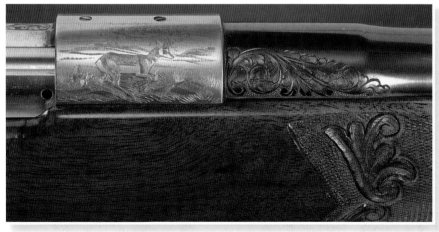

Detail right receiver. Courtesy Rock Island Auction.

R. Greco factory-engraved Olympian High Power Rifle in .338 Winchester Magnum. Courtesy Rock Island Auction.

Floorplate detail. Courtesy Rock Island Auction.

Trigger guard detail. Courtesy Rock Island Auction.

Left receiver detail. Courtesy Rock Island Auction.

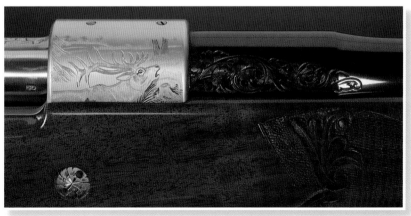

Right receiver detail. Courtesy Rock Island Auction.

NIB	EXC.	V.G.	GOOD	FAIR	POOR
7500	5000	4250	3250	2500	1500

THE MAGNIFICENT TWENTY

*I*n 1966 Robert C. Fessler, Sr. placed a special order with Browning for one of every caliber and barrel weight rifle the company made for that model year. The order was so special that it took four years to complete and was personally delivered to Mr. Fessler by John Val Browning, chairman of the board, and his son John M. Browning. The set consists of 20 presentation rifles, meticulously assembled and engraved by the very best of Browning's staff. The rifles are consecutively numbered with the smallest caliber, a .222 Remington Lightweight, having the lowest number and the largest bore gun, a .458 Winchester Magnum, the highest. One other caliber, a .264 Win. Magnum, was listed in the 1966 Browning catalog but it had been discontinued before Fessler's order was placed. Special arrangements were made and a .264 model, the last ever made by Browning, was included in the set known as "The Magnificent Twenty."

Only master and grand master engravers were allowed to work on the set and each rifle has at least two signatures and some have several more, all in highly visible locations. The top of each receiver is fully engraved and the bolts and handles are engraved where possible. The barrels of the .222 and the .458 are totally engraved. All normal markings, such as "Browning Arms Co." and the serial numbers that were usually hot stamped, are individually engraved in script in the Magnificent Twenty and the serial numbers on the right side of the receiver are inlaid with gold. More than 6,000 stock blanks of Claro walnut were examined before twenty were selected for their clarity and coloring for this one-of-a-kind matched set.

Six years after the delivery of the set, Fabrique Nationale purchased Browning Arms Corporation and all the original machinery, dies, tooling and jigs that were used to craft the Magnificent Twenty were replaced and scrapped. That assures that this set of spectacular rifles can never be duplicated.

The Magnificent Twenty was offered on the block on Saturday, April 30, 2005, at Rock Island Auction in Moline, Illinois. The sale of this lot was conducted in the "continental" style with each rifle offered individually. The sum of the individual winning bids, $260,000, became the opening bid for the entire set. A number of bidders joined the fray at the opening call but the pack quickly winnowed down to two resolute players. The winner stayed in on the phone to $430,000 plus the 15 percent buyer's premium, bringing the price of the set to $494,500. Included in the winning bid, in addition to the rifles, was complete documentation on manufacturing instructions, correspondence, life histories of the engravers and copies of the original purchase order and invoices as well as photos of the Browning facilities at Morgan, Utah and Liege, Belgium. *Courtesy Rock Island Auctions.*

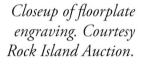

"Magnificent Twenty" Olympian High Power Rifle in .222 Remington, Lightweight barrel. Courtesy Rock Island Auction.

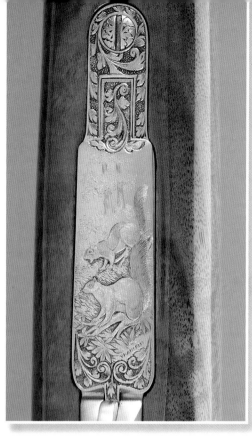

Closeup of floorplate engraving. Courtesy Rock Island Auction.

Closeup of left receiver engraving. Courtesy Rock Island Auction.

Closeup of right receiver. Courtesy Rock Island Auction.

Closeup front sight and muzzle. Courtesy Rock Island Auction.

Closeup of bottom of trigger guard. Courtesy Rock Island Auction.

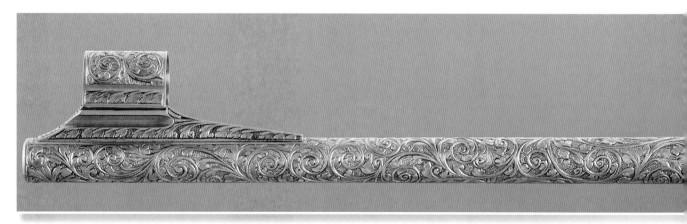

Barrel engraving. Courtesy Rock Island Auction.

"Magnificent Twenty" Olympian High Power Rifle in .222 Remington, Heavy barrel. Courtesy Rock Island Auction.

Closeup of floorplate. Courtesy Rock Island Auction.

Closeup of trigger guard. Courtesy Rock Island Auction.

Closeup of left receiver. Courtesy Rock Island Auction.

Closeup of right receiver. Courtesy Rock Island Auction.

Closeup left receiver. Courtesy Rock Island Auctions.

"Magnificent Twenty" Olympian High Power Rifle in .222 Remington Magnum, Lightweight barrel. Courtesy Rock Island Auction.

Closeup of floorplate. Courtesy Rock Island Auction.

Closeup of trigger guard. Courtesy Rock Island Auction.

Closeup of right receiver. Courtesy Rock Island Auction.

"Magnificent Twenty" Olympian High Power Rifle in .222 Remington Magnum, Heavy barrel. Courtesy Rock Island Auction.

Closeup of floorplate. Courtesy Rock Island Auction.

Closeup of trigger guard. Courtesy Rock Island Auction.

Closeup of right receiver. Courtesy Rock Island Auction.

Closeup of left receiver. Courtesy Rock Island Auction.

Closeup left receiver. Courtesy Rock Island Auction.

Closeup of right receiver. Courtesy Rock Island Auction.

Closeup of
floorplate.
Courtesy Rock
Island Auction.

Closeup of
trigger guard.
Courtesy
Rock Island
Auction.

*"Magnificent
Twenty" Olympian
High Power Rifle in
.22-250 Remington
Magnum,
Lightweight barrel.
Courtesy Rock
Island Auction.*

"Magnificent Twenty" Olympian High Power Rifle in .22-250 Remington, Heavy barrel. Courtesy Rock Island Auction.

Closeup of floorplate. Courtesy Rock Island Auction.

Closeup of trigger guard. Courtesy Rock Island Auction.

Closeup of right receiver. Courtesy Rock Island Auction.

Closeup of left receiver. Courtesy Rock Island Auction.

Closeup of left receiver. Courtesy Rock Island Auction.

Closeup of right receiver. Courtesy Rock Island Auction.

Closeup of floorplate. Courtesy Rock Island Auction.

Closeup of trigger guard. Courtesy Rock Island Auction.

"Magnificent Twenty" Olympian High Power Rifle in .243 Winchester, Lightweight barrel. Courtesy Rock Island Auction.

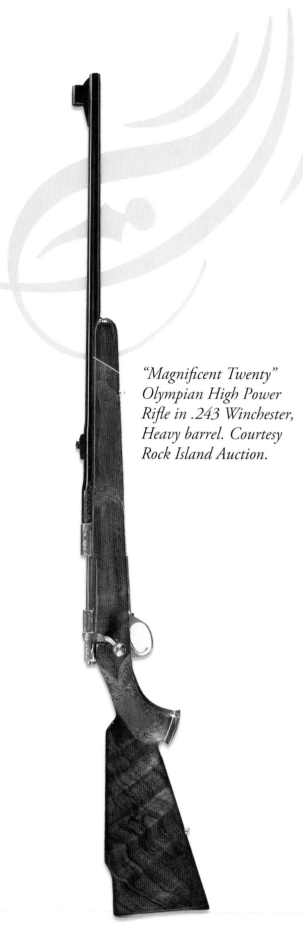

"Magnificent Twenty" Olympian High Power Rifle in .243 Winchester, Heavy barrel. Courtesy Rock Island Auction.

Closeup of floorplate. Courtesy Rock Island Auction.

Closeup of trigger guard. Courtesy Rock Island Auction.

Closeup of left receiver. Courtesy Rock Island Auction.

Closeup of right receiver. Courtesy Rock Island Auction.

Closeup of left receiver. Courtesy Rock Island Auction.

Closeup right receiver. Courtesy Rock Island Auction.

Closeup of floorplate. Courtesy Rock Island Auction.

Closeup of trigger guard. Courtesy Rock Island Auction.

"Magnificent Twenty" Olympian High Power Rifle in .284 Winchester. Courtesy Rock Island Auction.

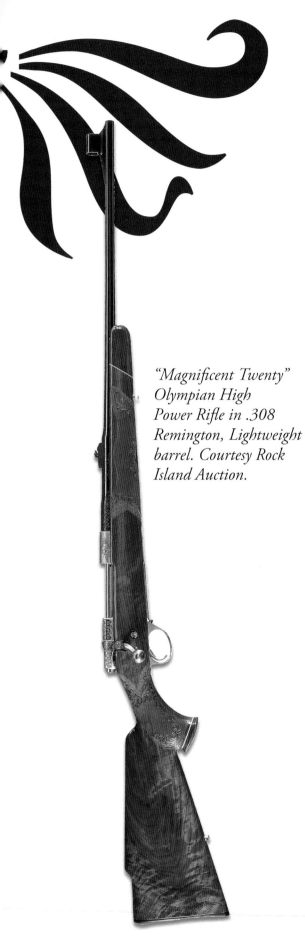

"Magnificent Twenty" Olympian High Power Rifle in .308 Remington, Lightweight barrel. Courtesy Rock Island Auction.

Closeup of floorplate. Courtesy Rock Island Auction.

Closeup of trigger guard. Courtesy Rock Island Auction.

Closeup of right receiver. Courtesy Rock Island Auction.

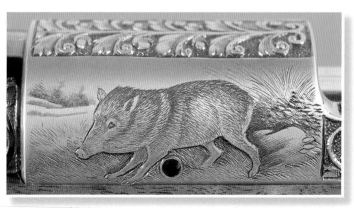

Closeup of left receiver. Courtesy Rock Island Auction.

Closeup of left receiver. Courtesy Rock Island Auction.

Closeup of right receiver. Courtesy Rock Island Auction.

"Magnificent Twenty" Olympian High Power Rifle in .270 Winchester, Standard barrel. Courtesy Rock Island Auction.

Closeup of floorplate. Courtesy Rock Island Auction.

Closeup of trigger guard. Courtesy Rock Island Auction.

"Magnificent Twenty" Olympian High Power Rifle in .30-06 Springfield, Standard barrel. Courtesy Rock Island Auction.

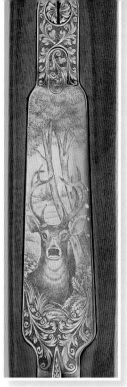

Closeup of floorplate. Courtesy Rock Island Auction.

Closeup of trigger guard. Courtesy Rock Island Auction.

Closeup of left receiver. Courtesy Rock Island Auction.

Closeup of right receiver. Courtesy Rock Island Auction.

Closeup of left receiver. Courtesy Rock Island Auction.

Closeup of right receiver. Courtesy Rock Island Auction.

Closeup of floorplate. Courtesy Rock Island Auction.

Closeup of trigger guard. Courtesy Rock Island Auction.

"Magnificent Twenty" Olympian High Power Rifle in .264 Winchester Magnum. Courtesy Rock Island Auction.

"Magnificent Twenty" Olympian High Power Rifle in 7mm Remington Magnum. Courtesy Rock Island Auction.

Closeup of floorplate. Courtesy Rock Island Auction.

Closeup of floorplate. Courtesy Rock Island Auction.

Left receiver detail. Courtesy Rock Island Auction.

Closeup of left receiver. Courtesy Rock Island Auction.

Closeup of left receiver. Courtesy Rock Island Auction.

Closeup of right receiver. Courtesy Rock Island Auction.

Closeup of floorplate. Courtesy Rock Island Auction.

Closeup of trigger guard. Courtesy Rock Island Auction.

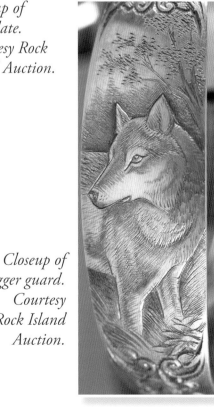

"Magnificent Twenty" Olympian High Power Rifle in .300 H&H Magnum. Courtesy Rock Island Auction.

*"Magnificent Twenty"
Olympian High Power
Rifle in .300 Winchester
Magnum. Courtesy
Rock Island Auction.*

*Closeup of floorplate.
Courtesy Rock
Island Auction.*

*Closeup of trigger
guard. Courtesy Rock
Island Auction.*

*Closeup of left receiver. Courtesy
Rock Island Auction.*

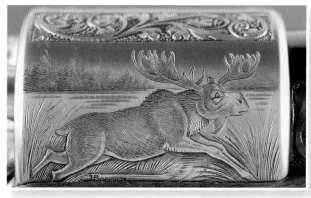

*Closeup of right receiver. Courtesy
Rock Island Auction.*

Closeup of left receiver. Courtesy Rock Island Auction.

Closeup of right receiver. Courtesy Rock Island Auction.

Closeup of floorplate. Courtesy Rock Island Auction.

Closeup of trigger guard. Courtesy Rock Island Auction.

"Magnificent Twenty" Olympian High Power Rifle in .308 Norma Magnum. Courtesy Rock Island Auction.

"Magnificent Twenty" Olympian High Power Rifle in .338 Winchester Magnum. Courtesy Rock Island Auction.

Closeup of floorplate. Courtesy Rock Island Auction.

Closeup of trigger guard. Courtesy Rock Island Auction.

Closeup of left receiver. Courtesy Rock Island Auction.

Closeup of right receiver. Courtesy Rock Island Auction.

Closeup left receiver. Courtesy Rock Island Auction.

Closeup of right receiver. Courtesy Rock Island Auction.

"Magnificent Twenty" Olympian High Power Rifle in .375 H&H Magnum. Courtesy Rock Island Auction.

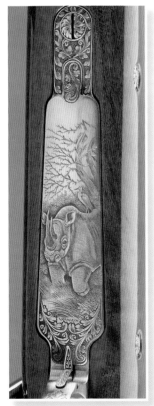

Closeup of floorplate. Courtesy Rock Island Auction.

Closeup of trigger guard. Courtesy Rock Island Auction.

"Magnificent Twenty" Olympian High Power Rifle in .458 Winchester Magnum. Courtesy Rock Island Auction.

Closeup of barrel engraving. Courtesy Rock Island Auction.

Closeup of left receiver. Courtesy Rock Island Auction.

Closeup of right receiver. Courtesy Rock Island Auction.

Closeup of floorplate. Courtesy Rock Island Auction.

Closeup of trigger guard. Courtesy Rock Island Auction.

Closeup right front barrel. Courtesy Rock Island Auction.

Closeup of muzzle. Courtesy Rock Island Auction.

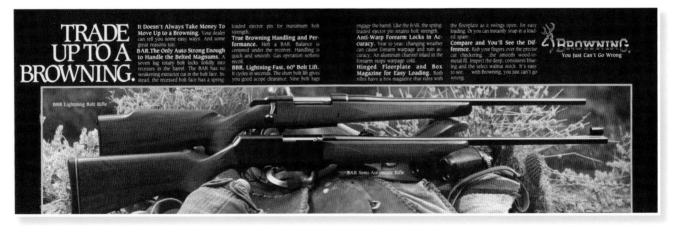

Period advertising for BBR and BAR Lightning. Courtesy Browning. Pricing no longer valid.

MODEL BBR

This is a bolt-action sporting rifle chambered for various popular calibers. It has a 24″ barrel with an adjustable trigger and fluted bolt. It features a detachable magazine under the floorplate and was furnished without sights. The finish is blued with a checkered, walnut, Monte Carlo stock. It was manufactured between 1978 and 1984 by Miroku.

EXC.	V.G.	GOOD	FAIR	POOR
525	400	350	275	200

BOSS™ SYSTEM

Introduced by Browning in 1994 this new accuracy system allows the shooter to fine-tune his Browning rifle to the particular load he is using. Consists of a tube on the end of the rifle muzzle that allows the shooter to select the best setting for the ammunition type; operates on the principle of adjustable harmonic vibration in the barrel. The system also reduces recoil.

BOSS stands for Ballistic Optimizing Shooting System. This option will add approximately $100 to $150 to the value of the particular Browning rifle on which it is fitted, depending upon the rarity of the caliber of the subject rifle. For some reason, the market has not readily accepted the BOSS system. I purchased one of the early BOSS equipped guns, in the Stainless Stalker variation, and was absolutely amazed at the accuracy that could be obtained. I am an avid hunter, but I am not an avid reloader. I would rather buy a case of the ammunition I want to shoot, loaded by the factory to factory specifications, and the BOSS system allows me to do this and then to get the accuracy out of that ammunition that I desire. I can pick the bullet and the load I want to shoot, and I can adjust the barrel harmonics to match the bullet, rather than the other way around. As a result, for me, this is just what the doctor ordered.

After this system had been on the market for a few years and I had observed that the BOSS system wasn't selling all that well, and because I have watched Browning for the past 30 years, I knew that sooner or later they would start to discontinue certain calibers that were not selling. I began accumulating a few of these rifles in the Stainless Stalker variation. And, I was right: after a period of time Browning started to discontinue certain calibers. As soon as they would discontinue a caliber, I would run out and buy one. In that way, I collected a complete set of these fantastically accurate rifles in all the calibers ever offered by Browning. Later on, a friend of mine became very interested in these rifles and started accumulating them. He, too, thought these rifles provided incredible accuracy and versatility of bullet selection. Almost immediately, he told me that some of the calibers were almost impossible to find. I began looking around too, and I was also amazed to find how difficult some of the calibers had become to find. I am wondering if there aren't quite a few individuals such as I who had started to accumulate these rifles in the various calibers. The calibers that I believe are hard-to-find are .22-250, .223, .243, .25-06, 7mm-08, .280 – with .223, .280, and .25-06 being the most difficult to find. This is the perfect illustration of how to find something that is fun to collect, is mechanically superior to anything else on the market, and provides a lot of pleasure to the collector.)

There's a split second in every sport that makes all the other seconds—the hours and days of preparation, the years of experience, worthwhile. The checkered flag in racing. Breaking the tape in running. The final bell in boxing.

In deer hunting that split second starts the instant the bullet leaves the muzzle. From here on the bullet is on its own. But flush up to the brink of that split second a lot of human skill is called on.

For the hunter a certain amount of steel in the nerves. A good shooting position. Steady hold, proper breathing, and above all, trigger squeeze.

And for the riflesmith, the rare skill to construct accuracy. The know-how to design perfect balance and a strong bolt lock-up. The cleverness to shorten the time between trigger let-off and primer cave-in . . . lock time. The experience to cut the rifling clean and true. And to marry the action to the stock. Then the rare knack—stoning the searing surfaces mirror smooth for a clean, crisp trigger pull . . . vital to accuracy.

That's how a Browning rifle is crafted. Because your skill depends first on our skill.

BROWNING
The difference in price is the smallest difference.

Split Second Skill

BLR lever action saddle or brush gun in .243W and .308W. **$174.50**

Browning Bolt Action, unsurpassed accuracy in 14 calibers. From **$276.50**

BAR, the soft recoil automatic in 4 regular and 3 magnum calibers. From **$229.50**
Browning Wide Angle Hunting Scopes, 5X fixed power and 2½X-8X variable power. From **$76.95**

Browning hunting knives, stainless steel blades and Brazilian rosewood handles. From **$24.95**

Browning ammunition, the constant, accurate rifle ammunition in all popular calibers.

Write for FREE 88-page full-color catalog.
Contains details on all Browning sporting arms, gun accessories, ammunition, hunting apparel & boots, archery equipment, plus practical shooting information.
Browning, Dept. 488, P.O. Box 500, Morgan, Utah 84050. In Canada: Browning Arms Co. of Canada, Ltd.   Copyright © Browning 1972

Period advertising for Browning big game rifles. Courtesy Browning. Pricing no longer valid.

A trio of A-Bolts, Browning's most successful bolt rifle series. Courtesy Browning.

A-BOLT SERIES

NOTE: All A-Bolt II Descriptions: "II" designation dropped from A-Bolt name in 2006.

A-BOLT HUNTER

This is the current bolt-action rifle manufactured by B.C. Miroku. It is chambered for various popular calibers and offered with a 22″, 24″, or 26″ barrel. It has either a short or long action, an adjustable trigger, and a detachable box magazine that is mounted under the floorplate. It is furnished without sights and is blued with a checkered walnut stock. It was introduced in 1985.

NIB	EXC.	V.G.	GOOD	FAIR	POOR
525	400	350	300	250	200

A-BOLT II HUNTER

Introduced in 1994 this new model features a newly designed anti-bind bolt and improved trigger system. In 2001 the .300 Winchester Short Magnum cartridge was offered for this model. In 2003 a left-hand model was introduced. A stainless version is also available; add 15 percent for stainless.

NIB	EXC.	V.G.	GOOD	FAIR	POOR
755	575	400	-	-	-

A-Bolt Hunter.
Courtesy Browning.

*A-Bolt II Hunter in .243
WSSM. Courtesy Browning.*

A-BOLT II HUNTER WSSM

Similar to the A-Bolt Hunter but chambered for the .223 WSM and .243 WSM cartridges. The stock design is also different from the A-Bolt Hunter with the addition of a longer pistol grip and thicker forearm. Weight is about 6.25 lbs. Introduced in 2003.

NIB	EXC.	V.G.	GOOD	FAIR	POOR
755	575	-	-	-	-

A-BOLT II MICRO HUNTER

Introduced in 1999, this model features a shorter length of pull and a shorter barrel length than the Hunter model. Offered in .22 Hornet, .22-250, 7mm-08, .308, .243, and .260 calibers. Weight is about 6 lbs. In 2003 the .270 WSM, 7mm WSM, and .300 WSM calibers were added for this model as well as a left-hand version.

NIB	EXC.	V.G.	GOOD	FAIR	POOR
625	525	400	325	-	-

NOTE: Add $30 for left-hand model and $30 for WSM calibers.

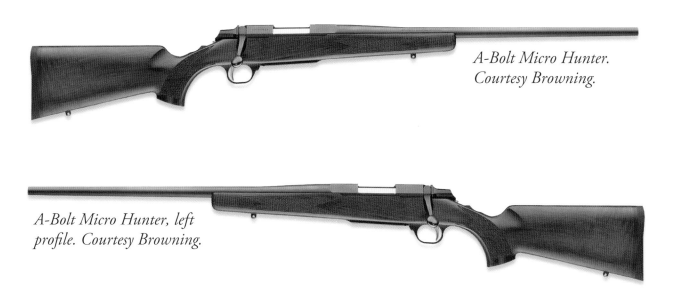

*A-Bolt Micro Hunter.
Courtesy Browning.*

*A-Bolt Micro Hunter, left
profile. Courtesy Browning.*

A-BOLT II CLASSIC HUNTER

This model features a Monte Carlo stock, low luster bluing, select walnut, and double bordered checkering. Offered in .30-06, .270, 7mm Rem. Mag., and .300 Win. Mag. No sights. Weight is about 7 lbs. Introduced in 1999.

NIB	EXC.	V.G.	GOOD	FAIR	POOR
625	500	335	300	-	-

A-Bolt safety, detail view. Courtesy Browning.

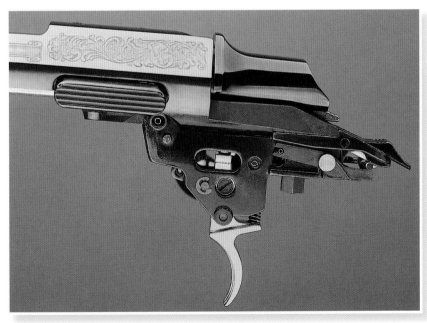

A-Bolt II trigger assembly. Courtesy Browning.

A-Bolt Classic Hunter. Courtesy Browning.

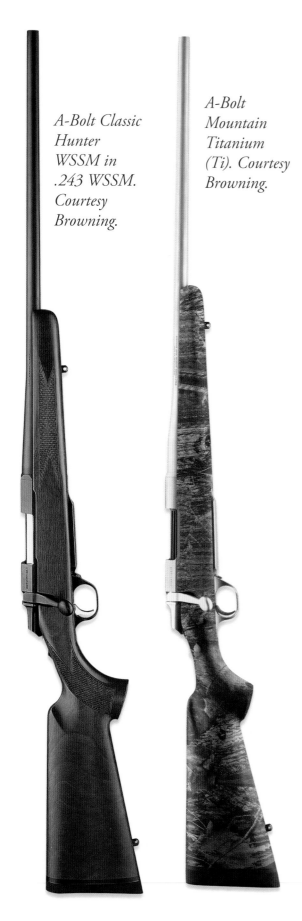

A-Bolt Classic Hunter WSSM in .243 WSSM. Courtesy Browning.

A-Bolt Mountain Titanium (Ti). Courtesy Browning.

A-BOLT CLASSIC HUNTER WSSM

As above but chambered for the .223 WSSM and .243 WSSM cartridges. Weight is about 6.25 lbs. Introduced in 2003.

NIB	EXC.	V.G.	GOOD	FAIR	POOR
760	600	-	-	-	-

A-BOLT MOUNTAIN TI-TANIUM (TI)

This model features a lightweight stainless steel 23″ barrel, titanium receiver, and lightweight fiberglass stock. Chambered for the .270 WSM, 7mm WSM, and the .300 WSM cartridges. Weight is about 5.5 lbs. Calibers: .243, 7mm-08, .308, .325 WSM. Introduced in 2004.

NIB	EXC.	V.G.	GOOD	FAIR	POOR
1620	1200	-	-	-	-

A-BOLT COMPOSITE STALKER

Supplied with composite stock and matte finish bluing. Offered in .338 Win. Mag., .300 Win. Mag., 7mm Rem. Mag., .25-06, .270, .280, .30-06. Introduced in 1988. In 2001 the .300 Winchester Short Magnum cartridge was offered for this model. Calibers: .223 WSSM, .243 WSSM, .25 WSSM, .223, .243, .7mm-08, .270 WSM, 7mm WSM, .300 WSM, .325 WSM, .25-06, .270, .280, .30-06, 7mm RM, .300 WM, .338 WM. Add 10 percent for BOSS or left-hand version.

NIB	EXC.	V.G.	GOOD	FAIR	POOR
450	350	300	250	200	150

A bolt from an A-Bolt in locked and unlocked (redlined) positions. Courtesy Browning.

A-BOLT II COMPOSITE STALKER

Same as above but with 1994 improvements.

NIB	EXC.	V.G.	GOOD	FAIR	POOR
670	525	400	300	250	200

NOTE: Add $80 for BOSS system.

A-BOLT COMPOS-ITE STALKER WSSM

As above but chambered for the .223 WSSM or the .243 WSSM cartridge. Weight is about 6 lbs. Introduced in 2003.

NIB	EXC.	V.G.	GOOD	FAIR	POOR
700	550	-	-	-	-

A-Bolt II Composite Stalker in .243 WSSM. Courtesy Browning.

A-Bolt II Composite Stalker with BOSS. Courtesy Browning.

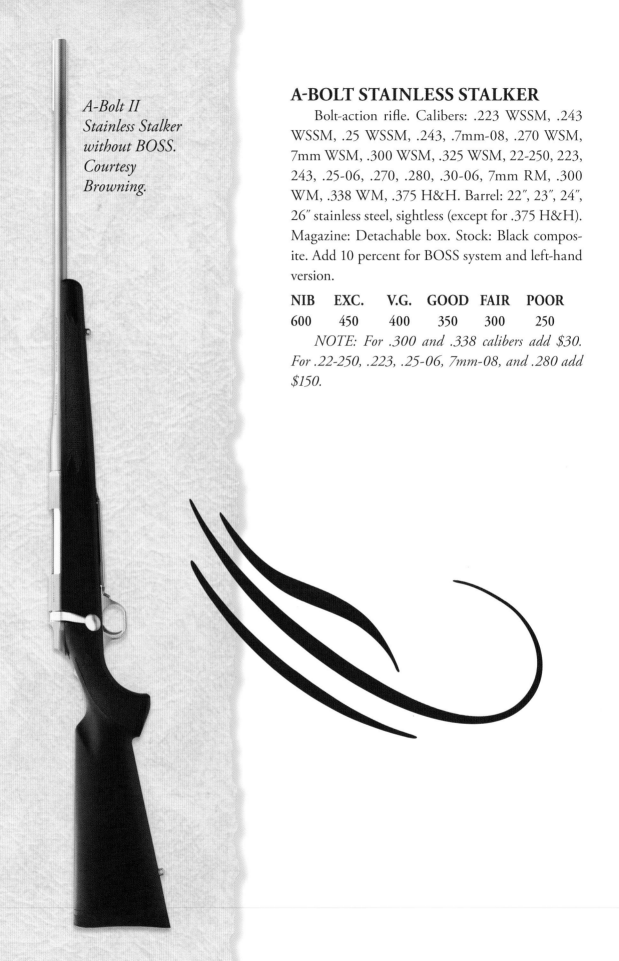

A-Bolt II Stainless Stalker without BOSS. Courtesy Browning.

A-BOLT STAINLESS STALKER

Bolt-action rifle. Calibers: .223 WSSM, .243 WSSM, .25 WSSM, .243, .7mm-08, .270 WSM, 7mm WSM, .300 WSM, .325 WSM, 22-250, 223, 243, .25-06, .270, .280, .30-06, 7mm RM, .300 WM, .338 WM, .375 H&H. Barrel: 22″, 23″, 24″, 26″ stainless steel, sightless (except for .375 H&H). Magazine: Detachable box. Stock: Black composite. Add 10 percent for BOSS system and left-hand version.

NIB	EXC.	V.G.	GOOD	FAIR	POOR
600	450	400	350	300	250

NOTE: For .300 and .338 calibers add $30. For .22-250, .223, .25-06, 7mm-08, and .280 add $150.

A-BOLT II COMPOSITE STAINLESS STALKER

Same as above but with 1994 improvements.

NIB	EXC.	V.G.	GOOD	FAIR	POOR
850	650	550	400	300	250

NOTE: For Magnum calibers add $30. For BOSS system add $110.

A-Bolt II Stainless Stalker with BOSS. Courtesy Browning.

A-Bolt II Stainless Stalker, left profile. Courtesy Browning.

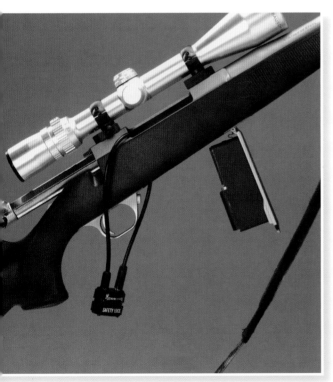

A-Bolt II Stainless Stalker with factory safety device. Courtesy Browning.

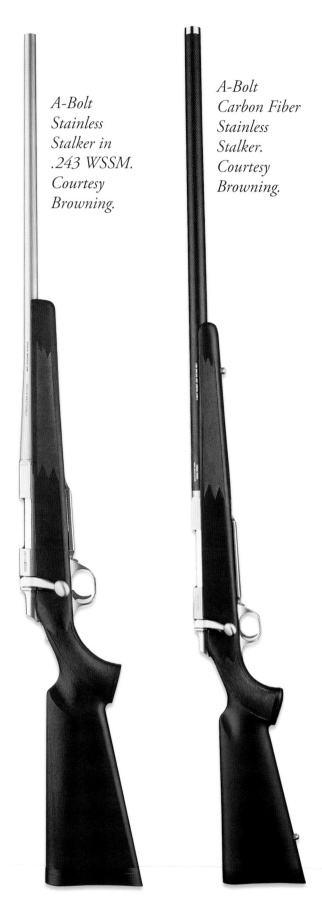

A-Bolt Stainless Stalker in .243 WSSM. Courtesy Browning.

A-Bolt Carbon Fiber Stainless Stalker. Courtesy Browning.

A-BOLT STAINLESS STALKER, WSSM

As above but chambered for the .223 WSSM and .243 WSSM calibers. Stock design is slightly different from standard A-Bolt Stalker. Weight is about 6 lbs. Introduced in 2003.

NIB	EXC.	V.G.	GOOD	FAIR	POOR
880	675	-	-	-	-

A-BOLT CARBON FIBER STAINLESS STALKER

This model features a Christensen Arms patent carbon barrel. Chambered for .22-250 or .300 Win. Mag. Weight is about 6.25 lbs. for short action and 7 lbs. for long action. Introduced in 2000. In 2001 the .300 Winchester Short Magnum cartridge was offered for this model.

NIB	EXC.	V.G.	GOOD	FAIR	POOR
1400	1200	1000	900	700	-

Cross section of a carbon fiber barrel. Courtesy Browning.

A-BOLT II HEAVY BARREL VARMINT

Introduced in 1994 this model features all of the A-Bolt II improvements in a heavy barrel varmint rifle. Offered in .22-250 and .223 Rem. calibers with 22″ barrel. Equipped with black laminated wood stock.

NIB	EXC.	V.G.	GOOD	FAIR	POOR
685	600	525	425	325	250

A-BOLT VARMINT STALKER

Introduced in 2002 this model features a new armor coated synthetic stock. Matte blue metal finish. Chambered for the .223 Rem. and .22-250 Rem. cartridges. Fitted with a 24″ barrel on the .223 and a 26″ barrel on the .22-250. Weight is about 8 lbs.

NIB	EXC.	V.G.	GOOD	FAIR	POOR
790	650	-	-	-	-

A-BOLT VARMINT STALKER WSSM

As above but chambered for the .223 WSSM and .243 WSSM cartridges. Weight is about 7.75 lbs. Introduced in 2003.

NIB	EXC.	V.G.	GOOD	FAIR	POOR
815	650	-	-	-	-

A-Bolt II Heavy Barrel Varmint. Courtesy Browning.

A-Bolt Varmint Stalker. Courtesy Browning.

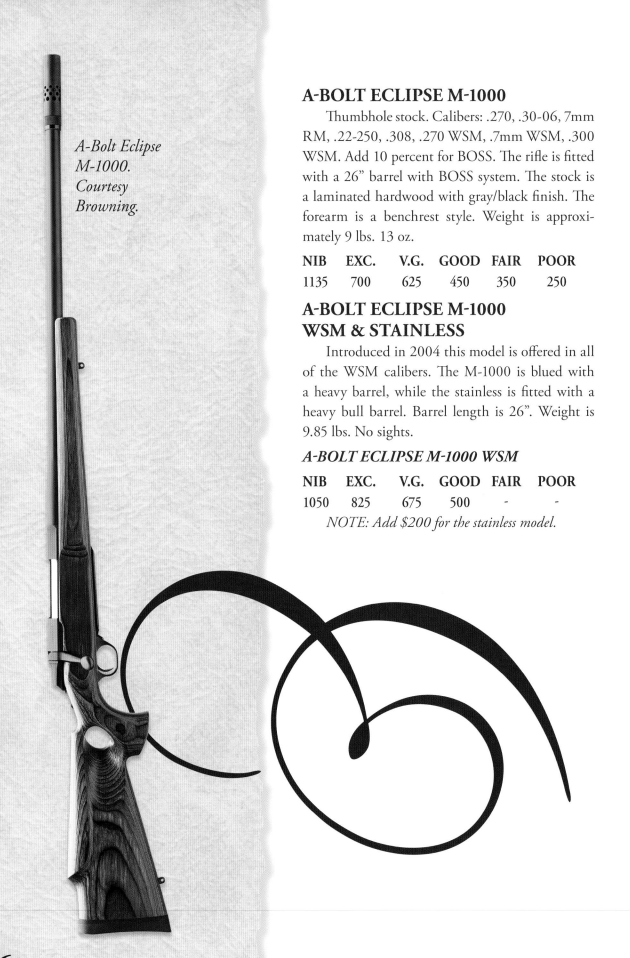

A-Bolt Eclipse M-1000. Courtesy Browning.

A-BOLT ECLIPSE M-1000

Thumbhole stock. Calibers: .270, .30-06, 7mm RM, .22-250, .308, .270 WSM, .7mm WSM, .300 WSM. Add 10 percent for BOSS. The rifle is fitted with a 26" barrel with BOSS system. The stock is a laminated hardwood with gray/black finish. The forearm is a benchrest style. Weight is approximately 9 lbs. 13 oz.

NIB	EXC.	V.G.	GOOD	FAIR	POOR
1135	700	625	450	350	250

A-BOLT ECLIPSE M-1000 WSM & STAINLESS

Introduced in 2004 this model is offered in all of the WSM calibers. The M-1000 is blued with a heavy barrel, while the stainless is fitted with a heavy bull barrel. Barrel length is 26". Weight is 9.85 lbs. No sights.

A-BOLT ECLIPSE M-1000 WSM

NIB	EXC.	V.G.	GOOD	FAIR	POOR
1050	825	675	500	-	-

NOTE: Add $200 for the stainless model.

A-BOLT ECLIPSE VARMINT

Introduced in 1996 this model features a thumbhole stock made from gray/black laminated hardwood. Offered in two version: a short-action, heavy-barrel version, and a long and short action with standard-weight barrel. Eclipse Varmint weighs about 9 lbs. and the standard-barrel version weighs about 7.5 lbs. depending on caliber.

Note: Add 10 percent for BOSS.

NIB	EXC.	V.G.	GOOD	FAIR	POOR
950	800	600	500	400	250

EURO-BOLT

First introduced in 1993 this A-Bolt variation features a rounded bolt shroud, Mannlicher-style bolt handle, continental-style stock with cheekpiece, schnabel-style forearm. The finish is a low-luster blue. Offered in .270, .30-06, and 7mm Rem. Mag. calibers. Weighs about 7 lbs.

NIB	EXC.	V.G.	GOOD	FAIR	POOR
550	500	450	350	250	150

A-BOLT II EURO BOLT

Same as above but with 1994 improvements.

NIB	EXC.	V.G.	GOOD	FAIR	POOR
550	500	450	350	250	150

A-BOLT MEDALLION MODEL

Calibers: .223 WSSM, .243 WSSM, .25 WSSM, .223, .243, .7mm-08, .270 WSM, 7mm WSM, .300 WSM, .325 WSM, .25-06, .270, .280, .30-06, 7mm RM, .300 WM, .338 WM. Add 10 percent for BOSS or left-hand version.

NIB	EXC.	V.G.	GOOD	FAIR	POOR
800	600	500	400	300	250

NOTE: Add $35 for .300 and .338 calibers.

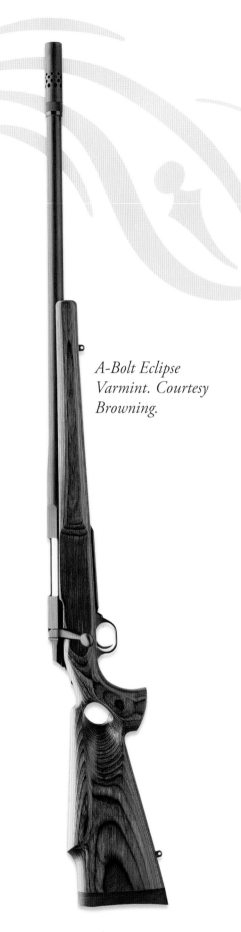

A-Bolt Eclipse Varmint. Courtesy Browning.

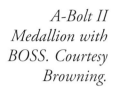

A-Bolt II Medallion with BOSS. Courtesy Browning.

A-BOLT II MEDALLION

Same as above but with 1994 improvements. In 2003 this model was offered in a left-hand version. Add 10 percent for BOSS.

NIB	EXC.	V.G.	GOOD	FAIR	POOR
765	600	450	350	300	250

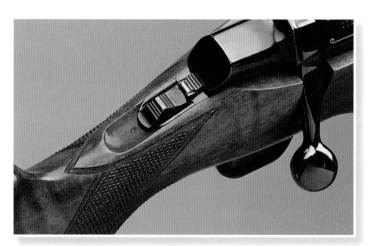

A-Bolt II Medallion tang safety, detail view. Courttesy Browning.

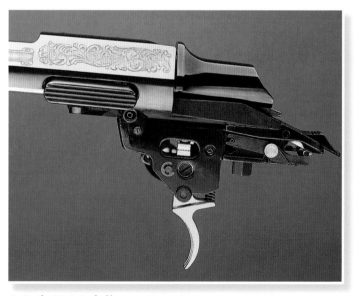

A-Bolt II Medallion trigger group, detail view. Courtesy Browning.

A-BOLT II MEDALLION WSSM

As above but chambered for the .223 WSSM or the .243 WSSM cartridge. Weight is about 6.25 lbs. Introduced in 2003.

NIB	EXC.	V.G.	GOOD	FAIR	POOR
795	650	525	-	-	-

A-BOLT GOLD MEDALLION

This version has a fancy grade walnut stock with a cheekpiece. It is lightly engraved and has gold-inlaid letters. It was introduced in 1988.

NIB	EXC.	V.G.	GOOD	FAIR	POOR
690	625	550	450	400	325

A-BOLT II GOLD MEDALLION

Same as above but with 1994 improvements.

NIB	EXC.	V.G.	GOOD	FAIR	POOR
690	625	550	450	400	325

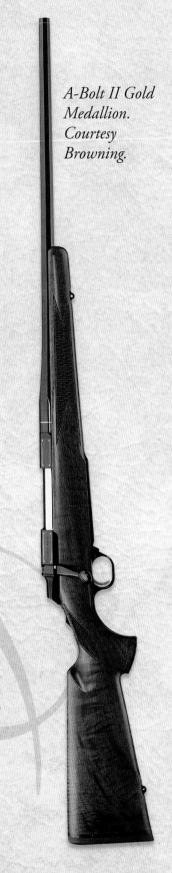

A-Bolt II Gold Medallion. Courtesy Browning.

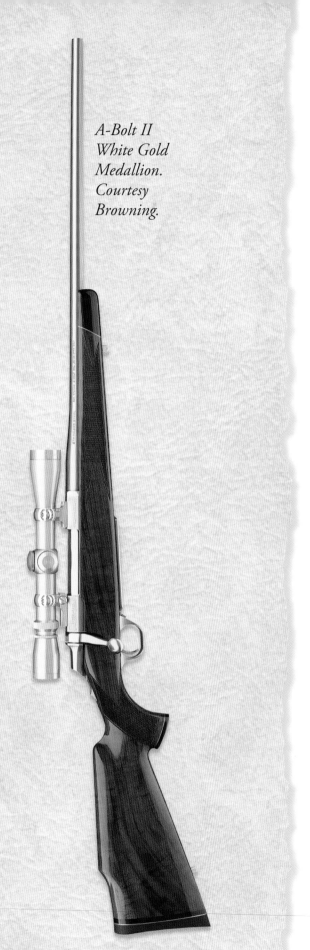

A-Bolt II White Gold Medallion. Courtesy Browning.

A-BOLT II WHITE GOLD MEDALLION

This model features a gold engraved stainless receiver and barrel, select walnut stock with brass spacers and rosewood caps. European-style cheekpiece. No sights. Introduced in 1999. Offered in .30-06, .270, 7mm Rem. Mag., and .300 Win. Mag. Weight is about 7 lbs. 8 ozs.

NIB	EXC.	V.G.	GOOD	FAIR	POOR
1100	800	650	500	300	200

A-BOLT WHITE GOLD MEDALLION, RMEF

Introduced in 2003 this model is a special edition for the Rocky Mountain Elk Foundation. Chambered for the 7mm Rem. Mag. and fitted with a 26″ barrel. Both action and barrel are stainless steel. Special RMEF logo on the grip cap. Weight is about 7.75 lbs. Add 5 percent for WSM calibers.

NIB	EXC.	V.G.	GOOD	FAIR	POOR
1200	950	-	-	-	-

A-BOLT CUSTOM TROPHY

Introduced in 1998 this model features gold highlights on the barrel and receiver, select walnut stock, with shadowline cheekpiece and skeleton pistol grip. The barrel is octagonal. Chambered for .270 and .30-06 with 24″ barrel and 7mm Rem. Mag. and .300 Win. Mag. with 26″ barrel. Weight varies from 7 lbs. 11 oz. to 7 lbs. 3 oz. depending on caliber.

NIB	EXC.	V.G.	GOOD	FAIR	POOR
1300	1000	800	-	-	-

NRA A-BOLT WILDLIFE CONSERVATION COLLECTION

Commemorates NRA's Environment Conservation and Hunting Outreach Program. Caliber: .243 Win. Barrel: 22″ blued sightless. Stock: Satin-finish walnut with NRA Heritage logo lasered on buttstock.

NIB	EXC.	V.G.	GOOD	FAIR	POOR
800	650	-	-	-	-

A-BOLT BIG HORN SHEEP ISSUE

This is a high-grade version of the A-Bolt chambered for the .270 cartridge. It features a deluxe skipline checkered walnut stock with a heavily engraved receiver and floorplate. It has two gold sheep inlays. There were 600 manufactured in 1986 and 1987.

NIB	EXC.	V.G.	GOOD	FAIR	POOR
1050	800	600	450	400	325

MICRO MEDALLION MODEL

This is a smaller version of the A-Bolt Hunter chambered for popular cartridges that fit a short action. It has a 20″ barrel without sights and a three-round magazine. It was introduced in 1988.

NIB	EXC.	V.G.	GOOD	FAIR	POOR
525	475	400	350	300	250

A-BOLT II MICRO MEDALLION

Same as above but with 1994 improvements.

NIB	EXC.	V.G.	GOOD	FAIR	POOR
525	475	400	350	300	250

A-BOLT PRONGHORN ISSUE

This is a deluxe version of the A-Bolt chambered for the .243 cartridge. It is heavily engraved and gold inlaid and features a presentation-grade walnut stock with skipline checkering and pearl-inlaid borders. There were 500 manufactured in 1987.

NOTE: These rifles are becoming more collectible, and that this time, I would give them a Collectibility Factor of #2.)

NIB	EXC.	V.G.	GOOD	FAIR	POOR
1300	1000	750	500	400	325

A-BOLT SPECIAL HUNTER RMEF

Similar to A-Bolt Hunter but honors Rocky Mountain Elk Foundation. Chambered in .325 WSM. Satin finish. Introduced 2007.

NIB	EXC	V.G.	GOOD	FAIR	POOR
800	600	-	-	-	-

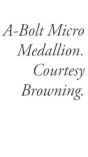

A-Bolt Micro Medallion. Courtesy Browning.

Browning Acera. Courtesy Browning.

A-BOLT WHITE GOLD RMEF

Similar to A-Bolt Special Hunter RMEF but with stainless barrel and receiver and glossy finish. Introduced 2007.

NIB	EXC	V.G.	GOOD	FAIR	POOR
1100	925	-	-	-	-

ACERA STRAIGHT PULL RIFLE

Introduced in 1999, this model features a straight action bolt system. It is chambered for the .30-06 with a 22″ barrel and the .300 Win. Mag. with 24″ barrel. Open sights are optional as is the BOSS system. Detachable box magazine. Checkered walnut stock. Prices listed are for .30-06 with no sights and no BOSS.

NIB	EXC	V.G.	GOOD	FAIR	POOR
1000	775	600	475	-	-

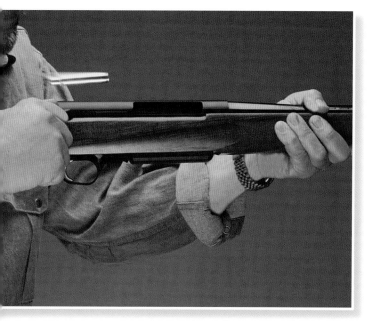

Cycling the action of an Acera. Courtesy Browning.

NOTE: Add $100 for .300 Win. Mag with no sights and no BOSS.

GRADE I A-BOLT .22

This is a bolt-action sporting rifle chambered for the .22 LR or .22 Magnum cartridges. It features a 60-degree bolt and a 22″ barrel available either with or without open sights. It has a five-round, detachable magazine and an the adjustable trigger. The finish is blued with a checkered walnut stock. It was introduced in 1986.

NIB	EXC.	V.G.	GOOD	FAIR	POOR
340	275	210	150	125	100

NOTE: .22 Magnum add 15 percent.

GOLD MEDALLION A-BOLT .22

This deluxe, high-grade version features a select stock with rosewood pistol-grip cap and forend tip. It is lightly engraved and has gold-filled letters. It was introduced in 1988.

NOTE: This weapon is becoming more collectible. At this time, I would award this model of browning a Collectibility Factor of #2.)

NIB	EXC.	V.G.	GOOD	FAIR	POOR
450	400	350	300	225	175

What's so NEW about the revolutionary BROWNING T-BOLT?

It's a lightning fast, straight-pull bolt action design, that combines fine accuracy with unmatched ease of operation!

The Browning T-BOLT is an entirely new concept in .22 caliber bolt action design.

Unique in mechanical function and handling qualities, the T-Bolt features nail-driving accuracy, a new experience in operating convenience, lifetime quality and handsome lines.

Unlike conventional bolt actions, the T-Bolt operates with a simple, quick, straight rearward and forward movement to complete the ejecting, cocking and loading cycle. Its new cross-bolt locking system is infallibly safe and so precisely orients the breech bolt for each firing that accuracy is unerringly consistent.

Clip fed, it shoots 6 long rifle cartridges, yet conveniently converts to a beginner-safe single shot with a handy adapter provided. As a single shot it also accepts .22 shorts and longs.

Available in two models. The *T-1* for the younger shooter or situations where rougher treatment might be expected. Weight 5 pounds 8 ounces. Barrel 22 inches. Walnut stock with a new, easily refurbished, oil finish, $54.50. The *T-2* is a more handsome version featuring select walnut, finely checkered and hand lacquered to a brilliantly polished finish. Weight 6 lbs. Barrel 24 inches. $74.50.

Other specifications: positive double extractors — side ejection — recessed muzzle — convenient manual safety which locks both bolt and trigger — fully adjustable receiver peep sight fits grooved receiver and is quickly interchangeable with telescope — clean, crisp trigger with no creep and maximum pull of 4 pounds. Both models will be available with left hand bolt by August.

T-2

Available through all Authorized Browning Dealers in the United States and Canada.

BROWNING
Finest in Sporting Arms

Write for FREE CATALOG

Write for catalog giving complete data on Browning guns and accessories **plus** special chapters containing valuable shooting information.
Browning Arms Co., Dept. 847, P.O. Box 450, St. Louis, Mo. 63166

Period advertising for T-Bolt. Courtesy Browning. Pricing no longer valid.

Two of the Finest .22 Rifles by a Long Shot!

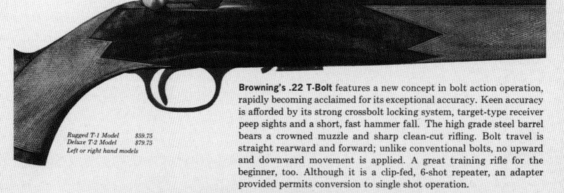

Rugged T-1 Model $59.75
Deluxe T-2 Model $79.75
Left or right hand models

Browning's .22 T-Bolt features a new concept in bolt action operation, rapidly becoming acclaimed for its exceptional accuracy. Keen accuracy is afforded by its strong crossbolt locking system, target-type receiver peep sights and a short, fast hammer fall. The high grade steel barrel bears a crowned muzzle and sharp clean-cut rifling. Bolt travel is straight rearward and forward; unlike conventional bolts, no upward and downward movement is applied. A great training rifle for the beginner, too. Although it is a clip-fed, 6-shot repeater, an adapter provided permits conversion to single shot operation.

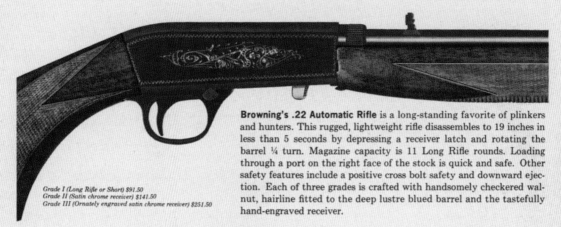

Grade I (Long Rifle or Short) $91.50
Grade II (Satin chrome receiver) $141.50
Grade III (Ornately engraved satin chrome receiver) $251.50

Browning's .22 Automatic Rifle is a long-standing favorite of plinkers and hunters. This rugged, lightweight rifle disassembles to 19 inches in less than 5 seconds by depressing a receiver latch and rotating the barrel ¼ turn. Magazine capacity is 11 Long Rifle rounds. Loading through a port on the right face of the stock is quick and safe. Other safety features include a positive cross bolt safety and downward ejection. Each of three grades is crafted with handsomely checkered walnut, hairline fitted to the deep lustre blued barrel and the tastefully hand-engraved receiver.

BROWNING
Finest in Sporting Arms

Write for FREE CATALOG	*Detailed information on all Browning guns and accessories, plus special illustrated section of practical shooting information.*

Browning Arms Co., Dept. 175, P.O. Box 500, Morgan, Utah 84050
In Canada—Browning Arms Company of Canada, Ltd.

Copyright© Browning Arms Company 1969   FFL #43-1156

Period advertising for T-Bolt T-2 and .22 Automatic. Courtesy Browning. Pricing no longer valid.

Scarce left-hand T-Bolt.
Courtesy Rock Island Auction.

T-BOLT MODEL T-1

This is a unique, straight-pull, bolt-action sporting rifle chambered for .22 caliber cartridges. It has a 22″ barrel with open sights and a five-round magazine. The finish is blued with a plain walnut stock. It was manufactured between 1965 and 1974 by FN. Many T-Bolt rifles were affected by salt wood. Proceed with caution. Reintroduced 2006 with rotary magazine.

NIB	EXC.	V.G.	GOOD	FAIR	POOR
550	395	350	150	100	

T-BOLT MODEL T-2

This version is similar to the T-1 with a select, checkered walnut stock and a 24″ barrel.

NOTE: I view this gun to be a potential sleeper, and as such, would give it a Collectibility Factor of #2.

NIB	EXC.	V.G.	GOOD	FAIR	POOR
600	450	375	250	200	

T-BOLT (2006)

Reintroduction of classic and collectible T-bolt straight-pull .22 rifle but with rotary magazine. Introduced 2006.

NIB	EXC	V.G.	GOOD	FAIR	POOR
600	475	-	-	-	-

T-BOLT TARGET/VARMINT

Similar to reintroduced T-Bolt but with floating heavy target barrel and other accurizing refinements. Introduced 2007.

NIB	EXC	V.G.	GOOD	FAIR	POOR
650	-	-	-	-	-

MODEL 52 LIMITED EDITION

This model is based on the design of the original Winchester Model 52 .22 caliber bolt-action rifle. Fitted with a 24″ barrel and walnut stock with oil finish. Metal pistol-grip cap and rosewood forend tip. Drilled and tapped for scope. Five-round detachable magazine. Blued finish. Weight is about 7 lbs. From 1991 to 1992, 5,000 Model 52s were built.

NOTE: These particular rifles are becoming more collectible. At this time, I would give this model of Browning a Collectibility Factor of #3.

NIB	EXC.	V.G.	GOOD	FAIR	POOR
700	435	325	225	-	-

TROMBONE MODEL

This is a slide-action rifle chambered for the .22 LR cartridge. It has a 24″ barrel with open sights and a takedown design. It has a tubular magazine and a hammerless action. There were approximately 150,000 manufactured by FN between 1922 and 1974. Approximately 3,200 were imported by Browning in the 1960s. They are marked with either the FN barrel address or the Browning Arms address. The Browning-marked guns are worth approximately 20 percent additional. The values given are for FN-marked guns.

NOTE: I believe this model is a real sleeper. I would recommend the accumulation of this weapon when priced reasonably, especially in NIB condition, and would give this model of Browning a Collectibility Factor of #1.

NIB	EXC.	V.G.	GOOD	FAIR	POOR
900	750	600	450	375	275

Grade II BPR-22 in .22 Magnum. Courtesy Rock Island Auction.

BPR-22

This is a short-stroke, slide action rifle chambered for the .22 LR and Magnum cartridges. It has a 20.25″ barrel with open sights and an 11-round, tubular magazine. The finish is blued with a checkered walnut stock. It was manufactured between 1977 and 1982.

EXC.	V.G.	GOOD	FAIR	POOR
400	300	215	125	95

NOTE: Add $100 for models chambered for .22 Magnum.

BPR-22 GRADE II

This version is engraved with a silvered receiver and has a select walnut stock.

EXC.	V.G.	GOOD	FAIR	POOR
500	375	275	225	150

NOTE: Add 20 percent for models chambered for .22 Magnum.

A RUGGED COMPACT FOR MEN OF ACTION

BROWNING
.22 Automatic

Bulk has been stripped away to achieve a slender compact, unencumbered by big gun size and weight. Yet every ounce of its bare 4¾ pounds is the finest steel and select walnut to assure toughness and reliability. Perfectly balanced and proportioned, it handles effortlessly but shoulders with the solidity and feel of a large bore.

Men like the precision machining and hand-fitting in evidence throughout and the genuine quality of hand-checkering and hand-engraving. Handsome? Yes sir, but just as much at home scaling a cliff or fording a river as in prize position in the gun rack. It will take the roughest treatment, then spit out rim fires faultlessly as fast as you can squeeze the trigger.

P.S. This is one rifle in your collection Junior can shoot like an expert too.

Available in three grades in .22 Short or Long Rifle from $82⁵⁰

Remember, it goes anywhere... takes down in just 3 seconds to fit suitcase or bedroll.

NOW — A companion-Browning 4-Power Scope to match. Only 9" long, 7 oz., with fine precision optics. Integral or separate mount models. From $29⁹⁵.

Lifetime Luggage Type Gun Cases to fit rifle and scope. From $23⁵⁰.

Prices subject to change without notice. Slightly higher in Canada.

Your **BROWNING** Dealer

Write for complete catalog describing all Browning Guns

Browning Arms Co., Dept. 632, St. Louis, Missouri 63103
—IN CANADA: Browning of Canada, Dept. 632, P. O. Box 991, Montreal 9, P.Q.

Period advertising for Browning .22 Automatic Rifle. Courtesy Browning. Pricing no longer valid.

John Browning with an early version of what would be known as the Browning .22 Caliber Semi-Auto Rifle or the SA-22. Courtesy Browning.

.22 CALIBER SEMI-AUTO

This is a blowback-operated, semi-automatic rifle chambered for the .22 Long Rifle or Short cartridge. It features a take-down barrel design with a 19.25″ barrel and an 11-round, tubular magazine inside the buttstock. It is loaded through a hole in the middle of the buttstock. The finish is blued with a checkered walnut stock and beavertail forearm. This lightweight, compact firearm was manufactured by FN between 1956 and 1974 for U.S. marked guns. There are a number of versions that differ in the amount of ornamentation and the quality of materials and workmanship.

NOTE: All of these .22 caliber semi-automatic Belgian-made Browning rifles are undergoing accumulation, and are very good merchandise, especially the high-grade guns. I recommend the purchase of these weapons when reasonably priced, especially those weapons which are NIB. I would give all of these weapons a Collectibility Factor of #1.

GRADE I

NIB	EXC.	V.G.	GOOD	FAIR	POOR
650	475	400	325	220	125

NOTE: For Grade I .22 Short add 20 percent. For early Wheel Sight manufactured 1956-1960, add 10 percent.

Belgian Browning Grade I .22 Semi-Automatic Rifle with box. Courtesy Rock Island Auction.

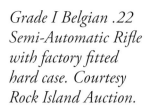

Grade I Belgian .22 Semi-Automatic Rifle with factory fitted hard case. Courtesy Rock Island Auction.

Cased Belgian Browning Grade II .22 Semi-Automatic Rifle. Courtesy Rock Island Auction.

GRADE II-FRENCH GRAYED RECEIVER

NIB	EXC.	V.G.	GOOD	FAIR	POOR
1500	1200	900	700	300	200

NOTE: For Grade II .22 Short add 300 percent.

Closeup of receiver engraving. Courtesy Rock Island Auction.

Marechals, anyone? Grade III Belgian .22 Semi-Automatic Rifle, factory engraved by A. Marechal. Courtesy Rock Island Auction.

Grade III Belgian .22 Semi-Automatic Rifle, factory engraved by F. Marechal. Courtesy Rock Island Auction.

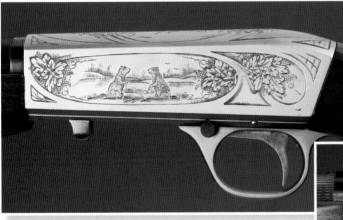

The work of two different Marechals. Compare this Grade III receiver work with by A. Marechal ...

GRADE III

Grayed receiver.

NIB	EXC.	V.G.	GOOD	FAIR	POOR
3000	2400	1900	1200	700	400

NOTE: For premium engravers add 40 percent to Grade III. For Grade III .22 Short add 800 percent. For unsigned Grade III, 1956-1960, deduct 20 percent.

... to that of F. Marechal on this Grade III receiver. Courtesy Rock Island Auction.

*Model SA-22.
Courtesy Browning.*

.22 SEMI-AUTO/MODEL SA-22 (MIROKU MFG.)

This model is similar to the Belgian FN except that it was produced as of 1976 by B.C. Miroku in Japan. Collector interest is not as high as for the FN version.

GRADE I

NIB	EXC.	V.G.	GOOD	FAIR	POOR
325	275	200	175	125	100

SA-22 taken down. Courtesy Browning.

SA-22 Grade II receiver detail.
Courtesy Browning.

GRADE II

NIB	EXC.	V.G.	GOOD	FAIR	POOR
475	400	325	275	225	150

GRADE III

NIB	EXC.	V.G.	GOOD	FAIR	POOR
750	675	500	400	300	200

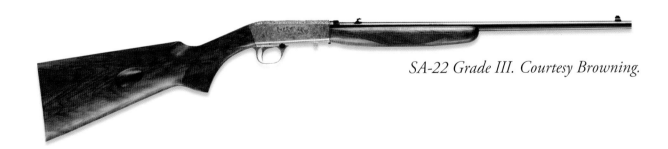

SA-22 Grade III. Courtesy Browning.

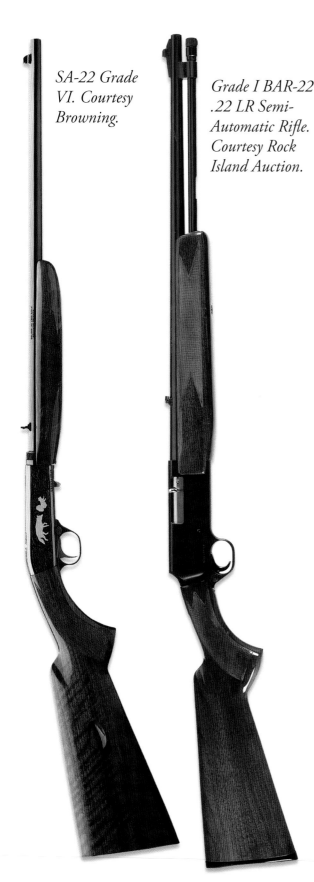

SA-22 Grade VI. Courtesy Browning.

Grade I BAR-22 .22 LR Semi-Automatic Rifle. Courtesy Rock Island Auction.

GRADE VI

Gold plated animals.

NIB	EXC.	V.G.	GOOD	FAIR	POOR
725	650	500	425	325	275

Receiver detail. Courtesy Browning.

BAR-22

This is a blowback-operated, semi-automatic rifle chambered for the .22 LR cartridge. It has a 20.25″ barrel with open sights and a 15-round, tubular magazine. It features a polished, lightweight alloy receiver. It was finished in blue with a checkered walnut stock. It is manufactured between 1977 and 1985 by Miroku.

EXC.	V.G.	GOOD	FAIR	POOR
475	325	190	160	125

BAR-22 GRADE II

This is a deluxe version with an engraved, silver-finished receiver. It has a select walnut stock. It was discontinued in 1985.

EXC.	V.G.	GOOD	FAIR	POOR
495	375	200	150	120

BUCK MARK RIFLE

This model uses the same design as the Buck Mark pistol. It is fitted with an 18″ barrel (heavy on the target model) and thumbhole pistol grip. Magazine capacity is 10 rounds. Integral rail scope mount. Introduced in 2001. Weight is about 4.25 lbs. for Sporter and 5.5 lbs. for the Target model.

SPORTER MODEL

NIB	EXC.	V.G.	GOOD	FAIR	POOR
570	450	325	250	-	-

TARGET MODEL

NIB	EXC.	V.G.	GOOD	FAIR	POOR
570	450	325	250	-	-

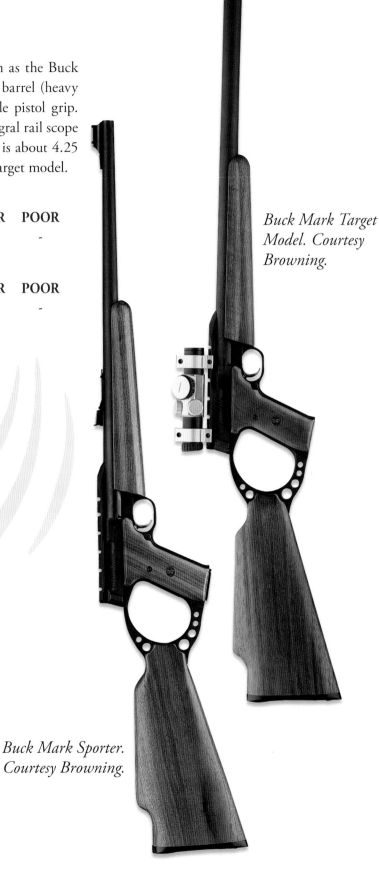

Buck Mark Target Model. Courtesy Browning.

Buck Mark Sporter. Courtesy Browning.

Buck Mark Field Target Gray Laminate Rifle, composite barrel. Courtesy Browning.

Buck Mark Field Target Gray Laminate Rifle, regular steel barrel. Courtesy Browning.

BUCK MARK FIELD TARGET GRAY LAMINATE RIFLE

Introduced in 2003 this model features either a lightweight carbon composite barrel or a regular steel barrel, gray laminate stock and integral scope rail. Chambered for the .22 cartridge and fitted with an 18″ barrel. Weight: 5.5 lbs. for standard; 3.75 lbs. for Lite model.

NIB	EXC.	V.G.	GOOD	FAIR	POOR
650	525	400	-	-	-

PATENT 1900 HIGH POWER RIFLE

NOTE: These weapons are very rare, and should be purchased in accumulated when reasonably priced. They deserve a Collectibility Factor of #1.

This is a semi-automatic sporting rifle chambered for the .35 Remington cartridge. It is similar in configuration to the Remington Model 8 rifle. It has a 22″ barrel with open sights and a five-round, integral magazine. The finish is blued with a plain walnut stock. There were approximately 5,000 manufactured between 1910 and 1931. A deluxe model with a ribbed barrel and checkered walnut stock was also available and would be worth approximately 15 percent additional.

EXC.	V.G.	GOOD	FAIR	POOR
675	600	500	375	300

you asked for it...
and you'll like it!

Grade I $164.50, Grade II $174.50

introducing the new high-power
Browning Automatic Rifle

You'll like the graceful, contemporary style hand engraving that distinguishes the Grade II.

You'll like the speed and convenience of its new "Trap-Door" attaching-detaching magazine.

You'll like its select French walnut stock, skillfully checkered and hand rubbed to a brilliant finish.

For years Browning users have asked us for a Semi-Automatic Sporter made the Browning way. Now ... here it is.

There are a lot of years of know-how represented in this new gas operated centerfire. In fact, John M. Browning invented the first successful one 77 years ago ... and automatic rifles, pistols, and shotguns have been synonymous with the name Browning ever since.

We believe you will like everything about this great new Browning rifle. Here are just a few of its special features:

Strong, one-piece receiver — Precision machined from a solid bar of the finest steel. Not a single exposed pin, screw, or hole in its entire surface, except those for scope mounting.

Much less recoil — Its fast, smooth, gas-operated action incorporates a specially buffered mechanism which so greatly softens recoil you won't believe you're shooting a high-power rifle.

Safe rotating bolt — Seven sturdy lugs provide strong, positive locking directly in the barrel just rearward of the chamber. You have bolt action strength and safety.

Four calibers — Chambered for four popular, extremely versatile, high-velocity calibers. First out, the .30/06, later the .270, .308 and .243.

Five capacity — Loading is unbelievably fast and convenient. The magazine swings downward and may either be detached or loaded in its handy attached position. Or you can snap in a spare in but a second.

Superb accuracy — An automatic rifle designed to give bolt action accuracy and reliability. There is the strong precision locking of *bolt to barrel* and the kind of crisp, clean trigger pull that gets the most out of a rifle.

Lightweight — Only 7 lbs. 6 oz. in the .30/06 and so nicely balanced you'll think it weighs much less.

Handsome and dependable — Made the way you expect a Browning to be made. Both its fine steel and select French walnut exhibit, in every detail, the personal attention and care of our skilled craftsmen.

see it at your Browning Dealer, U.S. or Canada

Write for FREE
64 page Catalog

BROWNING

You may have our fully illustrated, 64 page catalog without charge by writing: Browning Arms Co., Dept 953, P.O. Box 450, St. Louis, Mo. 63166

Copyright Browning Arms Company 1967

Introductory advertising for BAR, 1967. Courtesy Browning. Pricing no longer valid.

Grade I BAR 7mm Magnum with box. Courtesy Rock Island Auction.

BAR HIGH POWER RIFLE

This is a gas-operated, semi-automatic sporting rifle chambered for various popular calibers from the .243 up to the .338 Magnum cartridges. It was offered with either a 22″ or 24″ barrel with folding leaf sight until 1980. The finish is blued with a checkered walnut stock. The various grades offered differed in the amount of ornamentation and the quality of materials and workmanship utilized. Earlier models were manufactured in Belgium by FN; these guns would be worth approximately 15 percent additional over guns assembled in Portugal from parts manufactured by FN. The early .338 Magnum model is rarely encountered and would be worth approximately 25 percent additional. The Grade I values furnished are for Portuguese-assembled guns from 1977 until the introduction of the BAR Mark II in 1993. This model was introduced in 1967 and discontinued in 1977.

NOTE: These weapons are undergoing accumulation, and should be considered to be collectible. I give this model a Collectibility Factor of #1.

GRADE I

NIB	EXC.	V.G.	GOOD	FAIR	POOR
600	425	350	275	225	100

GRADE I MAGNUM

NIB	EXC.	V.G.	GOOD	FAIR	POOR
650	450	375	300	250	125

GRADE II DELUXE
1967-1974.

NIB	EXC.	V.G.	GOOD	FAIR	POOR
750	700	625	475	300	175

GRADE II DELUXE MAGNUM
1968-1974.

NIB	EXC.	V.G.	GOOD	FAIR	POOR
775	700	650	500	325	200

GRADE III

Discontinued 1984.

NOTE: *The Grade III was offered in two variations. The first was hand-engraved and produced in Belgium. The second was photo-etched and built in Belgium and assembled in Portugal. This second variation will not be as valuable as the first.*

NIB	EXC.	V.G.	GOOD	FAIR	POOR
1250	1000	700	550	375	250

Belgian Grade III hand-engraved BAR with box. Courtesy Rock Island Auction.

Right receiver detail. Courtesy Rock Island Auction.

Left receiver detail. Courtesy Rock Island Auction.

Photo-engraved Grade III BAR in 7mm Remington Magnum with box. Courtesy Rock Island Auction.

GRADE III MAGNUM

Discontinued 1984.

NIB	EXC.	V.G.	GOOD	FAIR	POOR
1400	1200	850	600	400	275

NOTE: Prices indicated above are for 1970 through 1974 production. For guns assembled in Portugal deduct 30 percent. .338 Win. Mag caliber is rare in Grade III; add 75 percent premium.

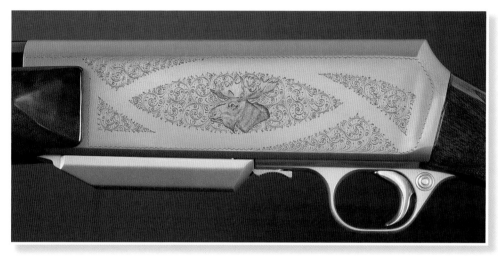

Left receiver detail. Courtesy Rock Island Auction.

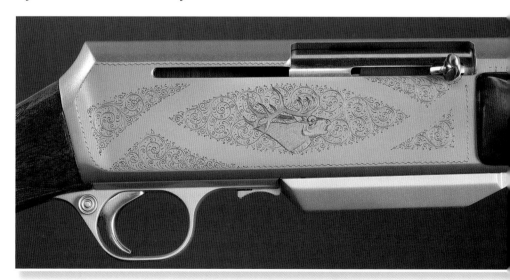

Right receiver detail. Courtesy Rock Island Auction.

GRADE IV

Gamescene engraved. This grade was hand-engraved from 1970 through 1976 then was etched thereafter. Grade IV rifles were discontinued in 1984.

NIB	EXC.	V.G.	GOOD	FAIR	POOR
1700	1300	950	800	650	400

NOTE: Pre-1977 rifles add 40 percent. Premium engraving add 10 percent.

GRADE IV MAGNUM

NIB	EXC.	V.G.	GOOD	FAIR	POOR
1800	1300	975	850	650	425

GRADE V

Gold Inlaid. 1971-1974.

NIB	EXC.	V.G.	GOOD	FAIR	POOR
3000	2700	2300	1800	1200	600

Factory-engraved Grade IV BAR in 7mm Remington Magnum with box. Courtesy Rock Island Auction.

Left receiver detail. Courtesy Rock Island Auction.

Right receiver detail. Courtesy Rock Island Auction.

L. Ernst factory-engraved Grade V BAR in .338 Winchester Magnum. Courtesy Rock Island Auction.

GRADE V MAGNUM

1971-1974.

NIB	EXC.	V.G.	GOOD	FAIR	POOR
3500	3200	2500	1850	1250	600

NOTE: For special order variations on Grade V rifles add up to 100 percent.

Left receiver detail. Courtesy Rock Island Auction.

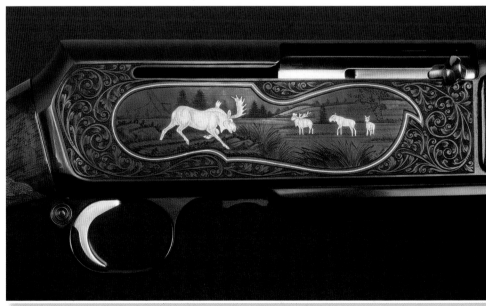

Right receiver detail. Courtesy Rock Island Auction.

Period advertising for Browning BAR. Courtesy Browning. Pricing no longer valid.

BAR Mark II Safari in .30-06 Springfield with iron sights. Courtesy Browning.

BAR Mark II Safari with BOSS. Courtesy Browning.

NORTH AMERICAN DEER RIFLE ISSUE BAR

This is a deluxe version of the BAR chambered for .30-06 only. It features a photo etched, silver-finished receiver and a deluxe, checkered walnut stock. There were 600 produced and furnished with a walnut case and accessories. This model was discontinued in 1983. As with all commemoratives, it must be NIB to command premium values.

NOTE: This model is very collectible and is undergoing accumulation. I recommend its purchase, but only in NIB condition. This model has a Collectibility Factor of #1.

NIB	EXC.	V.G.	GOOD	FAIR	POOR
2700	1800	1400	1000	450	250

BAR MARK II SAFARI RIFLE

This is an improved version of the BAR first introduced by Browning in 1967. Announced in 1993, this Mark II design uses a new gas system with a newly designed buffering system to improve reliability. This model also has a new bolt release lever, a new easily removable trigger assembly. Available with or without sights. Walnut stock with full pistol grip and recoil pad on magnum gun are standard. The receiver is blued with scroll engraving. Rifles with magnum calibers have a 24″ barrel while standard calibers are fitted with a 22″ barrel. Available in .243, .308, .270, .30-06, 7mm Rem. Mag., .300 Win. Mag., .338 Win. Mag. Standard calibers weigh about 7 lbs. 9 oz. and magnum calibers weigh about 8 lbs. 6 oz.

NIB	EXC.	V.G.	GOOD	FAIR	POOR
525	450	400	350	250	150

NOTE: Add 30 percent for .270 Wby. Mag., which was made for one year only.

BAR MARK II LIGHTWEIGHT

This version of the Mark II was introduced in 1997 and features a lightweight alloy receiver and shortened 20″ barrel. It is offered in .30-06, .270 Win., .308 Win., and .243 Win. calibers. It is not offered with the BOSS system. Weight is approximately 7 lbs. 2 oz.

NIB	EXC.	V.G.	GOOD	FAIR	POOR
700	550	400	300	-	-

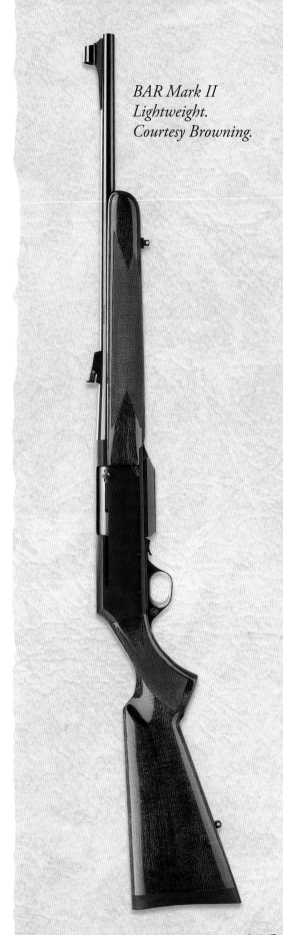

BAR Mark II Lightweight. Courtesy Browning.

BAR Composite Stalker, short action.

BAR Composite Stalker, long action. Courtesy Browning.

BAR LIGHTWEIGHT OR COMPOSITE STALKER

Introduced in 2001 this model features a composite buttstock and forend with removable magazine. It is offered in short action (.243 and .308) with sights, and in standard action (.270 and .30-06) with no sights. In magnum calibers (7mm, .330 Win., and .338) it is offered with no sights and with the BOSS system as well.

NIB	EXC.	V.G.	GOOD	FAIR	POOR
800	625	550	425	-	-

NOTE: For magnum calibers add $75, and for BOSS add $140.

High Grade BAR. Courtesy Browning.

BAR HIGH GRADE MODELS

These models will feature high grade walnut stock with highly polished blued barrel. Receivers will be grayed with game animals: mule deer and whitetail on the standard calibers (.270 and .30-06) and elk and moose on magnum calibers (7mm Magnum and .300 Win. Mag).

NOTE: This model of Browning rifle is particularly collectible, and I recommend its accumulation in NIB condition.

NIB	EXC.	V.G.	GOOD	FAIR	POOR
1825	1450	-	-	-	-

Right receiver detail. Courtesy Browning.

BAR Mark II D Grade. Courtesy Browning.

Left receiver detail. Courtesy Browning.

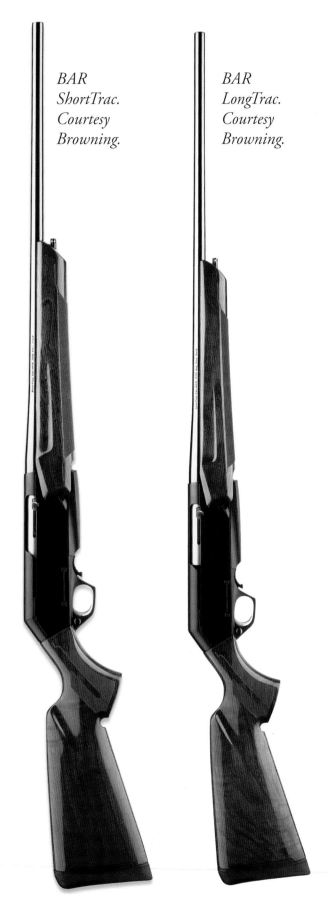

BAR ShortTrac. Courtesy Browning.

BAR LongTrac. Courtesy Browning.

BAR SHORTTRAC

Introduced in 2004 this model features the ability to chamber magnum cartridges. Offered in .270 WSM, 7mm WSM, and .300 WSM as well as .243 and .308. Fitted with a 23″ barrel in magnum calibers and 22″ barrel in non-magnum. Receiver is alloy steel. Redesigned stock adjustable length of pull. Weight is about 7.25 lbs. for magnum calibers and 6 75 lbs. for others. Add 10 percent for camo finish.

NIB	EXC.	V.G.	GOOD	FAIR	POOR
885	675	550	-	-	-

BAR LONGTRAC

Similar to the above model but made for long action calibers such as .270, .30-06, 7mm Rem. Mag, and .300 Win. Mag. Barrel length is 22″ for the .270 and .30-06 and 24″ for the other two calibers. Weight is about 7 lbs. for .270 and .30-06 and 7.5 lbs. for 7mm and .300. Introduced in 2004. Add 10 percent for camo finish.

NIB	EXC.	V.G.	GOOD	FAIR	POOR
885	675	550	-	-	-

NOTE: Add $75 for magnum calibers.

BAR SHORTTRAC STALKER

Similar to BAR ShortTrac but with matte blue barrel and composite stock. Introduced 2006.

NIB	EXC.	V.G.	GOOD	FAIR	POOR
850	670	-	-	-	-

BAR LONGTRAC STALKER

Long-action version of the BAR ShortTrac Stalker.

NIB	EXC.	V.G.	GOOD	FAIR	POOR
850	670	-	-	-	-

BAR SHORTTRAC LEFT-HAND

Similar to BAR ShortTrac but in left hand. Introduced 2007.

NIB	EXC	V.G.	GOOD	FAIR	POOR
950	-	-	-	-	-

BAR LongTrac Stalker. Courtesy Browning.

BAR ShortTrac Left Hand. Courtesy Browning.

BAR ShortTrac Stalker. Courtesy Browning.

BAR LongTrac Left Hand. Courtesy Browning.

BPR. Courtesy Browning.

BAR LONGTRAC LEFT-HAND

Similar to BAR Long-Trac but in left hand. Introduced 2007.

NIB	EXC	V.G.	GOOD	FAIR	POOR
950	-	-	-	-	-

MODEL BPR

The initials "BPR" stand for Browning Pump Rifle. It was introduced in 1997 and is similar in appearance to the BAR. Offered in both long action and short action calibers with barrel lengths from 22″ to 24″. Short action calibers include .243 Win., and .308 Win. Long action calibers include .270 Win., .30-06, 7mm Rem. Mag., and .300 Win. Mag. Weight is about 7 lbs. 3 oz. Discontinued 2003.

NIB	EXC.	V.G.	GOOD	FAIR	POOR
800	675	525	400	-	-

Top to bottom: Originals of the Winchester Models 86, 87, 92, 94, 95—invented by John M. Browning.

Promontory Point, Utah. Site of the completion of the first transcontinental railroad 100 years ago.

History repeats itself

BL-22 by Browning

The great levers of the past, invented by John M. Browning in Utah Territory between 1882 and 1895, are the forerunners of the new Browning BL-22. Capturing their classic lines and reminiscent of the ruggedness and adventure of the Old West, Browning's BL-22 features:

● **Short Lever Throw** — lever travels through an arc of only 33 degrees and carries the trigger with it, preventing finger pinch between lever and trigger on upward swing.

● **Safety** — an inertia firing pin, a half-cock hammer position, and a special disconnect system that prevents firing until the lever and breech are fully closed, leave nothing to chance.

● **Special Bullet Feed Track** — designed to feed Long Rifle, Long, and Short ammunition *in any combination* from its

tubular magazine. Capacity is 16 Long Rifles, 18 Longs, and 23 Shorts.

● **Forged and milled, solid steel receiver** — grooved to accept scope mounts. Precision open sights (folding leaf rear — bead front).

● **Accuracy** — a crisp trigger with no creep and a recessed muzzle add a final touch to this rifle's fine accuracy.

● **Fine Polished Walnut** — carefully fitted to specially processed, richly blued steels. All parts are machine finished and hand fitted.

● **Weight** — 5 pounds; **Length** — 36¾ inches; **Barrel** — 20 inches.

Examine the BL-22 in two grades at your Browning Dealer—U.S. or Canada. We are confident your judgment of quality will class this another "golden spike" milestone in Browning's lever action heritage.

Grade I, (illustrated) rugged and handsome — $67.50

Grade II, hand engraved and hand checkered — $84.50

BROWNING
Finest in Sporting Arms

| Write for FREE CATALOG | *Detailed information on all Browning guns and accessories plus special illustrated section of practical shooting information.* |

Browning Arms Company, Dept. 184, P.O. Box 500, Morgan, Utah 84050

In Canada—Browning Arms Company of Canada, Ltd.

Copyright© Browning Arms Company 1969

Period advertising for the BL-22. Courtesy Browning. Pricing no longer valid.

BL-22 Grade II.
Courtesy Browning.

BL-22 GRADE I

This is a lever-action rifle chambered for the .22 rimfire cartridge. It has an 18″ barrel with a tubular magazine and a folding leaf rear sight. It is a Western-style firearm that features an exposed hammer. The finish is blued with a walnut stock. It was introduced in 1970 by Miroku.

NIB	EXC.	V.G.	GOOD	FAIR	POOR
350	250	200	150	125	100

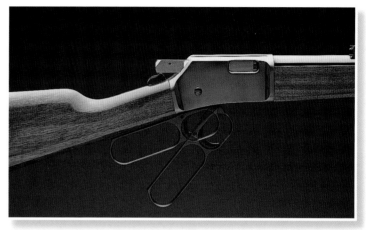

Short lever throw of BL-22. Courtesy Browning.

BL-22 GRADE II

This version is similar with a scroll-engraved receiver and a checkered, select walnut stock.

NIB	EXC.	V.G.	GOOD	FAIR	POOR
350	250	225	175	150	125

BL-22 FIELD SERIES GRADE I

Introduced in 2005 this rifle features a satin nickel receiver. Walnut stock with no checkering. Blued trigger. Magazine capacity is 16 rounds. Weight is about 5 lbs.

NIB	EXC.	V.G.	GOOD	FAIR	POOR
495	375	-	-	-	-

BL-17 FIELD SERIES GRADE I

As above but chambered for the .17 Mach 2 cartridge. Weight is about 5.2 lbs.

NIB	EXC.	V.G.	GOOD	FAIR	POOR
515	400	-	-	-	-

BL-22 FIELD SERIES GRADE II

As above but with checkered stock, gold trigger, and scroll engraving on the receiver.

NIB	EXC.	V.G.	GOOD	FAIR	POOR
555	425	-	-	-	-

BL-17 FIELD SERIES GRADE II

As above but chambered for the .17 Mach 2 cartridge.

NIB	EXC.	V.G.	GOOD	FAIR	POOR
545	425	-	-	-	-

BL-22 FIELD GRADE II OCTAGON

Introduced in 2005 this model has a 24" octagon barrel chambered for the .22 Long and Long Rifle cartridges. Receiver is silver nitride with scroll engraving and gold trigger. Magazine capacity is 16 rounds. Gold bead front sight. Weight is about 5.25 lbs.

NOTE: All of these octagon barreled models, although currently being produced, I predict are going to become collectible. At this time, I would give them a Collectibility Factor of #3.)

NIB	EXC.	V.G.	GOOD	FAIR	POOR
725	550	-	-	-	-

BL-17 FIELD GRADE II OCTAGON

As above but chambered for the .17 Mach 2 cartridge. Magazine capacity is 16 rounds. Weight is about 5.35 lbs. Introduced in 2005.

NIB	EXC.	V.G.	GOOD	FAIR	POOR
750	575	-	-	-	-

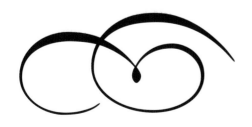

BL-17 Field Series Grade I. Courtesy Browning.

BL_22 Field Grade Octagon. Courtesy Browning.

BL-22 Classic. Courtesy Browning.

BL-22 CLASSIC

This model was introduced in 1999 and has the same features as the BL-22 Grade I.

NIB	EXC.	V.G.	GOOD	FAIR	POOR
425	375	275	200	175	-

BL-22 NRA GRADE 1

Similar to BL-22 Grade 1 but with NRA logo lasered on buttstock.

NIB	EXC.	V.G.	GOOD	FAIR	POOR
425	375	275	200	175	-

BL-22 GRAY LAMINATE STAINLESS

Similar to BL-22 but with gray laminated stock, nickeled receiver and stainless steel barrel. Introduced 2006.

NIB	EXC.	V.G.	GOOD	FAIR	POOR
675	575	-	-	-	-

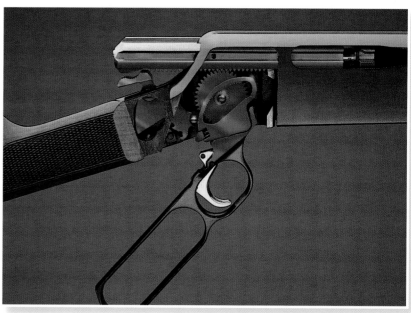

Cutaway view, BLR rack and pinion gear. Courtesy Browning.

*Left view of BLR "President" Commemorative Rifle;
Canadian commemorative issue inscribed with signature of
president of Browning Canada. Courtesy Rock Island Auction.*

*Right view of BLR "President."
Courtesy Rock Island Auction.*

MODEL 81 BLR

This is a contemporarily designed, lever-action sporting rifle chambered for various popular calibers from .22-250 up to .358 Winchester. In effect, it is a bolt-action rifle in which the bolt is operated with a lever. It has a 20″ barrel with adjustable sights. It features a 4-round, detachable magazine and a rotary locking bolt. The finish is blued with a checkered walnut stock and recoil pad. It was introduced in 1971 and manufactured that year in Belgium. In 1972 manufacture moved to Miroku in Japan. In 2003 a straight-grip stock was introduced and WSM calibers were added from .270 to .300. Weight is about 6.5 lbs. Originals had a steel receiver; these are increasingly collectible.

Closeup of inscribed signature, BLR "President." Courtesy Rock Island Auction.

NIB	EXC.	V.G.	GOOD	FAIR	POOR
850	6750	450	300	200	150

*BLR 81 with straight grip stock,
chambered in .308 Winchester.
Courtesy Rock Island Auction.*

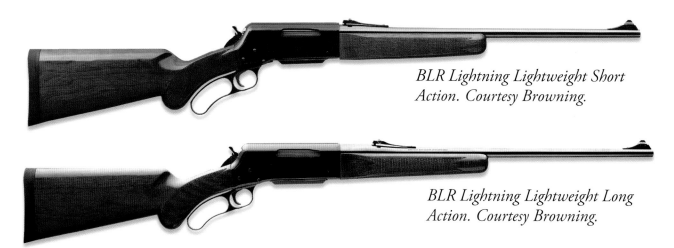

BLR Lightning Lightweight Short Action. Courtesy Browning.

BLR Lightning Lightweight Long Action. Courtesy Browning.

MODEL BLR LIGHTNING (LIGHTWEIGHT)

Introduced in 1996 this model features a lightweight aluminum receiver with walnut stock and checkered pistol grip. Offered in both long and short action calibers from .223 Rem. to 7mm Rem. Mag. Barrel length is 20" for short action calibers and 22" to 24" for long action calibers. Open sights are standard. Weight is about 7 lbs. depending on caliber. In 2003 a straight-grip stock was introduced.

NIB	EXC.	V.G.	GOOD	FAIR	POOR
740	600	450	300	200	150

MODEL BLR LIGHTWEIGHT '81

This model features a straight grip checkered walnut stock. Fitted with a 20" or 22" barrel depending on caliber. Magazine capacity is four or five rounds depending on caliber. Alloy receiver. Chambered for calibers .22-25-, .243, 7mm-08, .308, .358, .450 Marlin, .270 WSM, .300 WSM, and .325 WSM. Also offered in a long action version chambered for the .270, .30-06, 7mm Rem. mag, and the .300 Win. mag. Weight is from 6.5 lbs. to 7.75 lbs. depending on caliber.

NIB	EXC.	V.G.	GOOD	FAIR	POOR
730	550	425	325	-	-

NOTE: Add 20 percent for long action rifles and $70 for WSM calibers.

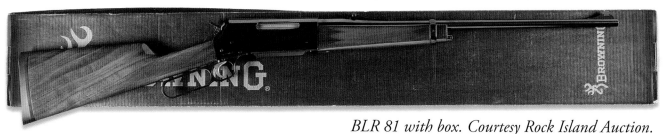

BLR 81 with box. Courtesy Rock Island Auction.

Scarce BLR Lightweight 81 in .223 Remington. Courtesy Rock Island Auction.

BLR LIGHTWEIGHT TAKEDOWN

Similar to BLR Lightweight but with take-down feature. Introduced 2007. Available with either straight grip or curved pistol grip.

NIB	EXC	V.G.	GOOD	FAIR	POOR
775	-	-	-	-	-

BLR Lightweight Takedown, pistol grip. Courtesy Browning.

BLR Lightweight Takedown, straight grip. Courtesy Browning.

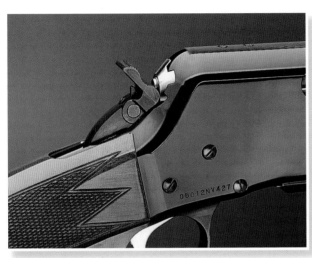

Closeup of BLR hammer safety. Courtesy Browning.

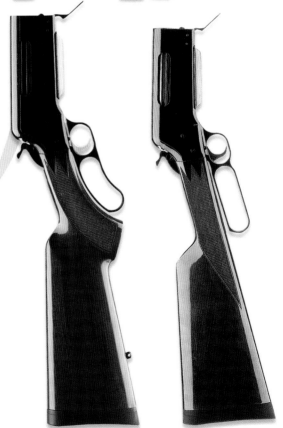

Two good reasons for becoming a Browning Man

NEW Browning 78
$247.50 Suggested retail

BAR from $229.50 Suggested retail

If you're the kind of guy who thinks sitting on top of the world glassing for a monarch buck, beats glassing the chorus at the opera hands down.

And you're the kind of guy who thinks a gun ought to be more than a gun...a trusty sidekick you'll be proud to carry through a lifetime of tough hunts.

You're a Browning Man.

Who's probably eager to shoulder the new Browning 78 Single Shot Rifle. Because it's fashioned after the old Model 85 Winchester High Wall, invented by John M. Browning and highly prized for its accuracy.

The "78" is gifted with a tight falling block action, a husky 26 inch barrel with clean-cut rifling and a forearm that attaches to a special receiver bracket—not the barrel. Add its recessed muzzle and grooved trigger with adjustable pull and one shot is all you should need.

Choose your "78" with a classic octagon barrel or round sporter barrel in .22/250, 6mm, .25/06 or .30/06.

Special scope mounts included with B-78

Want more than one shot? Then uncase a Browning Automatic Rifle on your next hunt.

What's unusual about the BAR? It's recoil is unusually soft and cushioned. Bolt lock-up is unusually strong. Accuracy is superb. A unique "trap-door" attaching-detaching

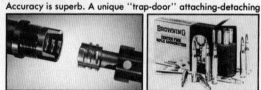

BAR rotary bolt head with 7 sturdy locking lugs

Squeeze every ounce of accuracy out of your rifle with Browning Ammo

magazine makes loading fast and convenient. (Carry a spare, loaded magazine in your pocket.) You can choose magnum calibers as well as standard calibers (7mmR Mag., .300W Mag., .338W Mag., .30/06, .270W, .308W or .243W)

Five beautiful BAR grades are available. From the rugged Grade I to a gold inlaid Grade V model.

Make this the year you become a Browning man.

FREE 104 page Browning catalog...on Guns, Ammo, Boots, Clothing, Archery, Knives, Backpacking Gear plus shooting tips. Write Browning, Dept. 513, Morgan, Utah 84050. In Canada: Browning Arms Co. of Canada, Ltd.

Copyright © Browning 1973.

Is this the year you trade up to a Browning? **BROWNING**

Period advertising for Browning Model 78 and BAR. Courtesy Browning. Pricing no longer valid.

Browning Model 53 in .32-20 Winchester. Courtesy Rock Island Auctionj.

MODEL B-78

Introduced in 1973 this single-shot, lever-action falling block was offered in several calibers from .22-250 to .45-70. Barrel lengths 24″ or 26″ in either round or octagonal shape with no sights except .45-70. Checkered walnut stock. First built in 1973 and discontinued in 1983. Add 15 percent for .45-70 caliber.

NOTE: These are very nice rifles, but in my opinion, they are not undergoing much accumulation.)

NIB	EXC.	V.G.	GOOD	FAIR	POOR
800	650	550	300	200	100

MODEL 53

Offered in 1990 this model is a reproduction of the Winchester Model 53 and like the original is chambered for the .32-20 cartridge. This is a limited edition offering confined to 5,000 rifles. It features hand-cut checkering, high-grade walnut stock with full pistol grip and semi-beavertail forend. Pistol grip is fitted with a metal grip cap. Barrel length is 22″ and the finish is blue.

NOTE: I believe these rifles are undergoing accumulation and should be purchased in the NIB condition only. I give this model a Collectibility Factor of #3.)

NIB	EXC.	V.G.	GOOD	FAIR	POOR
725	625	550	450	325	200

MODEL 65 GRADE I

This was a limited-edition, lever-action rifle chambered for the .218 Bee cartridge. It has a tapered, round, 24″ barrel with open sights. It was patterned after the Winchester Model 65 rifle. It has a seven-round, tubular magazine. The finish is blued with a plain walnut stock and metal buttplate. There were 3,500 manufactured in 1989.

NOTE: There is no question in my mind that this model is undergoing accumulation, and should be given a Collectibility Factor of #2. It should be purchased only in the NIB condition.

NIB	EXC.	V.G.	GOOD	FAIR	POOR
950	-	-	-	-	-

MODEL 65 HIGH GRADE

This is a deluxe version that features a silver-finished, scroll engraved receiver with gold animal inlays and a gold-plated trigger. It features a select, checkered walnut stock. There were 1,500 manufactured in 1989.

NIB	EXC.	V.G.	GOOD	FAIR	POOR
1150	-	-	-	-	-

*Model 71 in
.348 Winchester.
Courtesy Rock
Island Auction.*

MODEL 71 GRADE I

This was a reproduction of the Winchester Model 71, chambered for the .348 cartridge. It has either a 20″ or 24″ barrel with open sights and a four-round, tubular magazine. The finish is blued with a plain walnut stock. There were 4,000 20″ carbines and 3,000 24″ rifles manufactured in 1986 and 1987.

NOTE: I believe these weapons are becoming collectible but at this time are not undergoing a strong accumulation. The higher grade guns in NIB condition will become more collectible as time goes on.

EXC.	V.G.	GOOD	FAIR	POOR
950	750	-	-	-

MODEL 71 HIGH GRADE

This version was similar to the Grade I except that it had a scroll engraved, grayed receiver with a gold-plated trigger and gold inlays. There were 3,000 rifles and 3,000 carbines manufactured in 1986 and 1987.

EXC.	V.G.	GOOD	FAIR	POOR
1400	950	-	-	-

NOTE: For Belgian-manufactured version add 20 percent.

JONATHAN BROWNING CENTENNIAL MOUNTAIN RIFLE

This is a limited edition blackpowder rifle chambered for the .50 ball. It is fitted with a 30" octagon barrel with single set trigger. Figured walnut stock and engraved lock plate. Cased with powder horn. Limited to 1,000 rifles in 1978.

NOTE: These are very nice rifles, but in my opinion, are not undergoing strong accumulation and will take some time before they become highly collectible.

NIB	EXC.	V.G.	GOOD	FAIR	POOR
1250	750	-	-	-	-

Closeup of serial number pattern on centennial Jonathan Browning Mountain Rifle. Courtesy Rock Island Auction.

Closup of script on powder horn included with centennial Jonathan Browning Mountain Rifle.

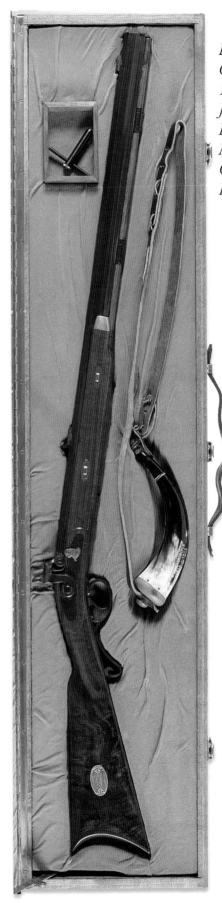

Browning Centennial 1878-1978 Jonathan Browning Mountain Rifle. Courtesy Rock Island Auction.

Model 1885 in .45-70 Government. Courtesy Rock Island Auction.

Model 1885 Low Wall. Courtesy Browning.

JONATHAN BROWNING MOUNTAIN RIFLE

Same as above but without fancy wood, case, or engraving. Also chambered for .45 or .54 caliber.

NIB	EXC.	V.G.	GOOD	FAIR	POOR
800	500	400	300	-	-

MODEL 1878

Based on John M. Browning's first patent ,this single-shot rifle was the only firearm manufactured by the Browning brothers. Offered in several calibers only a few hundred probably exist with the Ogden, Utah, barrel address. This design was later sold to Winchester and sold under that company's name as the Model 1885 High Wall. The much later Model 78 is loosely based on this very first Browning rifle.

NOTE: These are very rare rifles, and they certainly should be purchased whenever found, especially in better condition. They would certainly rate a Collectibility Factor of #1.

EXC.	V.G.	GOOD	FAIR	POOR
7500	5500	3500	2000	1000

MODEL 1885 HIGH WALL

This is a single-shot rifle with falling block action and octagonal free-floating barrel similar to the Model 78. Introduced in 1985. The stock is a high grade walnut with straight grip and recoil pad. Furnished with 28″ barrel it is offered in these calibers: .223, .22-250, .270, .30-06, 7mm Rem. Mag., .45-70 Gov't. Weighs about 8 lbs. 12 oz.

NOTE: As with other reproduction rifles, this particular model will become more collectible as time goes on. At this time, I would not recommend the accumulation of this rifle in terms of its being a good investment.

NIB	EXC.	V.G.	GOOD	FAIR	POOR
875	650	550	300	200	100

MODEL 1885 LOW WALL

Introduced in 1995 this rifle is similar to the above but in a more accurate version of the original Low Wall. The thin octagon barrel is 24″ in length. Trigger pull is adjustable. The walnut stock is fitted with a pistol grip and schnabel forearm. Offered in .22 Hornet, .223 Rem. and the .243 Win. calibers. Weight is about 6.4 lbs.

NIB	EXC.	V.G.	GOOD	FAIR	POOR
950	600	500	400	300	150

MODEL 1885 LOW WALL TRADITIONAL HUNTER

Introduced in 1998 this model is similar to the Low Wall but with a half-octagon half-round 24" barrel chambered for the .357 Magnum, .44 Magnum, and .45 Colt cartridges. Case colored receiver and crescent butt with tang sight are also features. Weight is approximately 6.5 lbs.

NIB	EXC.	V.G.	GOOD	FAIR	POOR
900	750	650	525	-	-

MODEL 1885 BPCR (BLACK POWDER CARTRIDGE RIFLE)

This model was introduced in 1996 for BPCR metallic silhouette shoots. Chambered for the .45-70 or .40-60 caliber the receiver is case colored and the 28" round barrel is fitted with vernier sight with level. The walnut stock has a checkered pistol grip and is fitted with a tang sight. Weight is approximately 11 lbs.

NIB	EXC.	V.G.	GOOD	FAIR	POOR
1500	1300	800	400	300	150

Browning Black Powder Cartridge Rifle (BPCR) Courtesy Browning.

BPCR tang sight. Courtesy Browning.

BPCR front spirit level sight. Courtesy Browning.

High Wall Traditional Hunter. Courtesy Browning.

MODEL 1885 BPCR CREEDMORE TYPE

Introduced in 1998 this model is chambered for the .45/90 cartridge and features a 34″ heavy half-round barrel with long range tang sight and wind gauge front sight. Weight is approximately 11 lbs. 13 oz.

NIB	EXC.	V.G.	GOOD	FAIR	POOR
1250	1000	875	750	-	-

MODEL 1885 HIGH WALL TRADITIONAL HUNTER

This variation of the Model 1885 series was introduced in 1997. It is fitted with an oil finish walnut stock with crescent buttplate. The barrel is octagonal and 28″ in length. The rear sight is buckhorn and the rifle is fitted with a tang-mounted peep sight. The front sight is gold bead classic style. The rifle is chambered for the .30-30, .38-55, and .45-70 cartridges. Weight is approximately 9 lbs. In 1998 the .454 Casull caliber was added to this rifle.

NIB	EXC.	V.G.	GOOD	FAIR	POOR
1100	900	700	575	-	-

MODEL 1886 GRADE I

This was a lever action sporting rifle patterned after the Model 1886 Winchester rifle. It was chambered for the .45-70 cartridge and has a 26″, octagonal barrel with a full-length, tubular magazine. The finish is blued with a walnut stock and crescent buttplate. There were 7,000 manufactured in 1986.

NOTE: There is no question that these Model 1886 reproduction rifles are undergoing accumulation, and if purchased in NIB condition at a good price should be a good investment. I would give the this model of Browning rifles a Collectibility Factor of #2.

NIB	EXC.	V.G.	GOOD	FAIR	POOR
1350	950	725	600	450	300

MODEL 1886 GRADE I CARBINE

NIB	EXC.	V.G.	GOOD	FAIR	POOR
950	650	550	400	325	250

MODEL 1886 HIGH GRADE

This deluxe version of the Model 1886 features game scene engraving with gold accents and a checkered, select walnut stock. "1 of 3,000" is engraved on the top of the barrel. There were 3,000 manufactured in 1986.

NIB	EXC.	V.G.	GOOD	FAIR	POOR
1600	1150	900	700	550	425

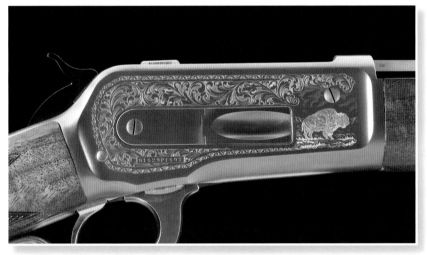

Model 1886 High Grade in .45-70, closeup of right receiver. Courtesy Rock Island Auction.

Model 1886 High Grade in .45-70, closeup of left receiver. Courtesy Rock Island Auction.

Model 1886 High Grade in .45-70. Courtesy Rock Island Auction.

Standard B-92 in .44 Magnum with box. Courtesy Rock Island Auction.

MODEL 1886 HIGH GRADE CARBINE

NIB	EXC.	V.G.	GOOD	FAIR	POOR
1200	950	750	600	450	300

MODEL 1886 MONTANA CENTENNIAL

This version is similar to the High Grade with a different engraving pattern designed to commemorate the centennial of the State of Montana. There were 2,000 manufactured in 1986. As with all commemoratives, it must be NIB with all supplied materials to command collector interest.

NIB	EXC.	V.G.	GOOD	FAIR	POOR
1300	950	750	600	450	375

B-92 CARBINE

This is a lever action sporting rifle patterned after the Winchester Model 92. It was chambered for the .357 Mag. or the .44 Mag. cartridge. It has a 20″ barrel with an 11-round, tubular magazine. The finish is blued with a walnut stock. It was discontinued in 1986.

EXC.	V.G.	GOOD	FAIR	POOR
650	425	295	150	120

NOTE: Add 10 percent for Centennial Model. For .357 Magnum add 30 percent.

Browning 1878-1978 Centennial B-92 Rifle in .44 Magnum. Courtesy Rock Island Auction.

MODEL 1895 GRADE I

This is a lever action sporting rifle chambered in .30-40 Krag and .30-06 cartridge. It was patterned after the Model 1895 Winchester rifle. It has a 24″ barrel and a 4-round, integral box magazine. It has a buckhorn rear sight and a blade front. The finish is blued with a walnut stock. There were 6,000 manufactured in .30-06 and 2,000 chambered for the .30-40 Krag. It was introduced in 1984.

EXC.	V.G.	GOOD	FAIR	POOR
950	675	475	375	275

MODEL 1895 HIGH GRADE

This is the deluxe engraved version of the Model 1895. It has gold-inlaid game scenes and a gold-plated trigger and features a checkered select walnut stock. There were 2,000 produced in 1984- 1,000 in each caliber.

EXC.	V.G.	GOOD	FAIR	POOR
1500	1250	900	700	400

EXPRESS RIFLE

This is an Over/Under, superposed rifle chambered for the .270 Winchester or the .30-06 cartridges. It has 24″ barrels with folding express sights and automatic ejectors. It features a single trigger. The receiver is engraved and is finished in blue with a deluxe checkered walnut stock. Introduced in 1980 and discontinued in 1986.

NOTE: These rifles, with or without the shotgun barrels, are big, big sleepers. At some point in time, in my opinion, these particular weapons will become very valuable. I believe they should be accumulated at reasonable prices, especially in the NIB condition. At this time, I would award to this model of Browning rifle a Collectibility Factor of #2.

NIB	EXC.	V.G.	GOOD	FAIR	POOR
5000	3200	2000	1500	1100	800

Browning Grade I Model 1895 in .30-40 Krag with factory box. Courtesy Rock Island Auction.

Browning Grade I Model 1895 in .30-06. Courtesy Browning.

CUSTOM SHOP EXPRESS RIFLES

Produced in two different models: the Herstall and the CCS 375. Both are custom-built with choice of engraving patterns.

NOTE: Collectibility Factor of #1.

NIB	EXC.	V.G.	GOOD	FAIR	POOR
35000	23000	17500	-	-	-

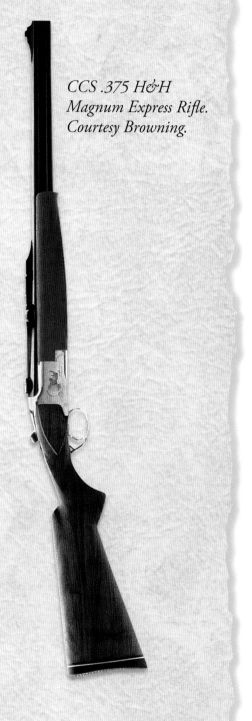

CCS .375 H&H Magnum Express Rifle. Courtesy Browning.

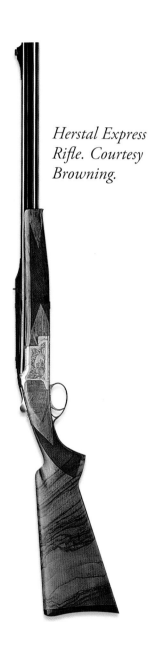

Herstal Express Rifle. Courtesy Browning.

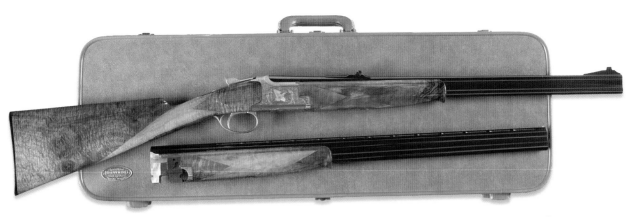

Browning Centennial Superposed Continental Rifle/Shotgun set, 20 ga. over/under shotgun and .30-06 Springfield over/under double rifle barrel set. Courtesy Rock Island Auction.

CONTINENTAL SET

This consists of an Express Rifle chambered for the .30-06 cartridge and furnished with an extra set of 20 gauge, Over/Under barrels. The shotgun barrels are 26.5″ in length. There is a single trigger, automatic ejectors, and a heavily engraved receiver. The select walnut stock is hand checkered and oil-finished. It was furnished with a fitted case. There were 500 manufactured between 1978 and 1986.

NOTE: These are weapons that should, under all conditions, be accumulated. They are somewhat rare and well worth the money. At some point in time, in my opinion, they will become quite valuable. At the time they were first introduced, they did not sell very well. I remember a time when these weapons could be purchased for $1700. That was a real bargain. I give to this set a Collectibility Factor of #1.

Left receiver detail. Courtesy Rock Island Auction.

NIB	EXC.	V.G.	GOOD	FAIR	POOR
7000	5500	3500	2250	1300	1000

Serial number pattern. Courtesy Rock Island Auction.

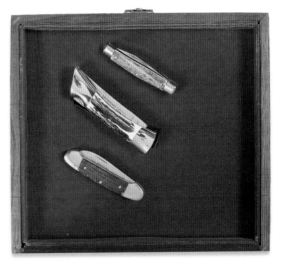

Browning 1878-1978 Centennial Knife Set, part of set with identical serial numbers to matching Centennial firearms (Browning Mountain Rifle, Super Centennial rifle/shotgun, B-92, and High Power pistol).

SECTION III

BROWNING
SHOTGUN VALUES

SUPERPOSED SHOTGUNS

This series of Over/Under, double-barrel shotguns is chambered for 12, 20, and 28 gauges, as well as the .410 bore and is offered with vent rib barrels from 26.5″ to 32″ in length. It features various choke combinations. This shotgun is built on a boxlock action and features either double or single-selective triggers and automatic ejectors. There were a number of versions offered that differ in the amount of ornamentation and the quality of the materials and workmanship utilized in manufacture. Values for small-bore models are generally higher. This series was introduced in 1930 and is manufactured by Fabrique Nationale in Belgium. For factory restored guns or very fine non-factory restorations Superposed guns will bring close to factory original prices. For extra factory installed barrels add $1000 to $2500 depending on the grade of the gun.

Period advertising for Browning shotguns. Courtesy Browning. Pricing no longer valid.

For many Americans, especially those who are not familiar with other European manufacturers, the Browning Superposed Shotguns were the ultimate in shotguns being offered for sale on a regular basis in the United States. These are the weapons that were purchased by the more wealthy and affluent Americans shotgun enthusiasts. There is no question that these weapons rate a Collectibility Factor of #1. These weapons are highly desirable and highly collectible, especially in the smaller gauges. However, it is my opinion that these weapons should only be purchased if they are in excellent plus condition or better unless your only interest is to have a very fine shotgun for hunting or breaking clays. They have become somewhat less desirable since the introduction of changeable chokes. Also, skeet and trap models are not as desirable or collectible as other models. The Browning Superposed is often seen with multiple barrels and even factory cases.)

PRE-WAR SUPERPOSED, 1930-1940

Browning Superposed shotgun prices are divided into three different categories. The first category is for pre-war guns built from 1930 to 1940. These pre-war Superposed guns were manufactured in 12 gauge only from serial number 1 to around 17,000. These shotguns were offered in four different grades: Grade I, Pigeon, Diana, and Midas.

GRADE I

NEW	EXC	GOOD	FAIR	POOR
2250	1750	1000	450	300

NOTE: Subtract $350 for 12 gauge magnum; add a premium of $1750 for 20 gauge; add a premium of 250 percent for 28 gauge; add a premium of $2500 for .410; subtract 20 percent for 12 gauge standard weight guns; add a premium of 25 percent for long tang, round knob guns (skeet guns excepted).

GRADE I SKEET GUNS

NEW	EXC.	V.G.	GOOD	FAIR	POOR
1700	1300	1100	600	–	–

NOTE: Add a premium of $800 for 20 gauge; add a premium of 250 percent for 28 gauge; add a premium of $1250 for .410.

GRADE I FOUR BARREL SKEET SET

NEW	EXC.	V.G.	GOOD	FAIR	POOR
5000	4500	3250	–	–	–

NOTE: Subtract 30 percent for new style barrels in 26 inch length.

PIGEON

NEW	EXC.	V.G.	GOOD	FAIR	POOR
6000	3500	2500	1500	500	400

NOTE: Add a premium of $2500 for 20 gauge; add a premium of 100 percent for 28 gauge; add a premium of $3000 for .410; add a premium of 30 percent for long tang stocks with round knobs, skeet guns excepted; subtract 25 percent for new skeet style.

DIANA

NEW	EXC.	V.G.	GOOD	FAIR	POOR
7900	6000	5200	3000	900	500

NOTE: Add a premium of $5,000 for 20 gauge; add a premium of 250 percent for 28 gauge; add a premium of 100 percent for .410; add a premium of 33 percent for long tang, round knob variation (an additional premium of 40 percent if in 28 gauge); add a premium of 40 percent if in Superlight variation

MIDAS

NEW	EXC.	V.G.	GOOD	FAIR	POOR
12,000	9000	7500	3700	1200	750

NOTE: Add a premium of 7000 for 20 gauge; add a premium of 100 percent for 28 gauge; add a premium of $7000 for .410 gauge; add an additional premium of 33 percent if in long tang round knob variation, skeet guns excepted; add a premium of 40 percent if in Superlight variation (add an additional 15 percent for 28 gauge variation); for twin-single triggers add 15 percent. For vent rib add 10 percent. For recoil pads or shorter than standard stocks deduct 25 percent.

SUPERPOSED FROM 1947-1959

The second category of Superposed was produced and sold from 1947 to 1959. These were built in 12 and 20 gauge as well as the 28 gauge and .410, which were introduced in 1959. These shotguns were graded using a Roman numeral system instead of names. They are: Grade I, Grade II, Grade III, Grade IV, Grade V, and Grade VI. The values listed are for 12 gauge. Add premiums or deductions as listed. The number of 28 gauge and .410 guns sold in late 1959 number fewer than 100.

NOTE: The number of Grade VIs sold in North America is unknown, but it was most likely very small. This is a very rare grade. Proceed with caution.

GRADE I

Marked Lightning on frame.

NIB	EXC.	V.G.	GOOD	FAIR	POOR
3000	2000	1100	900	300	250

NOTE: Add a premium of 50 percent for 20 gauge guns; add a premium of 100 percent for 28 gauge guns; add a premium of 80 percent for 410 gauge guns; add a premium of 40 percent for long tang round knob variation, skeet guns excepted; subtract 25 percent for new skeet style model.

GRADE II

NIB	EXC.	V.G.	GOOD	FAIR	POOR
4500	3300	2100	1200	600	375

NOTE: Add a premium of 60 percent for 20 gauge guns; add a premium of 125 percent for 28 gauge guns; add a premium of 100 percent for .410 guns; add a premium of 40 percent for long tang round knob variation, skeet guns excepted; subtract 25 percent for new skeet style model.

GRADE III

NIB	EXC.	V.G.	GOOD	FAIR	POOR
5750	5000	3500	2200	750	450

NOTE: Add a premium of 60 percent for 20 gauge guns; add a premium of 133 percent for 28 gauge guns; add a premium of 110 percent for .410 guns; add a premium of 40 percent for long tang round knob variation, skeet guns excepted; subtract 25 percent for new skeet style model.

Grade I Belgian Superposed 12-ga. with straight grip stock. Courtesy Rock Island Auction.

Belgian Browning Superposed 12-ga. Magnum. Courtesy Rock Island Auction.

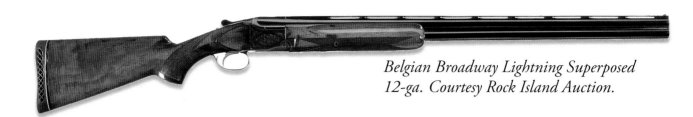

Belgian Broadway Lightning Superposed 12-ga. Courtesy Rock Island Auction.

GRADE IV

NIB	EXC.	V.G.	GOOD	FAIR	POOR
8500	7500	4000	2400	1200	550

NOTE: Add a premium of 60 percent for 20 gauge guns; add a premium of 125 percent for 28 gauge guns; add a premium of 100 percent for .410 guns; add a premium of 40 percent for long tang round knob variation, skeet guns excepted; subtract 25 percent for new skeet style model.

GRADE V

NIB	EXC.	V.G.	GOOD	FAIR	POOR
7500	6000	3800	2400	1200	650

NOTE: Add a premium of 60 percent for 20 gauge guns; add a premium of 125 percent for 28 gauge guns; add a premium of 100 percent for .410 guns; add a premium of 40 percent for long tang round knob variation, skeet guns excepted;; subtract 25 percent for new skeet style model.

GRADE VI

Built 1957 through 1959 only.

NIB	EXC.	V.G.	GOOD	FAIR	POOR
13000	11000	7000	4000	2200	850

NOTE: For 20 gauge add 45 percent; for 28 gauge add 90 percent (1959 only); for .410 add 45 percent (1959 only); for Trap deduct 40 percent; for standard weight 12 gauge Grade I deduct 10 percent.

SUPERPOSED FROM 1960-1976

Browning Superposed shotguns built from 1960 to 1976 revert back to the older grade names. They are Grade I, Pigeon, Pointer, Diana, and Midas. These shotguns were available in 12, 20, and 28 gauge as well as .410. This last production period is a little more complicated due to manufacturing changes that some collectors consider important such as round knobs and long tangs.

Prices listed reflect Superposed field guns produced from 1960 to 1965 in round pistol grip knob with long trigger guard tang in 12 gauge. For all other variations during this period one should consider:

- For salt wood damage deduct a minimum of 60 percent.
- For round knob short tang (circa 1966-1969) deduct 50 percent. For flat knob short tang (circa 1969-1971) deduct 50 percent.
- For flat knob long tang (circa 1971-1976) deduct 25 percent.
- For New Style Skeet and Lightning Trap (recoil pad, flat knob, full beavertail forearm) with long trigger guard tang (1971-1976) deduct 35 percent.
- For short trigger guard tang deduct 40 percent; if Broadway rib deduct an additional 10 percent.
- For skeet chokes on field guns deduct 5 percent.
- For recoil pads on 2-3/4″ chambered field guns deduct 20 percent.
- For Master engraver signed guns (Funken, Watrin, Vrancken, etc.) add 10 percent.
- For Standard weight Grade I guns deduct 10 percent.
- For shorter than standard stock length deduct 25 percent.
- For barrel lengths of 32″ add 10 percent.
- For 20 gauge add 50 percent.
- For 28 gauge add 100 percent.
- For .410 add 35 percent.

GRADE I

Lightning marked on frame.

NIB	EXC.	V.G.	GOOD	FAIR	POOR
3000	2250	1200	700	500	250

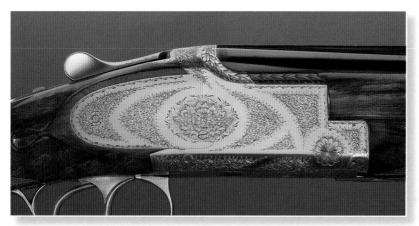

Right receiver detail. Courtesy Rock Island Auction.

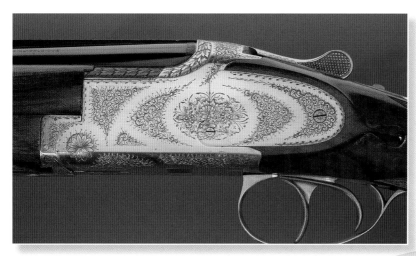

Left receiver detail. Courtesy Rock Island Auction.

Custom-engraved Superposed 20-ga. with extra-long forend. Courtesy Rock Island Auction.

1960s-vintage Belgian Pigeon Grade Superposed 20-ga. with Browning factory recoil pad. Courtesy Rock Island Auction.

PIGEON GRADE

NIB	EXC.	V.G.	GOOD	FAIR	POOR
5500	4500	3000	2000	1000	600

Left receiver detail. Courtesy Rock Island Auction.

Right receiver detail. Courtesy Rock Island Auction.

Bottom receiver detail. Courtesy Rock Island Auction.

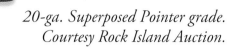

20-ga. Superposed Pointer grade.
Courtesy Rock Island Auction.

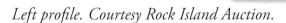

Left profile. Courtesy Rock Island Auction.

Left receiver profile.
Courtesy Rock
Island Auction.

POINTER GRADE-RARE

NIB	EXC.	V.G.	GOOD	FAIR	POOR
8500	7250	5000	3000	2000	1000

Right receiver profile.
Courtesy Rock Island Auction.

Bottom receiver
detail. Courtesy
Rock Island
Auction.

DIANA GRADE

NIB	EXC.	V.G.	GOOD	FAIR	POOR
8500	7250	5000	3000	2000	1000

MIDAS GRADE

NIB	EXC.	V.G.	GOOD	FAIR	POOR
11000	10000	8000	7000	5000	4000

NOTE: FN also built Exhibition Grades that were sold in this country under the Browning name. Collectors consider a true Exhibition Grade as one not having a "C" prefix in the serial number. These particular guns are considered quite desirable and should be appraised on an individual basis. Superposed shotguns in this catageory can range in price from $10,000 to $20,000 depending on gauge, engraving coverage, and options.

The second type of Exhibition Grade is known as the "C" type and was first sold in the United States from about 1973 to 1977. It is so called because of the "C" prefix in the serial number. There were about 225 of these guns sold in the United States They came in quite a few grades and some were specially ordered. Although the lower grades are not considered by some to be true Exhibitions (pre-C series), the highest "C" series grades are a match to the best of the older exhibitions. In 2000, an all-option Superlight two- barrel set with sideplates engraved by Vranken sold for $22,000. Generally, depending on the gun, prices will range between $6,000 and $25,000. These "C" grade guns should also be appraised individually.)

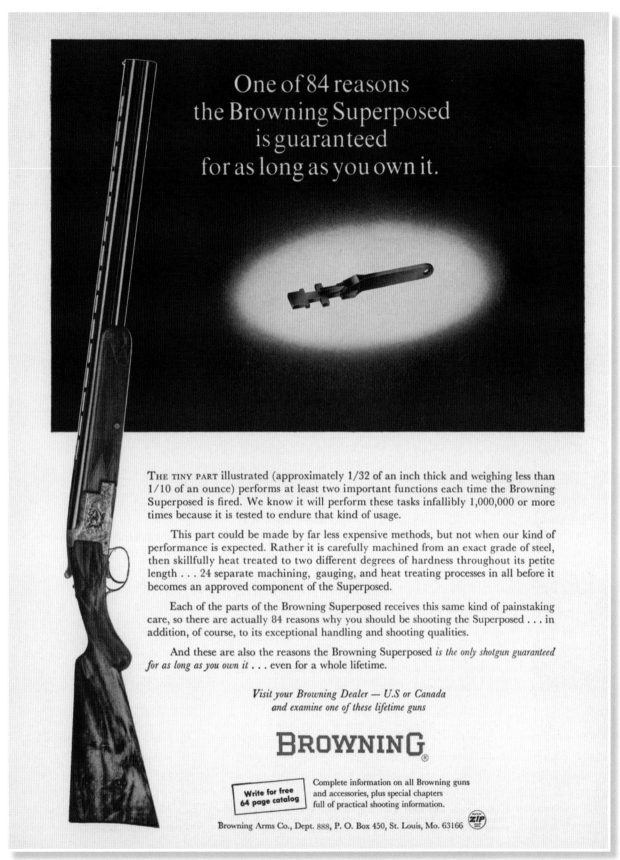

Period advertising for Superposed. Courtesy Browning. Pricing no longer valid.

SUPERPOSED SUPERLIGHT

This model was first introduced in 1967 in 12 gauge and in 1969 in 20 gauge. Special-order 28 gauge as well as .410 are also seen. It was offered in 26.5″ barrel lengths with 27.5″ barrls in 12 gauge and 28″ barrels in smaller bores available on special order. It features a rounded frame and straight grip stock with tapered solid or vent rib barrels. Regular production on the Superlight ended in 1976 for the grades listed. Production did continue for the Superlight in the P series begun in 1977.

The smaller the gauge and the higher the grades, for the most part, the more rare the weapon. The really rare variations of this model are rarely seen in the open market.

GRADE I

NIB	EXC.	V.G.	GOOD	FAIR	POOR
3250	2750	1700	600	400	250

NOTE: Add a premium of 60 percent for 20 gauge gun; add sa premium of 125 percent for 28 gauge guns; add a premium of 80 percent for .410 guns; add a premium of 40 percent for long tang round knob variation, skeet guns excepted; subtract 25 percent for new skeet style model.

PIGEON GRADE

NIB	EXC.	V.G.	GOOD	FAIR	POOR
5000	3900	3000	1500	1000	800

NOTE: Add a premium of 60 percent for 20 gauge guns; add a premium of 125 percent for 28 gauge guns; add a premium of 100 percent for .410; add a premium of 40 percent for long tang round knob variation, skeet guns excepted; subtract 25 percent for new skeet style model.

POINTER GRADE-RARE

NIB	EXC.	V.G.	GOOD	FAIR	POOR
9000	7000	4700	2500	1500	1000

NOTE: Add a premium of 60 percent for 20 gauge guns; add a premium of 125 percent for 28 gauge guns; add a premium of 100 percent for .410 gauge guns; add a premium of 40 percent for long tang round knob variation, skeet guns excepted; subtract 25 percent for new skeet style model.

DIANA GRADE

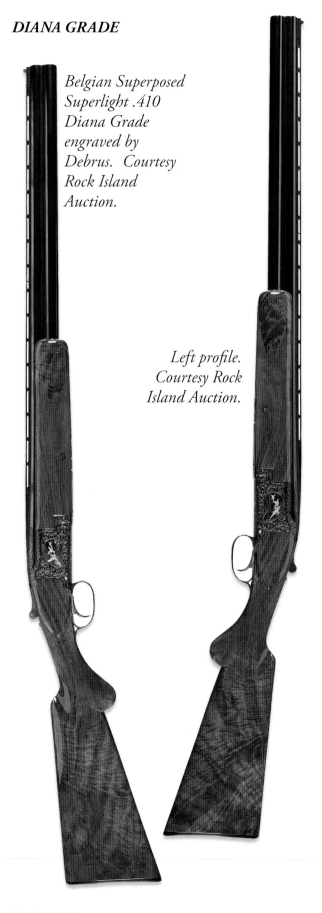

Belgian Superposed Superlight .410 Diana Grade engraved by Debrus. Courtesy Rock Island Auction.

Left profile. Courtesy Rock Island Auction.

Left receiver detail. Courtesy Rock Island Auction.

Right receiver view. Courtesy Rock Island Auction.

Bottom receiver detail. Courtesy Rock Island Auction.

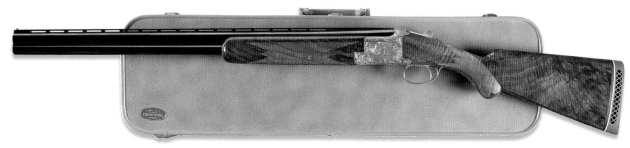

Diana Grade Superposed 12-ga. engraved by Vandermesseng, with factory case. Courtesy Rock Island Auction.

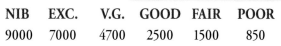

Right profile. Courtesy Rock Island Auction.

Bottom receiver detail. Courtesy Rock Island Auction.

Detail of engraver's signature. Courtesy Rock Island Auction.

Left receiver detail. Courtesy Rock Island Auction.

NIB	EXC.	V.G.	GOOD	FAIR	POOR
9000	7000	4700	2500	1500	850

NOTE: Add a premium of 50 percent for 20 gauge guns; a premium of 100 percent for 28 gauge guns; a premium of 80 percent for .410; a premium of 40 percent for long tang round knob variation, skeet guns excepted; subtract 25 percent for new skeet style model.

MIDAS GRADE

Midas Grade Superposed
12-ga. engraved by
Angelo Bee. Courtesy
Rock Island Auction.

Left profile.
Courtesy Rock
Island Auction.

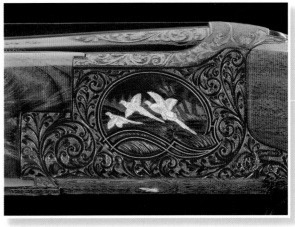

Left receiver detail. Courtesy
Rock Island Auction.

Right receiver detail. Courtesy
Rock Island Auction.

Bottom receiver detail. Courtesy
Rock Island Auction.

Cased Midas Upgrade Superposed Three-Barrel Set:
20-ga., 28-ga., and .410. Courtesy Rock Island Auction.

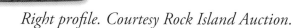

Right profile. Courtesy Rock Island Auction.

Left receiver detail. Courtesy
Rock Island Auction.

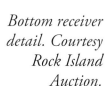

Bottom receiver
detail. Courtesy
Rock Island
Auction.

Right receiver detail. Courtesy
Rock Island Auction.

NIB	EXC.	V.G.	GOOD	FAIR	POOR
11000	9000	6500	3700	2000	1000

NOTE: For 20 gauge guns add a 50 percent premium.; for 28 gauge guns add a 100 percent premium; for .410 guns add 30 percent premium; for high grade guns and 30 percent for Grade I.

SUPERPOSED PRESENTA-TION GRADE SERIES

The Superposed shotguns listed were manufactured between 1977 and 1984 by FN in Belgium. The models listed differ in the amount of ornamentation and the quality of materials and workmanship utilized in construction. This series was also available in a Superlight configuration.

In my opinion, these are some of the most beautiful weapons that Browning ever manufactured. If a person had a lot of money and a lot of time, these weapons would surely be worth collecting, as many of them are so rare as to be virtually one-of-a-kind guns. The Collectibility Factor for these weapons would certainly be #1, and their desirability would also be very high. I know where a 28-gauge P3 is, in a very unique configuration, and I have tried to purchase it for the past 15 years, but to no avail. If it ever comes on the market, it will certainly be a gun that I will pursue.)

Due to the tremendous variation of P-Series guns, prices here reflect the Superlight configuration. An all option Superlight with a checkered butt, oil finish, and three piece forend will bring 25 to 30 percent more. For all other variations one should consider:

- For trap guns deduct 35 percent.
- For new style skeet deduct 30 percent.
- For skeet choked field guns deduct 5 percent.
- For recoil pads on field guns deduct 30 percent.
- For flat knob long tang hunting guns with no options deduct 35 percent.
- For flat knob long tang hunting guns with all options add 25 percent.
- For guns signed by J. Baerten add 5 percent.
- For P-4V guns with no gold deduct 20 percent.
- For hand filed vent rib add 5 percent.
- For Presentation Grade guns with extra sets of barrels add approximately $1,500 to $2,500 depending on gauge and combination.

- For P1, P2, and P3 grades add the premium listed:
- For 20 gauge guns, add 55 percent.
- For .28 gauge guns, add 115 percent.
- For .410 bore, add 65 percent.
- For the P4 grade, add the premium listed:
- For 20 gauge guns, add 55 percent.
- For 28 gauge guns, add 120 percent.
- For .410 bore, add 55 percent.

PRESENTATION I (WITHOUT GOLD INLAYS)

NIB	EXC.	V.G.	GOOD	FAIR	POOR
3500	2700	1200	1000	600	500

PRESENTATION 1 (GOLD INLAID)

NIB	EXC.	V.G.	GOOD	FAIR	POOR
5250	4000	2700	1400	700	500

PRESENTATION 2 (WITHOUT GOLD INLAYS)

NIB	EXC.	V.G.	GOOD	FAIR	POOR
5250	4250	3000	1800	1000	600

PRESENTATION 2 (GOLD-INLAID)

NIB	EXC.	V.G.	GOOD	FAIR	POOR
7500	6500	4250	2500	1500	1000

NOTE: For early hand-engraved P3 models (approximately 25 produced) add 40 percent. These early guns are rare, proceed with caution.

PRESENTATION 3 (GOLD-INLAID)

NIB	EXC.	V.G.	GOOD	FAIR	POOR
9500	8000	5800	4000	2000	1300

PRESENTATION 4 (GOLD-INLAID)

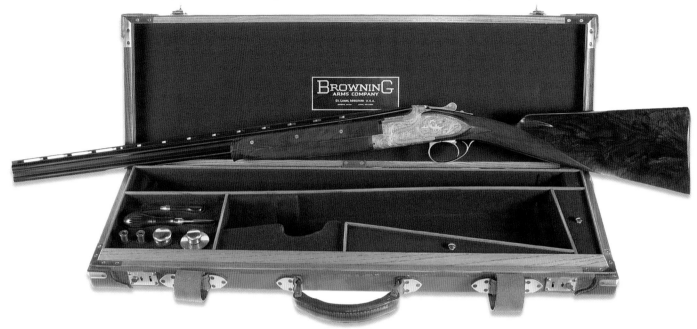

*Gold inlaid Presentation Grade IV .410 Superposed with factory fitted
case and engraving by J. M. Debrus. Courtesy Rock Island Auction.*

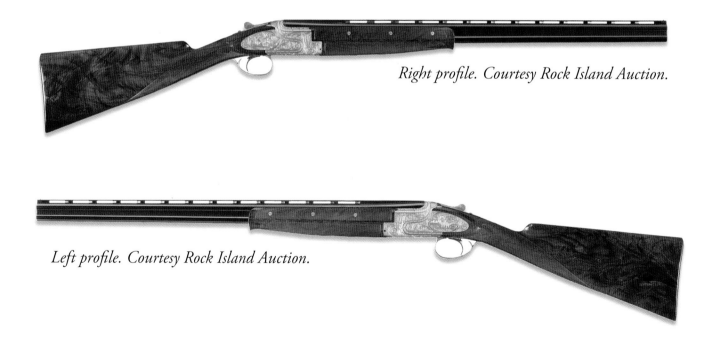

Right profile. Courtesy Rock Island Auction.

Left profile. Courtesy Rock Island Auction.

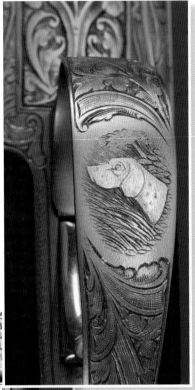

Trigger guard detail. Courtesy Rock Island Auction.

Engraver's signature. Courtesy Rock Island Auction.

Right receiver detail. Courtesy Rock Island Auction.

Underside detail. Courtesy Rock Island Auction.

NIB	EXC.	V.G.	GOOD	FAIR	POOR
13000	11500	9000	6750	5000	3500

NOTE: For P4 Grade guns with no gold deduct approximately 20 percent.

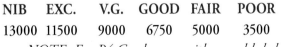

Left receiver detail. Courtesy Rock Island Auction.

SUPERPOSED WATERFOWL LIMITED EDITION SERIES

This model was issued in three different versions; Mallard, Pintail, and Black Duck. Each edition was limited to 500 guns, all in 12 gauge.

Once again, in this model, Browning has created a very beautiful weapon. Their limited production makes these guns uncommon. Almost all of these weapons, to this day, remain either in mint or unfired condition, and that's the way it should be. A friend of mine told me not too long ago that he would walk barefoot over 10 miles of broken glass to own one of the spectacular variations. If you ever go to the big shows, some of them are usually there for sale, on the tables of the bigger and more prosperous dealers. Take your time and look at them very closely. They are very beautiful.

1981 MALLARD ISSUE

NIB	EXC.	V.G.	GOOD	FAIR	POOR
7200	6000	4500	3300	1900	1100

1982 PINTAIL ISSUE

NIB	EXC.	V.G.	GOOD	FAIR	POOR
7200	6000	4500	3300	1900	1100

1983 BLACK DUCK ISSUE

NIB	EXC.	V.G.	GOOD	FAIR	POOR
7200	6000	4500	3300	1900	1100

BICENTENNIAL MODEL

Produced in 1976 to commemorate the 200-year anniversary of the United States of America. A total of 53 guns were built in this special edition. All of these Superposed were 12 gauge with 28″ barrels and each was numbered for one of the fifty states plus the District of Columbia. Two additional guns were built for the Smithsonian Institution and the Liege Firearms Museum. All were fitted with side plates with gold inlays. To reflect true value guns must be in unfired condition in their original case with all the papers.

There are so few of these guns in existence that if at any time you have a chance to look at them, it is time well spent.

NIB	EXC.	V.G.	GOOD	FAIR	POOR
10000	8000	5500	2750	1500	1000

NOTE: Price often depends on the state commemorated.

FN/BROWNING SUPERPOSED

A number of FN Browning Superposed B-25 shotguns were imported into this country by Browning in various grades. These Superposed were intended originally for FN's European market. There are a large number of variations and grades. It is strongly suggested that an expert appraisal be sought prior to the sale. As a general rule these prices for NIB guns are: A grade $1,200-1,600; B grade $1,600-2,500; C grade $2,500-3,500; D grade $3,500-5,000. These guns are marked with both the Browning and FN barrel address.

CLASSIC

Produced in 1986 this model was offered in 20 gauge with 26″ barrels. About 2,500 guns were produced. Silver gray receiver with engraving.

NIB	EXC.	V.G.	GOOD	FAIR	POOR
2500	1750	-	-	-	-

GOLD CLASSIC

This shotgun was similar to the above model but more finely finished and engraved with gold inlays. About 350 of these guns were built in 1986.

NIB	EXC.	V.G.	GOOD	FAIR	POOR
9500	6500	-	-	-	-

CUSTOM SHOP B25 & B125 SUPERPOSED

These special order Superposed are currently available with a delivery time of 6 to 8 months. A number of options are offered that affect price. B125 guns are assembled in Belgium with components made in other countries to hold down costs. The B25 is made entirely in Belgium and is the more expensive version of the Superposed. Prices listed are retail only.

NOTE: Retail prices for current production guns change often. Contact Browning for the present prices.

B-125

TRAP
Retail Price-$8,125

12 GAUGE SPORTING
A Style Retail Price-$4,475
B Style Retail Price-$4,800
C Style Retail Price-$5,275

12 & 20 GAUGE HUNTING AND SUPERLIGHT
A Style Retail price-$4,475
B Style Retail price-$4,800
C Style Retail price-$5,275

B-25

Browning B-25 Sporting, right profile. Courtesy Rock Island Auction.

Left receiver detail. Courtesy Rock Island Auction.

Bottom receiver detail. Courtesy Rock Island Auction.

B-25 Sporting, left profile. Courtesy Rock Island Auction.

B-25 Special Duck. Courtesy Browning.

GRADE I
   Retail price-$6,850

PIGEON GRADE
   Retail price-$8,625

POINTER GRADE
   Retail price-$9,950

DIANA GRADE
   Retail price-$10,350

MIDAS GRADE
   Retail price-$14,500

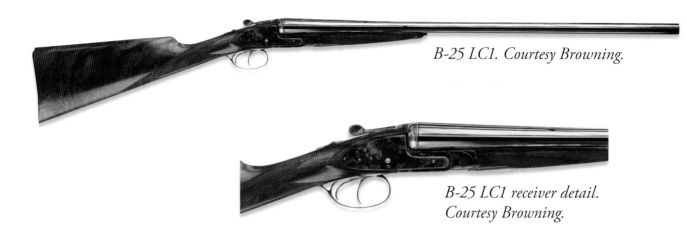

B-25 LC1. Courtesy Browning.

*B-25 LC1 receiver detail.
Courtesy Browning.*

CUSTOM SHOP BSL

This is a side-by-side shotgun is equiped with Browning sidelock barrel, Holland & Holland-type locks with double trigger and auto ejectors. The gun is assembled and finished by Labeau-Courally. It is offered in both 12 and 20 gauge. Engraved grayed receiver or case colored receiver. Introduced into the Browning product line in 2001.

In my opinion, if one is going to buy a late-production Browning double, these are the ones to own. They can be totally magnificent and outrageously beautiful.

CASE COLORED RECEIVER (BSL GRADE LC1)

NIB	EXC.	V.G.	GOOD	FAIR	POOR
10200	-	-	-	-	-

ENGRAVED GRAY RECEIVER (BSL GRADE LC2)

NIB	EXC.	V.G.	GOOD	FAIR	POOR
12275	-	-	-	-	-

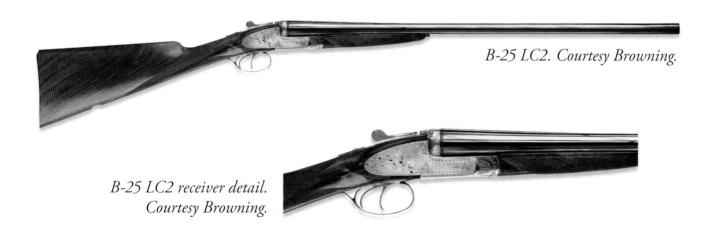

B-25 LC2. Courtesy Browning.

*B-25 LC2 receiver detail.
Courtesy Browning.*

Pick up a Liège and you'll find the tight, lifelong, receiver-to-barrel fit that comes from careful Browning handcraftsmanship.

The receiver is machined from a block of high grade steel. Then it's meticulously engraved and deeply blued to make the Liège look as good as it shoots.

Now shoulder the Liège ... effortlessly. It's got that perfect Browning balance shooters around the world swear by.

Plus all the conveniences:

SINGLE SELECTIVE MECHANICAL TRIGGER has a positive linkage that prevents misfires. Fast, crisp, certain.

BARREL SELECTOR is incorporated in the thumb safety for instant barrel selection.

AUTOMATIC EJECTORS throw out fired shells and elevate live rounds for easy removal.

CLEAN SIGHT PICTURE. Ventilated rib with matted surface breaks up heat waves and cools the barrels. Nickel silver sight bead.

FRENCH WALNUT STOCK, hand shaped from Europe's finest forests. The full pistol grip stock and sure-grip field forearm has sharp, 22-line checkering, and are hand rubbed and polished.

MODELS — Choose your Liège in a 12 gauge 3" magnum model with 30" barrels or a 12 gauge 2 3/4" model with 28" or 26 1/2" barrels, both in all popular choke combinations. The price: $472.50 suggested retail

AMMUNITION — New Browning "Power Rated" Shotgun Shells make selecting the right load a snap!

Liège
(Pronounced Lee-age)
$472.50*
You can tell it's a BROWNING by the way it shoots.

Shoulder the Liège at your Browning Dealer's. And Write for our FREE 104-page, full-color catalog, THE BROWNING MAN. It contains details and specifications on all Browning Sporting Arms, Gun Accessories, Ammunition, Clothing, Boots, Archery Equipment, New Browning Camping and Backpacking Equipment, plus 9 pages of helpful shooting tips. Browning, Dept. 506, Morgan, Utah 84050. In Canada: Browning Arms Co. of Canada, Ltd. Copyright © Browning 1973 *suggested retail price

Is this the year you trade up to a Browning?

Period advertising for Superposed Liege. Courtesy Browning. Pricing no longer valid.

B-27. Courtesy Rock Island Auction.

LIEGE

This is an Over/Under shotgun chambered for 12 gauge. It was offered with 26.5″, 28″, or 30″ vent rib barrels with various choke combinations. It features a boxlock action with a nonselective single trigger and automatic ejectors. The finish is blued with a checkered walnut stock. There were approximately 10,000 manufactured between 1973 and 1975. U.S. versions were marked Browning Arms Company on the barrel.

In my opinion, the quality of this model of Browning, for some reason, does not quite seem to meet standard. I have owned a few of these, but I have been happy when they have found a new home.

NIB	EXC.	V.G.	GOOD	FAIR	POOR
825	650	550	450	300	200

B-27

This improved version of the Liege was imported into the U.S., some without the Browning Arms Company markings and only the FN barrel address. Others may have both barrel addresses. It was offered in a number of variations that differed in the amount of ornamentation and quality of materials and workmanship utilized. It features the same action as the Liege Over/Under gun.

STANDARD

NIB	EXC.	V.G.	GOOD	FAIR	POOR
750	550	450	350	250	200

DELUXE

NIB	EXC.	V.G.	GOOD	FAIR	POOR
1100	900	650	500	350	250

DELUXE TRAP

NIB	EXC.	V.G.	GOOD	FAIR	POOR
1000	825	550	450	300	250

DELUXE SKEET

NIB	EXC.	V.G.	GOOD	FAIR	POOR
1000	825	550	450	300	250

GRAND DELUXE

NIB	EXC.	V.G.	GOOD	FAIR	POOR
1500	1100	775	650	500	400

CITY OF LIEGE COMMEMORATIVE

250 manufactured.

NIB	EXC.	V.G.	GOOD	FAIR	POOR
1500	1050	725	600	450	300

ST-100

This is an Over/Under trap gun that features separated barrels with an adjustable point of impact. It is chambered for 12 gauge and has a 30″ or 32″ barrel with full choke and a floating ventilated rib. It features a single trigger and automatic ejectors. The finish is blued with a checkered walnut stock. It was manufactured by FN between 1979 and 1981.

NIB	EXC.	V.G.	GOOD	FAIR	POOR
2750	1700	1400	1000	700	400

20-ga. Citori with adjustable comb. Courtesy Rock Island Auction.

CITORI SERIES

This is an Over/Under, double-barrel shotgun chambered for all gauges and offered with vent rib barrels of 26" through 30" in length. It has a boxlock action with a single-selective trigger and automatic ejectors. The various grades differ in the amount of ornamentation and the quality of materials and workmanship utilized in construction. This series is manufactured in Japan by B.C. Miroku and was introduced in 1973.

In my opinion, these are outstanding working guns. They shoot extremely well, and while they are a bit heavy, they seem to fit most people very well. I have a friend I hunt with who uses one of these on a daily basis when hunting, and I can tell you that he makes a formidable competitor. Today, the more basic models offer a great value, and the price of these weapons, for the most part, seem to be coming down. If you are going to purchase one of these weapons, I recommend that you only purchase those with adjustable chokes.

NOTE: For all Citori models, add a 15-20 percent premium for 28 gauge and .410.

GRADE I

NIB	EXC.	V.G.	GOOD	FAIR	POOR
900	800	725	550	425	300

NOTE: Add premium of 30 percent for 16 gauge guns.

UPLAND SPECIAL-GRADE I

Offered with straight-grip stock and 24" rib barrels. Available in 12 gauge or 20 gauge. Weighs 6 lbs. 11 oz. in 12 gauge and 6 lbs. in 20 gauge. Introduced in 1984.

NIB	EXC.	V.G.	GOOD	FAIR	POOR
1050	850	700	600	400	300

GRADE II-1978 TO 1983

EXC.	V.G.	GOOD	FAIR	POOR
1500	1200	1000	650	400

GRADE II-CHOKE TUBES

NIB	EXC.	V.G.	GOOD	FAIR	POOR
1600	1400	1000	775	650	400

GRADE V-1978 TO 1984

NIB	EXC.	V.G.	GOOD	FAIR	POOR
2600	2100	1600	950	750	400

GRADE V WITH SIDE-PLATES-1981 TO 1984

These are very nice guns given their somewhat modest price.

NIB	EXC.	V.G.	GOOD	FAIR	POOR
2900	2500	2100	1500	800	400

NOTE: Add 20 percent for small gauges.

GRADE VI-CHOKE TUBES

Introduced 1983.

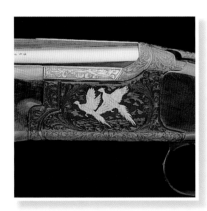

Citori Grade VI, receiver detail. Courtesy Browning.

NIB	EXC.	V.G.	GOOD	FAIR	POOR
1750	1500	1200	1000	750	500

CITORI HUNTER

This model features a full pistol-grip stock with beavertail forearm with high-gloss walnut. Chambered for 12 with 2.75″, 3″, or 3.5″ chambers and choice of 26″, 28″ or 30″ barrels in 12 gauge. The 20 gauge models have a choice of 26" or 28" barrels. Twelve gauge guns weigh from 7 lbs. 13 ozs. to 8 lbs. 9 ozs. depending on barrel length. Twenty gauge guns weigh about 6.75 lbs.

NIB	EXC.	V.G.	GOOD	FAIR	POOR
1300	1000	850	650	550	450

NOTE: Add $75 for 3.5″ models.

Citori Hunter. Courtesy Browning.

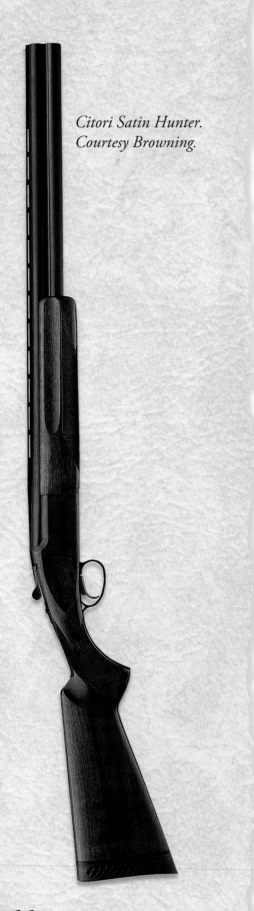

Citori Satin Hunter.
Courtesy Browning.

CITORI SPORTING HUNTER

This model has the same features as the Hunting model with the exception of the stock configuration. The Sporting Hunter has a Sporting model buttstock and a Superposed style forearm. Fitted with a contoured sporting recoil pad. Introduced in 1998.

NIB	EXC.	V.G.	GOOD	FAIR	POOR
1400	1300	1050	750	550	450

NOTE: Add $75 for 3.5" models.

CITORI SATIN HUNTER

This model is chambered for 12 gauge shells, has a hunting-style stock, choice of 26" or 28" barrels, and a special satin wood finish with matte black receiver and barrels. Offered in Grade I only. Weight is about 8 lbs. Introduced in 1999.

NIB	EXC.	V.G.	GOOD	FAIR	POOR
1250	1000	825	700	-	-

NOTE: Add $100 for 3.5" chamber.

Citori extractors, detail view. Browning.

Citori Lightning Grade I. Courtesy Browning.

CITORI LIGHTNING

This is a lightweight version that features a slimmer profile and has a checkered, round-knob, pistol-grip stock. It is offered in all gauges and in the same barrel lengths as the standard Citori. It features screw-in choke tubes known as Invectors. It was introduced in 1988. Offered in 12, 20 and 28 gauge and .410 bore. Weights are 6.5 lbs. to 8 lbs. depending on gauge and barrel length. The models differ in the amount of ornamentation and quality of materials and workmanship utilized.

These are my personal choice for hunting. I own one in almost all the grades and all the different configurations. If I want to impress someone who doesn't know a lot about guns, I take out a Grade VI.

GRADE I

NIB	EXC.	V.G.	GOOD	FAIR	POOR
1645	1200	900	600	450	375

GRADE III

NIB	EXC.	V.G.	GOOD	FAIR	POOR
2450	1900	1400	975	-	-

GRADE IV

Introduced in 2005.

NIB	EXC.	V.G.	GOOD	FAIR	POOR
2610	1950	-	-	-	-

GRADE VI

NIB	EXC.	V.G.	GOOD	FAIR	POOR
3800	3000	2250	1500	-	-

Citori Lightning Grade III. Courtesy Browning.

Citori Lightning Grade III receiver detail. Courtesy Browning.

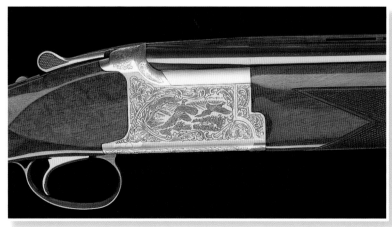

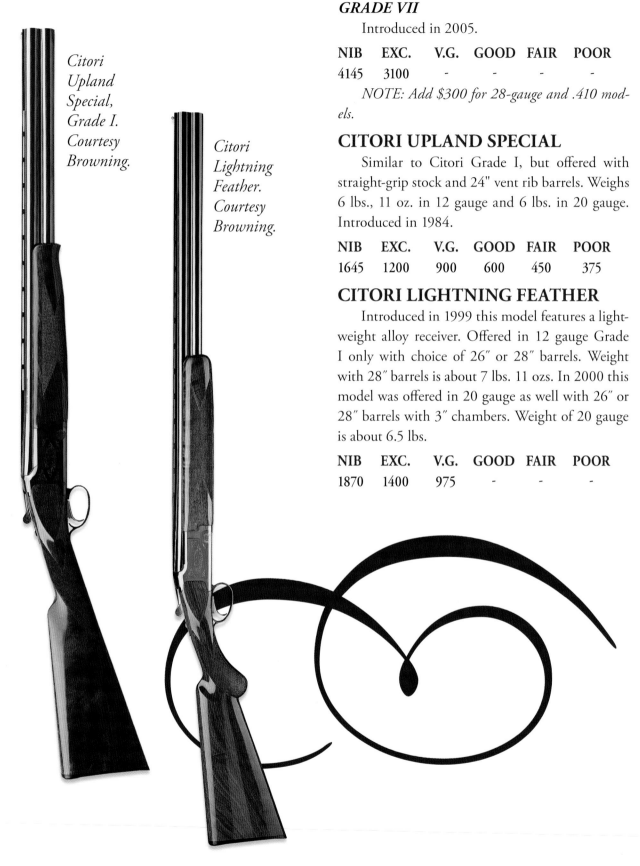

Citori Upland Special, Grade I. Courtesy Browning.

Citori Lightning Feather. Courtesy Browning.

Introduced in 2005.

NIB	EXC.	V.G.	GOOD	FAIR	POOR
4145	3100	-	-	-	-

NOTE: Add $300 for 28-gauge and .410 models.

CITORI UPLAND SPECIAL

Similar to Citori Grade I, but offered with straight-grip stock and 24" vent rib barrels. Weighs 6 lbs., 11 oz. in 12 gauge and 6 lbs. in 20 gauge. Introduced in 1984.

NIB	EXC.	V.G.	GOOD	FAIR	POOR
1645	1200	900	600	450	375

CITORI LIGHTNING FEATHER

Introduced in 1999 this model features a lightweight alloy receiver. Offered in 12 gauge Grade I only with choice of 26″ or 28″ barrels. Weight with 28″ barrels is about 7 lbs. 11 ozs. In 2000 this model was offered in 20 gauge as well with 26″ or 28″ barrels with 3″ chambers. Weight of 20 gauge is about 6.5 lbs.

NIB	EXC.	V.G.	GOOD	FAIR	POOR
1870	1400	975	-	-	-

Citori Lightning Feather Combo. Courtesy Browning.

CITORI LIGHTNING FEATHER COMBO

This model features a 20 gauge and 28 gauge barrel, both 27″ long. The 20 gauge with 3″ chambers the 28 gauge with 2.75″ chambers. Pistol grip stock. Weight is about 6.25 lbs. Supplied with Browning luggage case. Introduced in 2000.

NIB	EXC.	V.G.	GOOD	FAIR	POOR
3035	2250	1700	1250	-	-

Lightning Feather Combo in factory fitted case. Courtesy Browning.

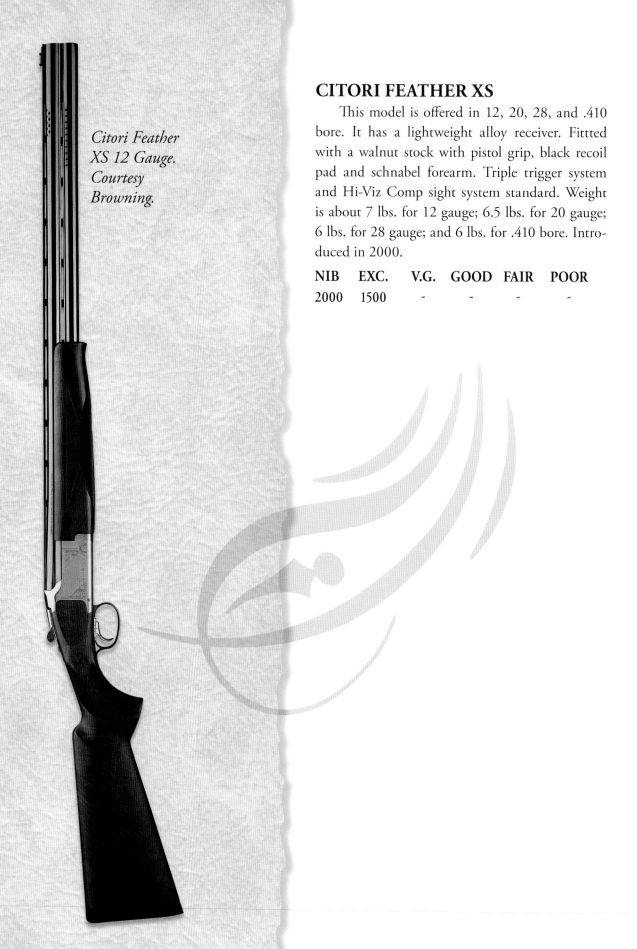

Citori Feather XS 12 Gauge. Courtesy Browning.

CITORI FEATHER XS

This model is offered in 12, 20, 28, and .410 bore. It has a lightweight alloy receiver. Fittted with a walnut stock with pistol grip, black recoil pad and schnabel forearm. Triple trigger system and Hi-Viz Comp sight system standard. Weight is about 7 lbs. for 12 gauge; 6.5 lbs. for 20 gauge; 6 lbs. for 28 gauge; and 6 lbs. for .410 bore. Introduced in 2000.

NIB	EXC.	V.G.	GOOD	FAIR	POOR
2000	1500	-	-	-	-

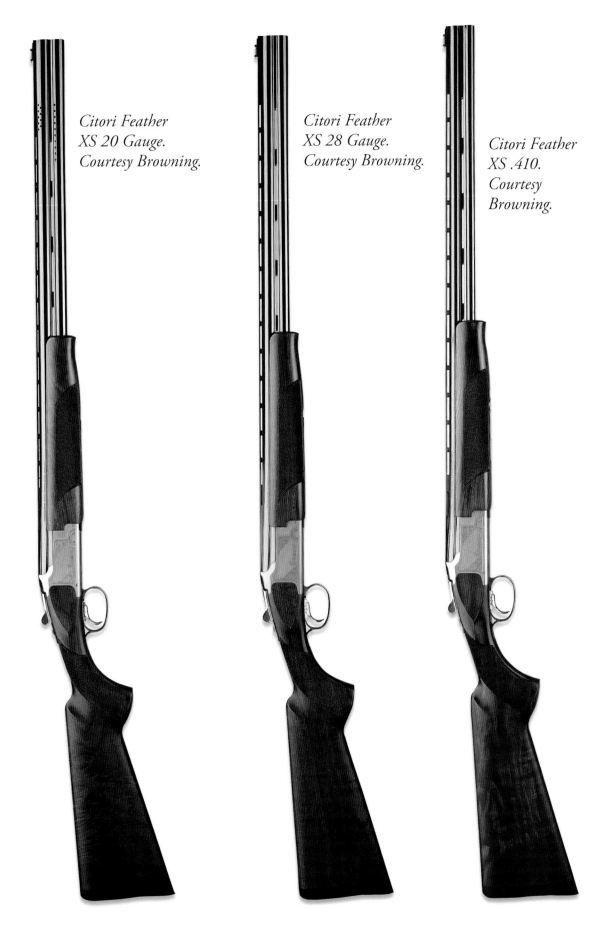

*Citori Feather
XS 20 Gauge.
Courtesy Browning.*

*Citori Feather
XS 28 Gauge.
Courtesy Browning.*

*Citori Feather
XS .410.
Courtesy
Browning.*

CITORI SUPERLIGHT FEATHER

Chambered for the 12 or 20 gauge with straight grip stock and schnabel forearm. This model has an alloy receiver. Checkered walnut stock. Offered with 26″ barrels. Weight is about 6 lbs. Introduced in 2002.

NIB	EXC.	V.G.	GOOD	FAIR	POOR
1940	1450	1100	-	-	-

CITORI SUPER LIGHT-NING GRADE I

Introduced in 2005 this 12 or 20 gauge model features a blued receiver with gold line border. Checkered satin finished select walnut stock with pistol grip and Schnabel forearm. Barrels are 26″ or 28″ with choke tubes. Recoil pad on 12 gauge. Weight is about 8 lbs. for the 12 gauge and 6.75 lbs. for the 20 gauge.

NIB	EXC.	V.G.	GOOD	FAIR	POOR
1865	1400	1050	-	-	-

Citori Superlight Feather. Courtesy Browning.

Period advertising for Citori. Courtesy Browning. Pricing no longer valid.

Citori Classic Lightning Grade I. Courtesy Browning.

Citori Classic Lightning Feather Grade I 20 Gauge. Courtesy Browning.

CITORI CLASSIC LIGHTNING GRADE I

Offered in 12 or 20 gauge with choice of 26″ or 28″ vent rib barrels with choke tubes. Receiver is scroll engraved on a silver nitride finish. Checkered select walnut stock with oil finish. Forearm is Lightning style. Recoil pad on 12 gauge. Weight is about 8 lbs. for 12 gauge and about 6.75 lbs. for the 20 gauge.

NIB	EXC.	V.G.	GOOD	FAIR	POOR
1890	1425	-	-	-	-

CITORI CLASSIC LIGHTNING FEATHER GRADE I

This model, introduced in 2005, features a high relief engraved alloy receiver. Chambered for the 12 or 20 gauge and fitted with 26″ or 28″ vent rib barrels with choke tubes. Checkered select stock with schnabel forearm. Recoil pad on 12 gauge. Weight is about 7 lbs. for 12 gauge and about 6.25 lbs. for 20 gauge.

NIB	EXC.	V.G.	GOOD	FAIR	POOR
1950	1450	-	-	-	-

CITORI 525 FEATHER

Similar to above but with alloy receiver, grade II/III select walnut stock, and 26" or 28" barrels. Available in 12, 20, and 28 gauge and .410. Weight from 6 lbs., 3 oz. (20-ga. magnum) to 7 lbs. (12 ga. magnum).

NIB	EXC.	V.G.	GOOD	FAIR	POOR
2320	1750	1250	-	-	-

CITORI 525 SPORTING

Introduced in 2002 this model is chambered for the 12 or 20 gauge and fitted with a choice of 28″ or 30″ vent rib ported barrels. The stock is redesigned with a Euro checkering pattern and more pronounced palm swell. Weight is about 8 lbs. for the 12 gauge and 7 lbs. for the 20. In 2003 this model was offered in both 28 gauge and .410 bore.

NIB	EXC.	V.G.	GOOD	FAIR	POOR
2320	1750	1250	-	-	-

NOTE: Add $275 for adjustable comb.

Citori 525 Sporting. Courtesy Browning.

Citori 525 Feather. Courtesy Browning.

Citori 525 Field Combo. Courtesy Browning.

CITORI 525 FIELD

As above but with a choice of 26″ or 28″ barrels. Barrels are unported. Ventilated recoil pad. Introduced in 2002. In 2003 this model was offered in both 28 gauge and .410 bore. Add 50 percent for combo.

NIB	EXC.	V.G.	GOOD	FAIR	POOR
1980	1475	950	-	-	-

CITORI 525 GOLDEN CLAYS SPORTING

This model has the same features as the 525 Sporting but with an oil-finished high stock and engraved receiver with gold inlays. In 2003 this model was offered in both 28 gauge and .410 bore.

NIB	EXC.	V.G.	GOOD	FAIR	POOR
4450	3250	2600	-	-	-

CITORI ESPRIT

Introduced in 2002 this model features removable decorative sideplates, schnabel forearm, and high-grade walnut stock. Offered in 12 gauge only with 28″ vent rib barrels. Weight is about 8.25 lbs.

NIB	EXC.	V.G.	GOOD	FAIR	POOR
2450	1900	-	-	-	-

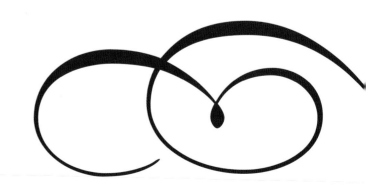

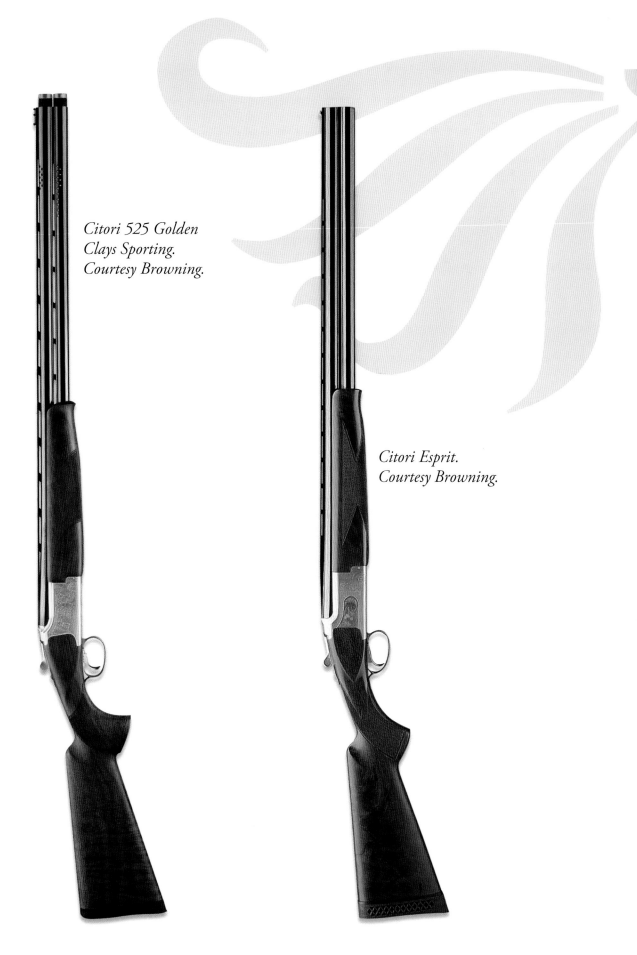

*Citori 525 Golden
Clays Sporting.
Courtesy Browning.*

*Citori Esprit.
Courtesy Browning.*

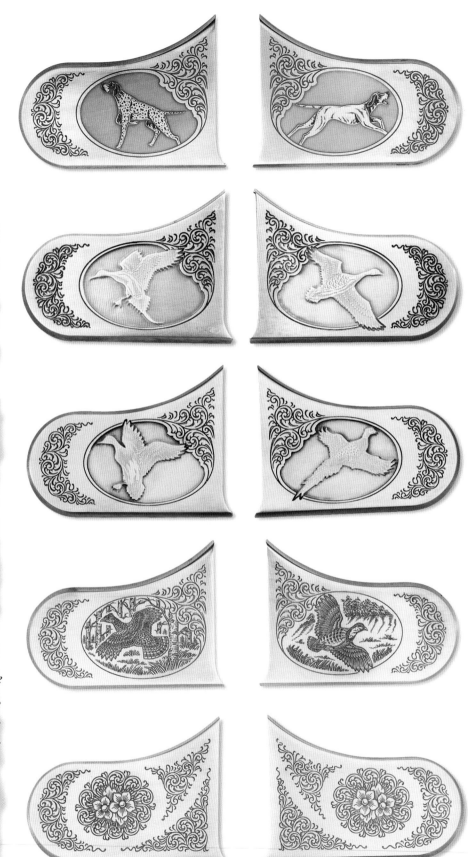

Citori Esprit sideplate engraving patterns, left and right view. Courtesy Browning.

CITORI LIGHTNING SPORTING CLAYS

Specifically designed for sporting clays shooting. Offered in 12 gauge only, each model is backbored, ported and fitted with Invector-Plus choke tubes. Barrels are chrome-plated. Receiver is blued with gold inscription. Pigeon Grade has gold detailing and high grade gloss round knob walnut stock. Signature Grade features a red and black print on the stock with gold decals. Trigger is adjustable to three length of pull positions. Comes with three interchangeable trigger shoes. Each model is fitted with rubber recoil pad.

NIB	EXC.	V.G.	GOOD	FAIR	POOR
2450	1900	-	-	-	-

LIGHTNING SPORTING MODEL

This model features a rounded pistol grip and Lightning forearm with choice of high or low vent rib. Chambered for 3″ shells. Offered in 28″ or 30″ barrels. Weighs about 8.5 lbs. Introduced in 1989.

NIB	EXC.	V.G.	GOOD	FAIR	POOR
1200	1000	800	600	450	300

PIGEON GRADE

NIB	Exc.	V.G.	Good	Fair	Poor
1350	1100	900	650	450	300

GOLDEN CLAYS

First introduced in 1994.

NIB	EXC.	V.G.	GOOD	FAIR	POOR
2600	2250	1650	900	450	300

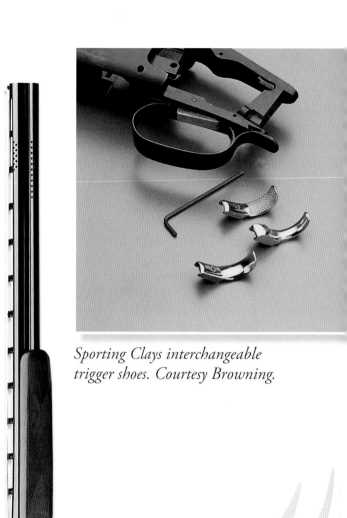

Sporting Clays interchangeable trigger shoes. Courtesy Browning.

Citori Lightning Sporting Clays. Courtesy Browning.

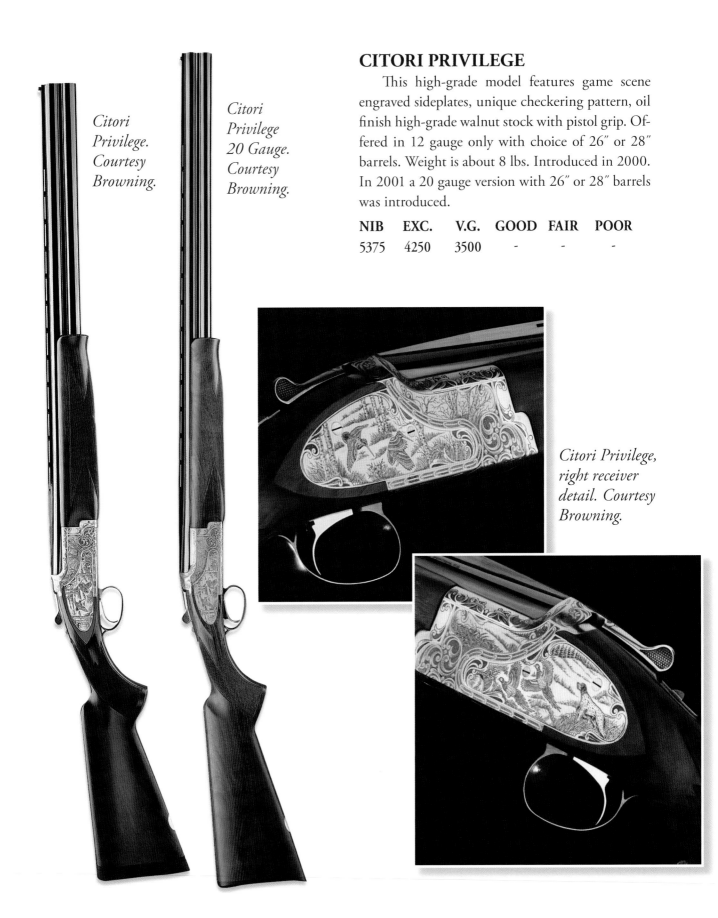

Citori Privilege. Courtesy Browning.

Citori Privilege 20 Gauge. Courtesy Browning.

CITORI PRIVILEGE

This high-grade model features game scene engraved sideplates, unique checkering pattern, oil finish high-grade walnut stock with pistol grip. Offered in 12 gauge only with choice of 26″ or 28″ barrels. Weight is about 8 lbs. Introduced in 2000. In 2001 a 20 gauge version with 26″ or 28″ barrels was introduced.

NIB	EXC.	V.G.	GOOD	FAIR	POOR
5375	4250	3500	-	-	-

Citori Privilege, right receiver detail. Courtesy Browning.

CITORI XS SPORTING CLAYS

Introduced in 1999, this model features silver nitride receiver with gold accents and European-style stock with schnabel forend. Available in 12 or 20. Choice of 28″, 30″ or 32″ barrels. Weight varies from 8 lbs. in 12 gauge to 7 lbs. for the 20 gauge.

NIB	EXC.	V.G.	GOOD	FAIR	POOR
2470	1850	1350	-	-	-

CITORI ULTRA XS SKEET

This model is offered in 12 gauge only with choice of 28″ or 30″ ported barrels chambered for 2.75″ shells. Semi-beavertail forearm. Triple trigger system standard. Adjustable comb optional. Walnut stock with pistol grip and black recoil pad. Weight is about 7.75 lbs. Introduced in 2000. In 2001 a 20 gauge version was introduced with a choice of 28″ or 30″ barrels.

NIB	EXC.	V.G.	GOOD	FAIR	POOR
2435	1800	-	-	-	-

NOTE: Add $275 for adjustable comb.

CITORI XS SPECIAL

This is a 12 gauge 2.75″ chamber gun with choice of 30" or 32" vent rib barrels with porting and extended choke tubes. Checkered walnut stock with adjustable comb and pistol grip. Semi-beavertail forearm. Silver engraved receiver. Weight is about 8.7 lbs.

NIB	EXC.	V.G.	GOOD	FAIR	POOR
2725	2050	-	-	-	-

CITORI PLUS

This model features an adjustable point of impact from 3″ to 12″ above point of aim. Receiver on Grade I is blued with scroll engraving. Walnut stock is adjustable and forearm is a modified beavertail style. Available in 30″ or 32″ barrels that are backbored and ported. Non-ported barrels are optional. Weighs about 9 lbs. 6 oz. Introduced in 1989.

NOTE: In terms of technological advancement, these are extraordinary weapons.

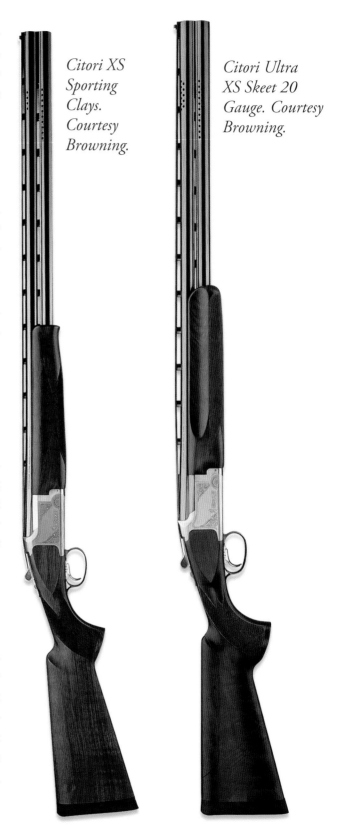

Citori XS Sporting Clays. Courtesy Browning.

Citori Ultra XS Skeet 20 Gauge. Courtesy Browning.

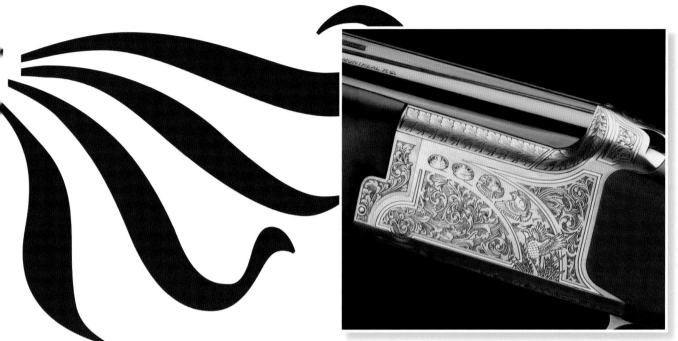

Citori Plus Sporting Clays receiver detail. Courtesy Browning.

GRADE I

NIB	EXC.	V.G.	GOOD	FAIR	POOR
1200	1000	750	500	400	300

PIGEON GRADE

NIB	EXC.	V.G.	GOOD	FAIR	POOR
1750	1500	950	700	500	300

Signature Grade

NIB	EXC.	V.G.	GOOD	FAIR	POOR
1650	1450	950	700	500	300

GOLDEN CLAYS

First introduced in 1994.

NIB	EXC.	V.G.	GOOD	FAIR	POOR
2750	2250	1500	900	450	300

CITORI PLUS COMBO

This model features a single-barrel trap and an interchangeable Over/Under set of barrels. Other features are similar to Citori Plus Grade 1. Barrel combinations are 32″ Over/Under with 34″ single barrel or 30″ Over/Under barrel with 32″ or 34″ single barrel. Introduced in 1989.

NIB	EXC.	V.G.	GOOD	FAIR	POOR
2500	2100	1750	1100	700	450

CITORI TRAP COMBINATION SET

This version is offered in Grade I only and features a 34″ single barrel and a 32″ set of Over/Under barrels. It is furnished in a fitted case and has been discontinued.

EXC.	V.G.	GOOD	FAIR	POOR
1200	1050	950	800	700

GTI MODEL

This model features a 13mm wide rib, ventilated side ribs, pistol-grip stock, semi-beavertail forearm. Offered in 28″ or 30″ barrel. Weighs about 8 lbs. This model not offered in Pigeon Grade. Introduced in 1989.

GRADE I

NIB	EXC.	V.G.	GOOD	FAIR	POOR
1100	900	750	600	450	300

SIGNATURE GRADE

NIB	EXC.	V.G.	GOOD	FAIR	POOR
1100	900	750	600	450	300

GOLDEN CLAYS

First introduced in 1994.

NIB	EXC.	V.G.	GOOD	FAIR	POOR
2350	1900	1250	900	450	300

ULTRA SPORTER-SPORTING CLAYS

This model was introduced in 1995 and replaces the GTI model. It features a 10mm to 13mm tapered rib and is offered with either a blued or gray receiver with walnut stock with pistol grip and semi-beavertail forearm. Fitted with adjustable comb. Adjustable length of pull. Offered in 12 gauge only with 28″ or 30″ barrels. Average weight is 8 lbs.

NIB	EXC.	V.G.	GOOD	FAIR	POOR
1450	1100	800	550	400	300

ULTRA SPORTER SPORTING CLAYS-GOLDEN CLAYS

NIB	EXC.	V.G.	GOOD	FAIR	POOR
2750	2200	1600	1100	750	400

NOTE: For Ultra Sporters with adjustable comb add $200 to NIB price.

CITORI SUPERLIGHT

This is a lighter-weight version of the Citori chambered for all gauges and offered with the same features as the Lightning Series. The grades differ in the amount of ornamentation and quality of materials and workmanship utilized. This series was introduced in 1983.

MICRO LIGHTNING

Offered in 20 gauge only and has reduced dimensions for smaller shooters. Available with 24″ vent rib barrels. Weighs 6 lbs. 3 oz. Introduced in 1991.

NIB	EXC.	V.G.	GOOD	FAIR	POOR
950	850	700	600	400	300

Citori Micro Lightning. Courtesy Browning.

Citori Gran Lightning. Courtesy Browning.

Citori White Lightning. Courtesy Browning.

GRAN LIGHTNING

This is essentially a Grade I Lightning with a high grade select walnut stock with satin finish. Receiver and barrels are blued. Offered in 12 gauge and 20 gauge with choice of 26" or 28" vent rib barrels. Choke tubes standard. Weighs about 8 lbs. in 12 gauge and 6 lbs. 11 oz. in 20 gauge. Introduced in 1990. In 2004 the 28 gauge and .410 bore were added.

NIB	EXC.	V.G.	GOOD	FAIR	POOR
2430	1800	1300	975	650	350

CITORI WHITE LIGHTNING

Introduced in 1998 this model features a silver nitride scroll engraved receiver. Offered in 3" 12 and 3" 20 gauge with choice of 26" or 28" barrels. In 2004 this model is also available in 28 gauge as well as .410 bore. Weight is approximately 8 lbs. for 12 gauge models and 6.8 lbs. for 20 gauge models. Invector-Plus chokes standard. Lightning-style stock.

NIB	EXC.	V.G.	GOOD	FAIR	POOR
1715	1300	950	700	-	-

NOTE: Add $75 for 28 and .410 models.

CITORI WHITE UPLAND SPECIAL

Introduced in 2000 this model features a shortened straight-grip stock, schnabel forearm, and 24″ barrel. Fitted with 2.75″ chambered for 12 gauge and 20 gauge only. Weight is about 6.75 lbs.

NIB	EXC.	V.G.	GOOD	FAIR	POOR
1650	1200	975	-	-	-

Citori White Upland Special. Courtesy Browning.

Citori Skeet 20 Gauge. Courtesy Browning.

CITORI SKEET

This series of guns was chambered for all gauges and was designed for competition skeet shooting. It is similar to the standard Citori with a high-post target rib and 26″ or 28″ barrels. The versions differ in the amount of engraving and the quality of materials and workmanship utilized.

GRADE I

NIB	EXC.	V.G.	GOOD	FAIR	POOR
1000	925	750	550	425	350

GRADE II

Discontinued 1983.

EXC.	V.G.	GOOD	FAIR	POOR
1000	900	750	450	300

GRADE III

NIB	EXC.	V.G.	GOOD	FAIR	POOR
1500	1200	900	750	450	300

GRADE V

Discontinued 1984.

NIB	EXC.	V.G.	GOOD	FAIR	POOR
1600	1200	900	750	450	300

GRADE VI

NIB	EXC.	V.G.	GOOD	FAIR	POOR
2000	1750	1200	900	450	300

GOLDEN CLAYS

First introduced in 1994.

NIB	EXC.	V.G.	GOOD	FAIR	POOR
2400	2000	1500	900	450	300

Citori XT Trap. Courtesy Browning.

CITORI 3 GAUGE SET

Consists of 20 gauge, 28 gauge, and .410 bore interchangeable 28" vent rib barrels. Introduced in 1987.

GRADE I

NIB	EXC.	V.G.	GOOD	FAIR	POOR
2100	1950	1700	1250	900	700

GRADE III

NIB	EXC.	V.G.	GOOD	FAIR	POOR
2500	2250	1900	1400	1100	800

GRADE VI

NIB	EXC.	V.G.	GOOD	FAIR	POOR
2950	2500	2000	1500	1200	900

CITORI 4 GAUGE SET

This set has a 12 gauge, 20 gauge, 28 gauge, and .410 bore interchangeable vent rib barrels in either 26" or 28" lengths. Introduced in 1981.

GRADE I

NIB	EXC.	V.G.	GOOD	FAIR	POOR
3300	2750	2250	1700	1250	900

GRADE III

NIB	EXC.	V.G.	GOOD	FAIR	POOR
3400	2900	2500	1900	1350	900

GRADE VI

NIB	EXC.	V.G.	GOOD	FAIR	POOR
3800	3300	2900	2250	1400	950

CITORI TRAP

This version is similar to the standard Citori, offered in 12 gauge only with 30" or 32" barrels. It features a high rib and a Monte Carlo-type stock with recoil pad. The versions differ as to the amount of ornamentation and the quality of materials and workmanship utilized.

GRADE I

NIB	EXC.	V.G.	GOOD	FAIR	POOR
1000	900	750	550	425	350

PLUS TRAP

Adjustable rib and stock. Introduced in 1989.

NIB	EXC.	V.G.	GOOD	FAIR	POOR
1500	1350	1000	750	600	500

Grade II

DISCONTINUED 1983.

EXC.	V.G.	GOOD	FAIR	POOR
1000	850	675	450	350

GRADE III

NIB	EXC.	V.G.	GOOD	FAIR	POOR
1500	1350	1000	750	600	500

GRADE V

Discontinued 1984.

EXC.	V.G.	GOOD	FAIR	POOR
1400	1250	900	650	450

GRADE VI

NIB	EXC.	V.G.	GOOD	FAIR	POOR
2100	1800	1550	1250	1000	800

CITORI XT TRAP

Introduced in 1999, this Trap model is fitted with contoured beavertail with Monte Carlo stock with or without adjustable comb. The grayed receiver is highlighted in gold with light scroll work. Choice of 32" or 30" barrels. Weight is approximately 8 lbs. 11 ozs.

NIB	EXC.	V.G.	GOOD	FAIR	POOR
2275	1700	1200	-	-	-

NOTE: Add $275 for adjustable comb.

Citori 425 Sporting Clays. Courtesy Browning.

GOLDEN CLAYS

First introduced in 1994.

NIB	EXC.	V.G.	GOOD	FAIR	POOR
2750	2250	1500	900	450	300

SIGNATURE GRADE

NIB	EXC.	V.G.	GOOD	FAIR	POOR
1150	950	800	600	450	300

CITORI XT TRAP GOLD

Introduced in 2005 this model features a gold game scene engraving pattern on a silver receiver. Choice of 30″ or 32″ vent rib ported barrels with choke tubes. Checkered select walnut stock with adjustable comb and semi-beavertail forearm. Stock also has adjustable length of pull and recoil reduction system. Weight is about 9 lbs.

NIB	EXC.	V.G.	GOOD	FAIR	POOR
4220	3150	-	-	-	-

MODEL 325 SPORTING CLAYS

Introduced in 1993 this model has a European design that features a scroll-engraved, grayed receiver schnabel forearm, 10mm wide vent rib, three interchangeable and adjustable trigger shoes, and back-bore barrels that are ported and fitted with choke tubes. Available in 12 gauge and 20 gauge. The 12 gauge is offered with 28″, 30″, or 32″ barrels while the 20 gauge is offered with 28″ or 30″ barrel fitted with conventional chokes. The 12 gauge weighs about 7 lbs. 14 oz., while the 20 gauge weighs about 6 lbs. 12 oz.

NIB	EXC.	V.G.	GOOD	FAIR	POOR
1350	1200	900	700	450	300

SPECIAL SPORTING

Similar to the Sporting model but fitted with a 2-3/4″ chamber and choice of 28″, 30″, or 32″ barrels. Barrels are ported. Barrels are also fitted with a high post rib. Stock has a full pistol grip and optional adjustable comb. Depending on barrel length weighs about 8.3 lbs.

GRADE I

NIB	EXC.	V.G.	GOOD	FAIR	POOR
1150	900	750	600	450	300

SIGNATURE GRADE

NIB	EXC.	V.G.	GOOD	FAIR	POOR
1150	900	750	600	450	300

PIGEON GRADE

NIB	EXC.	V.G.	GOOD	FAIR	POOR
1300	1100	850	600	450	300

GOLDEN CLAYS

NIB	EXC.	V.G.	GOOD	FAIR	POOR
2400	1900	1250	900	450	300

MODEL 425 SPORTING CLAYS

This Citori over-and-under gun is offered in both 12 and 20 gauge with a choice of 28″ and 30″ barrel with 32″ barrels available on the 12 gauge as well. The 425 is adjustable for length of pull and has an adjustable comb. Barrels are fitted with a 10mm wide rib. Invector chokes are standard. Average weight is 7 lbs. 14 oz. Introduced in 1995.

NIB	EXC.	V.G.	GOOD	FAIR	POOR
1550	1200	850	600	450	300

Model 425 Golden Clays. Courtesy Browning.

Light Sporting 802ES. Courtesy Browning.

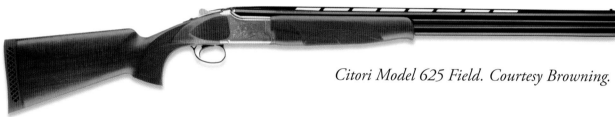

Citori Model 625 Field. Courtesy Browning.

MODEL 425 GOLDEN CLAYS

Same as above but with high-grade wood and engraved receiver.

NIB	EXC.	V.G.	GOOD	FAIR	POOR
2950	2350	1650	1100	600	300

NOTE: For Model 425 with adjustable comb add $200 to NIB price.

LIGHT SPORTING 802ES (EXTENDED SWING)

Introduced in 1996 this model features a 28″ vent rib barrel with 2″ stainless steel extension tubes for an extended swing of 30″. An additional 4″ extension is also included. Thus the barrel can be 28″, 30″ or 32″ according to needs. Chambered for 12 gauge with adjustable length of pull. Walnut stock with pistol grip and schnabel forearm. Weight is about 7.5 lbs.

NIB	EXC.	V.G.	GOOD	FAIR	POOR
1700	1400	900	700	500	250

CITORI 625 FIELD

Introduced in 2008. This model has a single selective trigger, back-bored barrels, select walnut stock, and Invector Plus choke tubes. Silver nitride finish, high relief engraving and schnabel forend.

NIB	EXC.	V.G.	GOOD	FAIR	POOR
2650	–	–	–	–	–

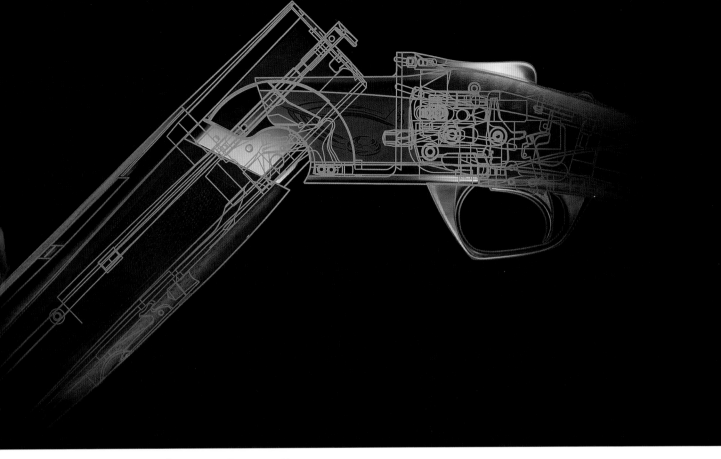

Cynergy CAD schematic. Courtesy Browning.

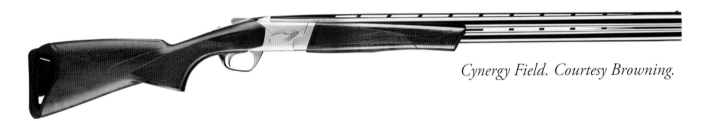

Cynergy Field. Courtesy Browning.

CYNERGY SERIES

This series was introduced in 2004. Browning calls it the third generation over-and-under gun. The Cynergy has a number of new design features such as a monoblock hinge system for a lower profile, an inflex recoil pad, a new mechanical trigger system, an adjustable comb, back-bored barrels, and impact ejectors.

NOTE:These are great guns, but they have not been particularly well accepted by the market. Converting one of these to cash at a good price, in my opinion, would take some time.)

CYNERGY FIELD

This 12 gauge 3″ model features a checkered walnut stock and forearm. Silver nitrate receiver with engraving. Choice of 26″ or 28″ vent rib barrels with choke tubes. Weight is about 7.75 lbs. A synthetic stock with adjustable comb is also offered.

NIB	EXC.	V.G.	GOOD	FAIR	POOR
2050	1500	-	-	-	-

NOTE: Deduct $40 for synthetic stock.

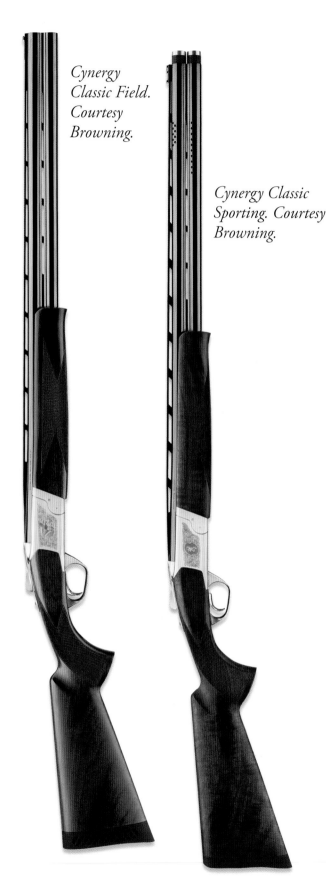

Cynergy Classic Field. Courtesy Browning.

Cynergy Classic Sporting. Courtesy Browning.

CYNERGY CLASSIC FIELD

This more traditionally styled 12 gauge was added to the Cynergy line in 2006. It features a steel receiver with silver nitride finish and game bird scenes on each side. Satin finish walnut stock and schnabel style forend. Three choke tubes. Available in barrel lengths of 26″ and 28″ with an average weight of 7.75 lbs.

NIB	EXC.	V.G.	GOOD	FAIR	POOR
2150	-	-	-	-	-

CYNERGY FIELD SMALL GAUGE

Introduced in 2005 this model is chambered for the 20 or 28 gauge. Choice of 26″ or 28″ vent rib barrels. Weight is about 6.25 lbs.

NIB	EXC.	V.G.	GOOD	FAIR	POOR
2060	1600	-	-	-	-

CYNERGY SPORTING

As above but with higher grade walnut stock and choice of 28″, 30″, or 32″ vent rib barrels with choke tubes. Ported barrels. Hi-Viz front sight. Weight is about 8 lbs. A synthetic stock with adjustable comb is also offered.

NIB	EXC.	V.G.	GOOD	FAIR	POOR
2690	2100	-	-	-	-

NOTE: For synthetic stock deduct $40.

CYNERGY CLASSIC SPORTING

New for 2006, this traditionally styled version of the Cynergy Sporting is available in 12 gauge with 28″, 30″ or 32″ ported barrels. Oil finish walnut stock with Schnabel forend and Browning logo on steel receiver with silver nitride finish. Three Invector-Plus Midas Grade choke tubes. Average weight 7.75 lbs.

NOTE: Technically speaking, these shotguns outclass anything that I have seen in the marketplace, for the money.

NIB	EXC.	V.G.	GOOD	FAIR	POOR
2500	-	-	-	-	-

CYNERGY SPORTING, ADJUSTABLE COMB

Similar to Cynergy Sporting but with a comb adjustable for cast and drop. Average weight 8.2 lbs. Introduced 2006.

NIB	EXC.	V.G.	GOOD	FAIR	POOR
2800	-	-	-	-	-

CYNERGY SPORTING SMALL GAUGE

As above but in 20 or 28 gauge. Choice of 28″, 30″, or 32″ ported barrels in 20 gauge and 28″ or 30″ ported barrels in 28 gauge. Weight is about 6.25 to 6.5 lbs. depending on barrel length. Introduced in 2005.

NIB	EXC.	V.G.	GOOD	FAIR	POOR
3080	2300	-	-	-	-

CYNERGY CLASSIC FIELD SMALL GAUGE

The 20 and 28 gauges and .410 bore models were added to the Classic Field line in 2007. All offer choice of 26" or 28" barrels. 3" chambers in 20 gauge and .410 bore; 2-3/4" chambers in 28 gauge. Average weight 6.5 lbs.

NIB	EXC.	V.G.	GOOD	FAIR	POOR
2200	-	-	-	-	-

CYNERGY CLASSIC FIELD GRADE III

High-grade model added in 2007 features a steel receiver with silver-nitride finish and high-relief engraving on trigger guard, tang and lever. Gloss finish Grade III/IV walnut and 3 Invector Plus chokes. Available in 12 and 20 gauge with 26" or 28" barrels. Weight is about 8 lbs. in 12 gauge and 6.4 lbs. in 20 gauge.

NIB	EXC.	V.G.	GOOD	FAIR	POOR
3200	-	-	-	-	-

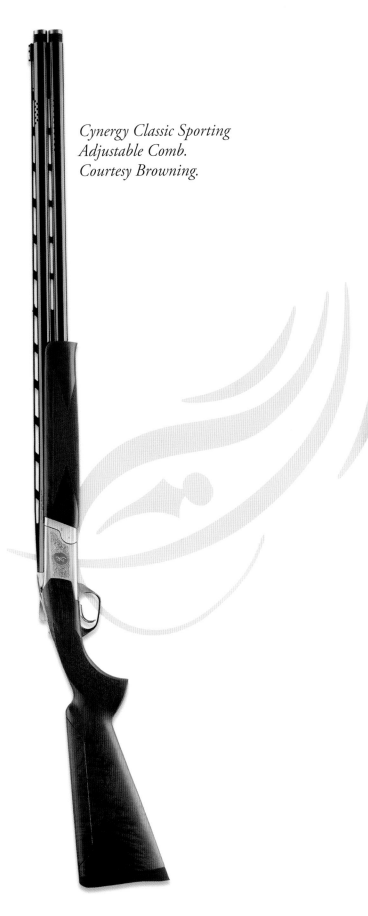

Cynergy Classic Sporting Adjustable Comb. Courtesy Browning.

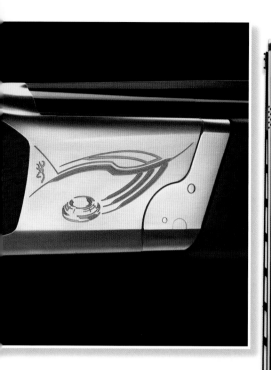

Cynergy receiver, detail view. Courtesy Browning.

CYNERGY CLASSIC FIELD GRADE VI

AS ABOVE, BUT WITH GOLD ENHANCED ENGRAVING AND GRADE V/VI WALNUT.

NIB	EXC.	V.G.	GOOD	FAIR	POOR
4750	-	-	-	-	-

CYNERGY CLASSIC SPORTING SMALL GAUGE

Seven small gauge offerings were added to the Classic Sporting line in 2007. The 23/4" 28 gauge and 3" .410 bore are available with 28" and 30" barrels with three Invector chokes. The 2-3/4" 20 gauge comes with 28", 30" or 32" barrels and three Invector Plus Midas Grade chokes. Average weight 6.5 lbs.

NIB	EXC.	V.G.	GOOD	FAIR	POOR
3200	-	-	-	-	-

CYNERGY CLASSIC SPORTING WITH ADJUSTABLE COMB

New in 2007 in 2-3/4" 12 and 20 gauge with 28", 30" or 32" barrels. Same features as Classic Sporting plus a comb adjustable for cast and drop. Weight about 8.5 lbs. in 12 gauge and 7.1 lbs. in 20 gauge.

12 GA.

NIB	EXC.	V.G.	GOOD	FAIR	POOR
3200	-	-	-	-	-

20 GA.

NIB	EXC.	V.G.	GOOD	FAIR	POOR
3500	-	-	-	-	-

CYNERGY CLASSIC TRAP

Trap model with 2-3/4" chambers features gloss finish Monte Carlo stock with right hand palm swell and modified semi-beavertail forend with finger grooves. Available with 30" or 32" barrels with three Invector Plus Midas Grade chokes. Average weight 8.75 lbs. Also available with Unsingle trap barrel. Add 20 percent for Unsingle.

NIB	EXC.	V.G.	GOOD	FAIR	POOR
3250	-	-	-	-	-

Cynergy Classic Trap. Courtesy Browning.

CYNERGY CLASSIC TRAP
WITH ADJUSTABLE COMB

SAME FEATURES AS ABOVE BUT WITH COMB ADJUSTABLE FOR CAST AND DROP.

NIB	EXC.	V.G.	GOOD	FAIR	POOR
3500	-	-	-	-	-

CYNERGY EURO SPORTING

New in 2007, this Euro-styled 2-3/4" chambered Cynergy is offered with 28", 30" or 32" ported barrels, Inflex recoil pad and three Invector Plus Diamond Grade chokes. Average weight is 8 lbs.

NIB	EXC.	V.G.	GOOD	FAIR	POOR
3400	-	-	-	-	-

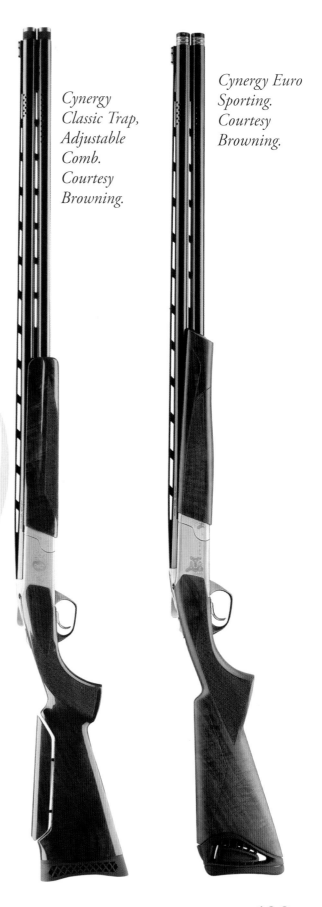

Cynergy Classic Trap, Adjustable Comb. Courtesy Browning.

Cynergy Euro Sporting. Courtesy Browning.

Cynergy Euro Sporting, Adjustable Comb. Courtesy Browning.

CYNERGY EURO SPORTING WITH ADJUSTABLE COMB

Same features as above but with comb adjustable for cast and drop. Average weight 8.25 lbs.

NIB	EXC.	V.G.	GOOD	FAIR	POOR
3700	-	-	-	-	-

CYNERGY EURO SPORTING COMPOSITE

Same features as Euro Sporting but with black composite stock and rubber overmolding in grip areas. Average weight 7.75 pounds.

NIB	EXC.	V.G.	GOOD	FAIR	POOR
3200	-	-	-	-	-

Cynergy Euro Sporting Composite. Courtesy Browning.

Cynergy, receiver detail. Courtesy Browning.

Cynergy Feather. Courtesy Browning.

Cynergy Feather Composite. Courtesy Browning.

Cynergy Camo. Courtesy Browning.

Cynergy nickel tin. Courtesy Browning.

CYNERGY FEATHER

Introduced in 2007, the Feather is based on the Cynergy Field but features a lightweight alloy with steel breech face and gold enchanced gray finish. It has 3" chambers and is offered with 26" and 28" barrels. Weight is 6.75 lbs.

NIB	EXC.	V.G.	GOOD	FAIR	POOR
2350	-	-	-	-	-

CYNERGY FEATHER COMPOSITE

Same features as above but with black composite stock and rubber overmoldings in grip areas. Weight is about 6.6 lbs.

NIB	EXC.	V.G.	GOOD	FAIR	POOR
2300	-	-	-	-	-

CYNERGY CAMO

Camouflage, synthetic stocked 12 gauge models with 3.5" chambers based on the Cynergy Field. Three different Mossy Oak® camo patterns with 26" or 28" barrels. Three Invector Plus choke tubes.

NIB	EXC.	V.G.	GOOD	FAIR	POOR
2250	-	-	-	-	-

CYNERGY NICKEL TIN

New in 2007, this 3.5" 12 gauge Cynergy features a steel receiver with matte grey nickel tin finish. The stock is black composite with rubber overmolding in grip areas. Barrels are 26" or 28". Three Invector Plus chokes. Weight is about 7.8 lbs.

NIB	EXC.	V.G.	GOOD	FAIR	POOR
2200	-	-	-	-	-

The Complete Competitor.

The BT-99 Competition is one of the fiercest competing shotguns on the line today. A high post rib places the center of your pattern a nominal 9 inches high at 40 yards so you can see those claybirds clearly all the way back to 27 yards. This point-of-impact means you won't have to blot out a bird to hit it—even at handicap positions. The bird you can see is the bird you can hit.

You can also count on your point-of-impact to stay put through even the longest, hottest shoots. This is because that high rib **floats** on all posts. The barrel is free to expand naturally, without interference from the rib. Your point-of-impact will be the same for your 200th bird as it was for your 2nd.

With a BT-99, you can choose from two grades. Grade I features rosette and scroll designs on a blued receiver fitted to a stock of select French walnut hand checkered 18 lines to the inch. The Pigeon Grade BT-99 has a greyed steel receiver engraved with pigeons on an ornate fleur-de-lis background and a high grade American walnut stock skillfully hand checkered 22 lines to the inch.

Other features include a choice of conventional or Monte Carlo stocks specially dimensioned for trap, a full pistol grip and broad wedge-shaped forearm for positive pointing and swinging control, and interchangeable barrels for the versatility of different barrel lengths and/or different chokes (32" or 34" choked F, IM, or M).

But the line isn't the only place a BT-99 Competition is competitive. It's just as strong on your dealer's rack. At $589.95, suggested retail, the Grade I Competition has no competition. Pigeon Grade guns are priced from $1275.00, suggested retail. See both at your authorized Browning dealer today.

Send a postcard to Browning, Dept. 98D , Morgan, Utah 84050. Distributed in Canada by Browning Canada Sports Ltd/Ltée.

FREE CATALOG

BROWNING
Make A BT-99 Part Of Your Family

Period advertising for BT-99. Courtesy Browning. Pricing no longer valid.

BT-99

This is a break-open, single-barrel trap gun chambered for 12 gauge only. It is offered with a 32″ or 34″, vent rib barrel with screw-in choke tubes. It features a boxlock action with automatic ejectors. The finish is blued with a checkered walnut stock and beavertail forearm. It was introduced in 1968 by B.C. Miroku.

NIB	EXC.	V.G.	GOOD	FAIR	POOR
800	700	600	500	400	350

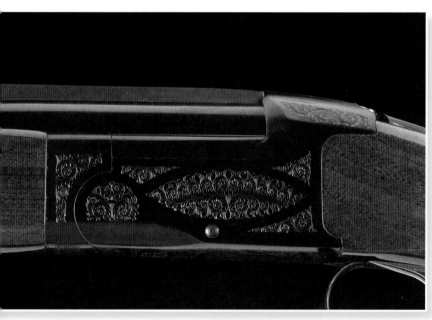

Left receiver detail. Courtesy Rock Island Auction.

BT-99 Trap Gun with adjustable butt. Courtesy Rock Island Auction.

Before you spend over $500 for a single barrel trap gun, look what you can get for under $500. Way under.

The Browning BT-99 $414.50*.

Every design component of the BT-99 exists to serve one end only—to help you shoot the best scores you are capable of. Special trap stock dimensions and high post rib design make the BT-99 impact above aiming point. You don't have to block out your birds. The bird you see is the bird you hit.

You get a special, **floating** trap rib that won't bind the barrel and change your point of impact as the barrel heats. Its wide 11/32 inch surface is matted to reduce reflection and has front and center ivory sight beads for precision pointing.

To soften recoil you get a low center of gravity, a thick deluxe, trap recoil pad, and a beavertail forearm with a special rearward taper so your pointing hand and arm absorbs some of the recoil before it gets to your shoulder.

You get a clean, crisp trigger letoff followed with a very fast lock time.

Ejection is automatic. And there is **no manual safety** to interrupt your rhythm and concentration. Close the breech and you're ready to fire.

Your BT-99 will break in easily. It fits most shooters perfectly, points quickly and swings smoothly. A BT-99 will bring out your best.

What more can you ask for in a single barrel trap gun? Ask for the BT-99 at your Browning dealer. 32" or 34" barrel, choked Mod, Imp Mod or Full.

Copyright © Browning 1976 *suggested retail price

BROWNING

FREE Catalog on all Browning Guns and Sports Equipment. Write Browning, Dept. 751, Morgan, Utah 84050.

Period advertising for BT-99 Pricing no longer valid. Courtesy Browning.

BT-99 STAINLESS

First introduced in 1993.

NIB	EXC.	V.G.	GOOD	FAIR	POOR
1275	1150	900	700	550	350

BT-99 SIGNATURE GRADE I

First introduced in 1993.

NIB	EXC.	V.G.	GOOD	FAIR	POOR
975	850	700	600	500	300

BT-99 PIGEON GRADE

First introduced in 1993.

NIB	EXC.	V.G.	GOOD	FAIR	POOR
1200	950	800	650	500	300

*BT-99 Grade III.
Courtesy Rock
Island Auction.*

Browning gauge reducers in a BT-99. Courtesy Browning.

BT-99 Plus.
Courtesy Browning.

BT-99 GOLDEN CLAYS

First introduced in 1994. In 2003 this model was offered with an adjustable comb. Weight is about 9 lbs. Available with either a 32″ or 34″ barrel.

NIB	EXC.	V.G.	GOOD	FAIR	POOR
3500	2500	1750	1100	500	300

BT-99 PLUS

This version features an adjustable vent rib and a recoil reduction system. It has an adjustable stock and recoil pad, as well as a back-bored barrel. It was introduced in 1989.

NIB	EXC.	V.G.	GOOD	FAIR	POOR
1350	1200	900	700	500	300

BT-99 PLUS-PIGEON GRADE

NIB	EXC.	V.G.	GOOD	FAIR	POOR
1500	1200	900	800	550	350

BT-99 PLUS-SIGNATURE GRADE

NIB	EXC.	V.G.	GOOD	FAIR	POOR
1400	1100	850	700	500	300

BT-99 PLUS STAINLESS-GRADE I

Same as standard version but offered in stainless steel. First introduced in 1993. Available in 32″ and 34″ barrels. Weighs about 8 lbs. 11 oz.

NIB	EXC.	V.G.	GOOD	FAIR	POOR
1600	1350	900	700	500	350

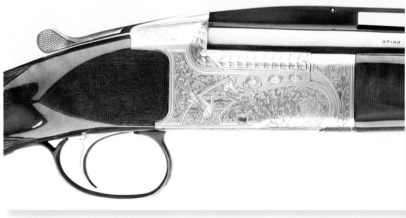

BT-99 receiver detail. Courtesy Browning.

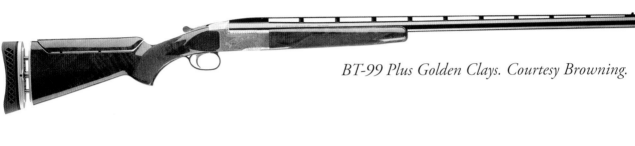

BT-99 Plus Golden Clays. Courtesy Browning.

BT-99 Plus Micro. Courtesy Browning.

BT-100. Courtesy Browning.

BT-99 PLUS-GOLDEN CLAYS

First introduced in 1994.

NIB	EXC.	V.G.	GOOD	FAIR	POOR
2600	2250	1750	900	450	300

BT-99 PLUS MICRO

Slightly reduced dimensions and offered in barrel lengths from 28″ to 34″. Weighs about 8 lbs. 6 oz. Introduced in 1991.

NIB	EXC.	V.G.	GOOD	FAIR	POOR
1350	1100	900	700	500	300

MODEL BT-100

First introduced in 1995 this single-barrel trap features an adjustable trigger pull and length of pull. The stock is either a Monte Carlo version or an adjustable comb version. Barrel is either 32″ or 34″. Choice of blue or stainless finish. Weight is about 8.9 lbs.

NIB	EXC.	V.G.	GOOD	FAIR	POOR
1850	1200	900	700	500	300

BT-100 Stainless with Monte Carlo stock. Courtesy Browning.

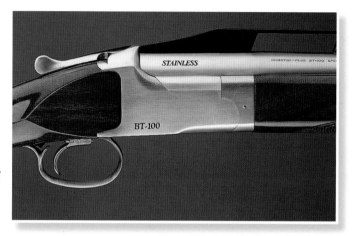

BT-100 Stainless receiver, detail view. Courtesy Browning.

BT-100 Satin. Courtesy Browning.

MODEL BT-100 STAINLESS

Introduced in 2000, this model is similar to the above but with stainless receiver and barrel.

NIB	EXC.	V.G.	GOOD	FAIR	POOR
1850	1500	1250	-	-	-

MODEL BT-100 SATIN

Introduced in 1999, this model features a matte black receiver and barrels without ejector selector. Available in 32″ or 34″ barrels. Available in Grade I only.

NIB	EXC.	V.G.	GOOD	FAIR	POOR
1650	1300	1050	-	-	-

MODEL BT-100 THUMBHOLE

This model is the same as the standard BT-100, but with the additional feature of a thumbhole stock. Offered in both blue and stainless.

NIB	EXC.	V.G.	GOOD	FAIR	POOR
2375	1900	1350	-	-	-

RECOILLESS TRAP

First introduced in 1993 this model features an advanced design that eliminates recoil up to 72 percent. The receiver is a special bolt-action single-shot. Receiver is black anodized. It is fitted with an adjustable ventilated rib so the point of impact can be moved. Adjustable length of pull. The Standard Model is a 12 gauge with 30″ barrel while the Micro Model is fitted with 27″ barrels. Choke tubes are supplied. Standard Model weighs 9 lbs. 1 oz., while the Micro Model weighs 8 lbs. 10 oz.

NIB	EXC.	V.G.	GOOD	FAIR	POOR
1500	1300	900	700	500	350

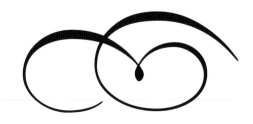

Side-By-Side Success.

For young and old alike, an upland hunt is always exciting. Somehow, you never quite get used to a peaceful thicket that suddenly erupts with a flurry of wild wings straining against the bond of gravity. Only a second or two stands between an empty bag and a savory upland feast.

This kind of shooting takes a gun with quick reflexes. A gun that mounts instantly, swings smoothly, and points by a special instinct all its own. A gun like the Browning B-SS.

The reason the B-SS responds so quickly is the built-in balance. The weight is tucked neatly between your hands. Whether you prefer a B-SS Standard with a hand-filling beavertail forearm and full pistol grip stock or a more traditional B-SS Sporter with a classic straight

grip stock and slimmed down forearm, you'll be in complete control.

Other B-SS advantages include 3 inch chambers, a selective firing mechanism that lets you choose which barrel and which choke you want to fire first, a selective ejector system that automatically throws spent hulls free of the gun while simply elevating unfired shells for easy removal, and a choice of two grades of hand engraving.

No matter which grade or style B-SS you choose, you'll possess a gun finished in the finest Browning tradition. You'll find the metal richly blued, and the wood to metal fits exact, and the hand checkering sharp and crisp. Priced from $419.95, suggested retail, the Browning B-SS is an outstanding field gun that responds in grand style to the demands of upland hunting.

Send a postcard to Browning, Dept. 17D, Morgan, Utah 84050. Distributed in Canada by Browning Canada Sports Ltd/Ltée.

FREE CATALOG

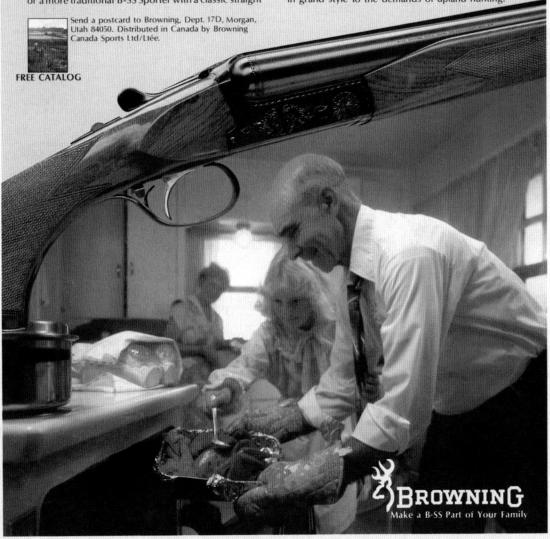

BROWNING
Make a B-SS Part of Your Family

Period advertising for BSS. Courtesy Browning. Pricing no longer valid.

BSS. Courtesy Rock Island Auction.

BSS

This is a side-by-side, double-barrel shotgun chambered for 12 or 20 gauge. It was offered with a 26″, 28″, or 30″ barrel with various choke combinations. It features a boxlock action and automatic ejectors. Early guns had a nonselective single trigger; late production, a selective trigger. The finish is blued with a checkered walnut stock and beavertail forearm. It was manufactured between 1978 and 1987 by B.C. Miroku.

NOTE: These particular Browning weapons, when first introduced, had nonselective triggers, and were not particularly popular or well received. They were competing with several other side-by-sides, e.g., the SKB. But slowly they began to become more appreciated, and today they have reached some degree of decent acceptance. I give them a Collectibility Factor of #2.

EXC.	V.G.	GOOD	FAIR	POOR
1400	1050	775	650	400

NOTE: Single-selective trigger add 20 percent. 20 gauge add 20 percent.

BSS SPORTER

This version features an English-style, straight-grip stock and a splinter forearm. The stock was oil-finished. It was offered with a 26″ or 28″ barrel.

EXC.	V.G.	GOOD	FAIR	POOR
1200	950	775	650	400

NOTE: For 20 gauge add 20 percent.

BSS GRADE II

This version features game scene engraving and a satin, coin finished receiver. It was discontinued in 1984.

NOTE: These are rare, and their rarity gives them some modest collector's interest.)

EXC.	V.G.	GOOD	FAIR	POOR
1750	1350	1100	850	500

BSS SIDELOCK

This version features an engraved sidelock action and was offered in 12 or 20 gauge. It was offered with a 26″ or 28″ barrel and has a straight-grip stock and splintered forearm. It was manufactured in Korea between 1983 and 1987.

NOTE: The last few dozen 12 gauge sidelocks produced were an uncatalogued version of earlier guns. These guns had very finely engraved game scenes with English scroll. Add a 30 percent premium for this variation. If I were going to buy a BSS, this is the one I would buy. They are extremely beautiful, and extremely rare, and my prediction is that their values will only continue to rise.

NIB	EXC.	V.G.	GOOD	FAIR	POOR
2750	2100	1600	1250	800	500

NOTE: Add 30 percent to above prices for 20 gauge guns.

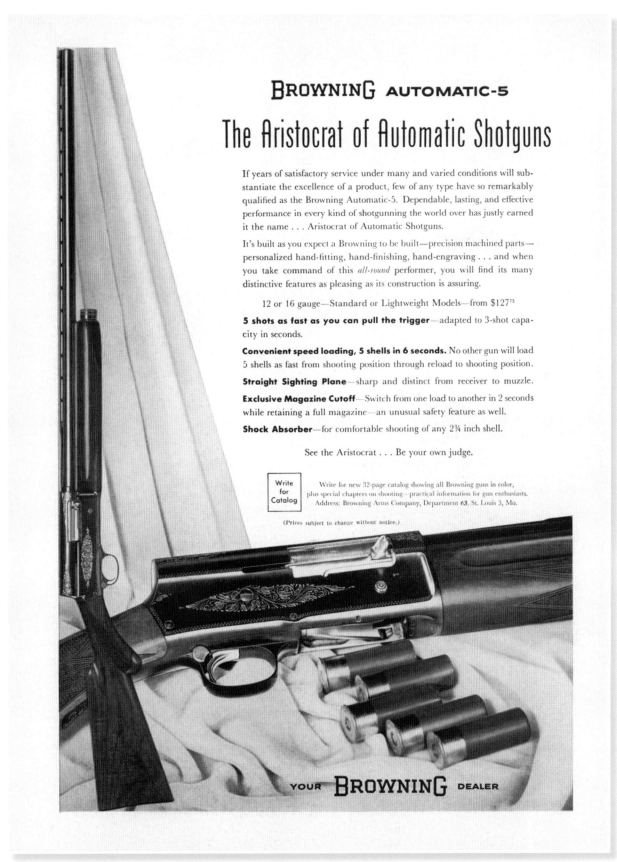

Period advertising for Browning Auto-5. Courtesy Browning. Pricing no longer valid.

AUTO-5 SHOTGUN

EARLY PRODUCTION AUTO-5

This series of recoil-operated, semi-automatic shotguns was designed by John M. Browning and was offered in 12 or 16 gauge. The barrel lengths were 26″, 28″, 30″, or 32″ with various chokes and ribs. It has a unique, square-back action that has become instantly recognizable. The finish is blued with a checkered, walnut, round-knob stock. The various versions differ in the amount of ornamentation, type of rib, and quality of materials and workmanship utilized in construction. This series was manufactured in Belgium by FN between 1903 and 1939. The first example appeared in the United States in 1923. Pre-WWII 16 gauge guns, introduced in 1936, had 2-9/16″ chambers; early models should be inspected by a qualified gunsmith before firing.

John Browning with one of the greatest shotguns of all time, his legendary Auto-5. Courtesy Browning.

A familiar sight to lovers of the Auto-5. Courtesy Rock Island Auction.

NOTE: For 16 gauge not converted to 2-3/4″ chamber deduct 30 percent. Grade III or Grade IV prices are not nearly as affected by chamber length because of their rarity. Original pre-war barrels were serial numbered to the gun. For extra barrels serial numbered to the gun add $100 for plain barrels, $200 for matte rib barrels, $275 for vent rib barrels. For extra barrels on Grade IV guns add an additional 30 percent to these barrel prices. Prices given are for guns with original barrels serial numbered to the gun. Remember the safety is located in front of the trigger guard.

NOTE: These shotguns, while somewhat strange appearance, were the rage, especially after their introduction. Many older shotgunners tell stories of how well these gun shoot and operate. There is no reason why I would not accumulate a few of these at the right price, especially in the more rare configurations. These weapons deserved a Collectibility Factor of #1. In addition, although, technically speaking, these guns are considered to be somewhat antiquated, it's amazing how well they sell and how much demand there is for them.

GRADE I-PLAIN BARREL

NEW	EXC.	V.G.	GOOD	FAIR	POOR
800	500	400	300	250	150

GRADE I-MATTE RIB

NEW	EXC.	V.G.	GOOD	FAIR	POOR
1000	850	575	450	300	175

Belgian Auto-5 16-ga. round knob with "suicide safety" in ON position at front of trigger guard. This is not a Sweet Sixteen. Courtesy Rock Island Auction.

Belgian 12-ga. Auto-5 with suicide safety in OFF position. Manufactured in 1950. Courtesy Rock Islad Auction.

Auto-5 20-ga. with fitted factory case and extra barrel. Courtesy Rock Island Auction.

Right receiver detail. Courtesy Rock Island Auction.

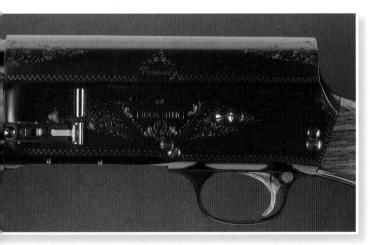

Left receiver detail. Courtesy Rock Island Auction.

GRADE I-VENT RIB

NEW	EXC.	V.G.	GOOD	FAIR	POOR
1200	825	650	475	375	200

GRADE II-PLAIN BARREL

NEW	EXC.	V.G.	GOOD	FAIR	POOR
1000	750	450	300	250	150

GRADE II-MATTE RIB

NOTE: I believe that these prices these guns should be accumulated and will continue to appreciate at a better than average ratee.)

NEW	EXC.	V.G.	GOOD	FAIR	POOR
1250	825	650	450	350	175

GRADE II-VENT RIB

NEW	EXC.	V.G.	GOOD	FAIR	POOR
1650	1400	850	600	400	200

GRADE III-PLAIN BARREL

NEW	EXC.	V.G.	GOOD	FAIR	POOR
2500	1900	1500	850	500	250

GRADE III-MATTE RIB

NOTE: These are extremely rare and beautiful guns and are currently priced at what I believe they are worth, and what I believe the market will recognize as their value for some time to come.

NEW	EXC.	V.G.	GOOD	FAIR	POOR
3500	3000	2500	1350	600	250

GRADE III-VENT RIB

NEW	EXC.	V.G.	GOOD	FAIR	POOR
4500	3500	2500	1350	600	300

Belgian Auto-5 round knob 12-ga. with vent rib and factory box. Courtesy Rock Island Auction.

GRADE IV-PLAIN BARREL

NEW	EXC.	V.G.	GOOD	FAIR	POOR
4500	4000	3250	2250	850	350

GRADE IV-MATTE RIB

NEW	EXC.	V.G.	GOOD	FAIR	POOR
5700	4850	4150	3000	1000	400

GRADE IV-VENT RIB

NEW	EXC.	V.G.	GOOD	FAIR	POOR
7500	5500	4750	3500	1500	500

AMERICAN BROWNING AUTO-5

This recoil-operated, semi-automatic shotgun was another variation of the early-production Auto-5. It was chambered for 12, 16, or 20 gauge and was manufactured by the Remington Company for Browning. It is quite similar to Remington's Model 11 shotgun but features the Browning logo and a different type of engraving. There were approximately 45,000 manufactured between 1940 and 1942.

EXC.	V.G.	GOOD	FAIR	POOR
675	575	450	375	200

NOTE: Vent rib add 20 percent. 20 gauge add 10 percent.

MID-PRODUCTION AUTO-5 FN MANUFACTURE STANDARD WEIGHT

This version of the recoil-operated, semi-automatic Auto-5 shotgun was manufactured by FN in Belgium between 1952 and 1976. It was offered in 12 or 16 gauge with 26″ through 32″ barrels with various chokes. The finish is blued with a checkered walnut stock and a black buttplate that was marked "Browning Automatic" with "FN" in center oval. Guns made prior to 1967 will be found with round knob pistol grips. The flatbottom variation was introduced in 1967.

PLAIN BARREL

NIB	EXC.	V.G.	GOOD	FAIR	POOR
850	650	475	400	250	175

MATTE RIB

NIB	EXC.	V.G.	GOOD	FAIR	POOR
1000	750	500	400	275	200

VENT RIB

NIB	EXC.	V.G.	GOOD	FAIR	POOR
1200	800	600	450	300	250

NOTE: Add 25 percent for guns with round-knob pistol grip and 35 percent for straight-grip stock. Add 20 percent for 20 gauge guns. Add 50 percent for 16 and add 33 percent for 20 gauge guns NIB.

AUTO-5 LIGHTWEIGHT

This version was chambered for 12 or 20 gauge and featured a lighter-weight, scroll-engraved receiver. It was manufactured between 1952 and 1976 by FN. The 20 gauge was not introduced until 1958.

NIB	EXC.	V.G.	GOOD	FAIR	POOR
895	750	600	450	275	200

NOTE: Vent rib add 20 percent. For 20 gauge add 20 percent.

Belgian flat knob 20-ga. Magnum Auto-5. Courtesy Rock Island Auction.

Belgian Auto-5 "Sweet Sixteen." Courtesy Rock Island Auction.

AUTO-5 MAGNUM

This version featured 3″ chambers and was offered with 26″ through 32″, full-choke barrels. It was manufactured between 1958 and 1976 by FN. The 12 gauge was introduced in 1958 and the 20 gauge brought out in 1967.

NIB	EXC.	V.G.	GOOD	FAIR	POOR
1000	850	650	500	375	200

NOTE: Vent rib add 20 percent.

AUTO-5 SKEET

This version is similar to the Lightweight Model, chambered for 12 or 20 gauge with a 26″ or 28″, vent rib, skeet-choked barrel.

EXC.	V.G.	GOOD	FAIR	POOR
795	575	525	425	250

AUTO-5 TRAP MODEL

This version is similar to the standard-weight model except chambered for 12 gauge only, with a 30″, vent rib, full-choke barrel. It was manufactured by FN until 1971.

EXC.	V.G.	GOOD	FAIR	POOR
675	550	475	300	225

SWEET SIXTEEN

This version is similar to the standard-weight and is chambered for 16 gauge only. It has a gold-plated trigger and was manufactured by FN between 1936 and 1976.

NOTE: Not all A-5 16-gauges are Sweet Sixteens. Look for the gold-plated trigger and the lack of a suicide safety. Matte rib add 25 percent. Vent rib add 50 percent. This is the one that everyone wants. They are extremely nice, lightweight, and a real pleasure to take hunting. The Matte rib variation is my very favorite.

NIB	EXC.	V.G.	GOOD	FAIR	POOR
1000	750	700	400	300	200

BUCK SPECIAL

This version features a 24″, cylinder-bore barrel with adjustable rifle sights. It was produced in 12 and 20 gauge 2-3/4″ and 3″ Magnum, and in 16 gauge with 2-3/4″ chambers. It was manufactured by FN between 1963 and 1976. Prices are for 12 gauge guns.

EXC.	V.G.	GOOD	FAIR	POOR
750	650	525	400	275

Serial No. 2,000,000

More than 2,000,000 Browning Automatic-5 shotguns from Browning's own production facilities now serve America's sportsmen. In addition, hundreds of thousands more have been produced by other gunmakers with no variation in basic design. What finer credentials for its inventor, John M. Browning, and his rare talent to design lifelong serviceability into a sporting arm?

Serial number 2,000,000 above commemorates this occasion. Valued at $8,350.00, this masterpiece features breathtaking, two-color gold inlaid engraving, the finest figured walnut hand-carved and checkered, accented by the brilliance of its deeply blued steel. It will be preserved as a symbol of the quality that has made it America's favorite shotgun for 67 years.

Special Two-Millionth Commemorative Model — As a gesture of thanks from us to you, the American sportsman, and your very real insistence on reliability and durability, we are producing a limited issue (2,500 only) special Automatic-5's for your collection of fine guns. Each features figured walnut brilliantly polished and hand-checkered, and hand-engraved steel, deeply blued and polished. The serial number, John M. Browning's profile and personal signature are hand-engraved in 24-karat gold. Specifications: 12 gauge, 28" Modified, ventilated rib with ivory sight, in plush lined fitted luggage case with commemorative medallion and historical collector's booklet. Serial number 2,000,000-1 to 2,000,000-2500. Price complete, $575.00.

Copyright © Browning Arms Company 1970

Win Serial Number 2,000,000-1 or other valuable prizes by registering with your Browning Dealer the lowest serial numbered Browning Automatic-5 still in service. He has complete details on the contest and prizes.

BROWNING

WRITE FOR FREE CATALOG containing detailed information on all Browning Guns and accessories, plus special illustrated section of practical shooting information. Browning Arms Company, Dept. 295 P. O. Box 500, Morgan, Utah 84050. In Canada — Browning Arms Co. of Canada, Ltd.

Period advertising for Auto-5 Two-Millionth limited edition. Pricing/offer no longer valid. Courtesy Browning.

Belgian Two Millionth Commemorative Auto-5. Courtesy Rock island Auction.

TWO MILLIONTH COMMEMORATIVE

This version commemorated the two millionth Auto-5 shotgun produced by FN. It was engraved with a special high-polish blue finish and high-grade, checkered walnut in the stock. It was furnished in a black fitted case along with a book on the Browning Company. There were 2,500 manufactured between 1971 and 1974. As with all commemoratives, it must be NIB to realize its top potential.

NIB	EXC.	V.G.	GOOD	FAIR	POOR
2750	1700	950	625	-	-

Left receiver detail. Courtesy Rock Island Auction.

Right receiver detail. Courtesy Rock Island Auction.

LATE PRODUCTION AUTO-5-B.C. MIROKU MANUFACTURE

In 1976 production of the Auto-5 shotgun was begun by B.C. Miroku in Japan. This move was accomplished after approximately 2,750,000 Auto-5 shotguns were manufactured by FN in Belgium between 1903 and 1976. The Japanese-manufactured guns, in the opinion of many knowledgeable people, show no less quality or functionality but are simply not as desirable from a collector's standpoint. In 1999 Browning discontinued production of the Auto-5 shotgun.

NOTE: These shotguns are starting to undergo accumulation, and will, in my opinion, become collectible. At this point, I give these weapons, especially the ones in the more rare variations, a Collectibility Factor of #3. Don't pass these up, especially the more rare ones, if they're cheap and come with a box.

AUTO-5 LIGHT 12

This version is chambered for 12 gauge 2-3/4" chamber only and is offered with a lightweight receiver. The barrel has a vent rib and choke tubes. It was introduced in 1975.

NIB	EXC.	V.G.	GOOD	FAIR	POOR
750	650	500	400	350	250

AUTO-5 LIGHT 20

This version is similar to the Light 12 except chambered for 20 gauge only.

NIB	EXC.	V.G.	GOOD	FAIR	POOR
800	650	550	425	350	250

AUTO-5 MAGNUM

This version features 3" chambers and is offered with 26", 28", 30", or 32" barrels. It was introduced in 1976 by Miroku and discontinued in 1996.

NIB	EXC.	V.G.	GOOD	FAIR	POOR
775	625	575	450	325	250

Miroku-made flat knob Light 12 with aftermarket recoil pad. Courtesy Rock Island Auction.

AUTO-5 BUCK SPECIAL

This version has a 24″ barrel cylinder-bored with adjustable sights. It was introduced by Miroku in 1976.

NIB	EXC.	V.G.	GOOD	FAIR	POOR
725	625	500	425	300	200

AUTO-5 SKEET

This is a competition model that features 26″ or 28″, skeet-bored barrels with a vent rib. It was manufactured between 1976 and 1983 by Miroku.

NIB	EXC.	V.G.	GOOD	FAIR	POOR
825	550	450	350	275	200

SWEET SIXTEEN

This version is similar to the Belgian-produced Sweet Sixteen, but is offered standard with a vent rib and screw-in Invector choke tubes. It was introduced in 1988 by Miroku and discontinued in 1992.

NOTE: I recommend the accumulation of these weapons if found in the box, at a reasonable price and in new condition. Notice how the price for these has already started to increase. It is my opinion that this trend will continue.

NIB	EXC.	V.G.	GOOD	FAIR	POOR
1150	950	750	550	375	225

A-5 DU 50TH ANNIVERSARY

This was a high-grade version of the Auto-5 produced to commemorate the 50th anniversary of Ducks Unlimited. It is highly engraved and features high-gloss bluing and a fancy checkered walnut stock. There were approximately 5,500 manufactured by Miroku in 1987. They were auctioned by the Ducks Unlimited chapters to raise money for the organization, and because of this fact, it is difficult to furnish an accurate value. This is a commemorative firearm and, as such, must be NIB with all furnished materials to command premium collector value. We furnish what we feel is a general value.

NIB	EXC.	V.G.	GOOD	FAIR	POOR
1550	1000	800	600	450	300

A-5 DU SWEET SIXTEEN

This was a special version of the Miroku-manufactured Sweet Sixteen that was auctioned by the Ducks Unlimited chapters in 1988. There were 5,500 produced. All specifications and cautions that were furnished for the 50th Anniversary gun also apply here.

NOTE: This is another variation that should be accumulated, if found new in the box, and reasonably priced.

NIB	EXC.	V.G.	GOOD	FAIR	POOR
1350	105	0850	600	400	300

AUTO-5 CLASSIC

This is a special limited edition series of A-5 shotguns built in 12 gauge only. The Classic is photo-etched with game scenes on a silver gray receiver. 5,000 of these guns were manufactured in 1984. The Gold Classic is similar in appearance but features gold inlays and is limited to 500 guns.

CLASSIC

NIB	EXC.	V.G.	GOOD	FAIR	POOR
1750	1400	1050	775	600	400

Right receiver detail. Courtesy Rock Island Auction.

Left receiver detail. Courtesy Rock Island Auction.

Belgian Classic Auto-5, One of Five Thousand. Courtesy Rock Island Auction.

Auto-5 Gold Classic. One of 500 made 1986-7. Engraved by J. M. Debrus. Courtesy Rock Island Auction.

GOLD CLASSIC
Produced by FN.

NIB	EXC.	V.G.	GOOD	FAIR	POOR
4500	3250	2500	2000	1000	500

Engraver's signature. Courtesy Rock Island Auction.

Right receiver detail. Courtesy Rock Island Auction.

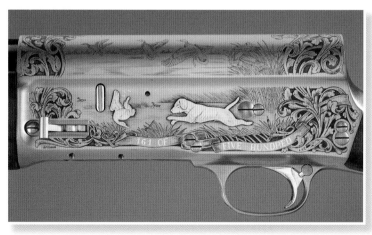

Left receiver detail. Courtesy Rock Island Auction.

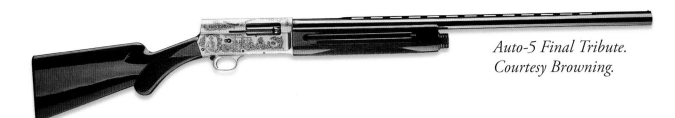

*Auto-5 Final Tribute.
Courtesy Browning.*

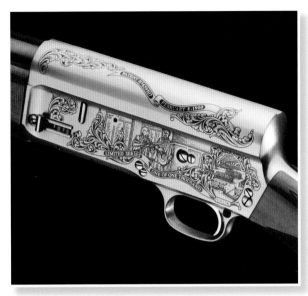

*Auto-5 Final Tribute, left receiver
detail. Courtesy Browning.*

*Auto-5 Final Tribute, right receiver
detail. Courtesy Browning.*

AUTO-5 LIGHT BUCK SPECIAL

This model is a lightweight version of the Buck Special. Chambered for the 2-3/4″ shell and fitted with a 24″ vent rib barrel. Conventional choked for slug or buckshot. Barrel has adjustable rear sight and ramp front sight. Weighs 8 lbs.

NIB	EXC.	V.G.	GOOD	FAIR	POOR
750	650	550	450	375	225

AUTO-5 STALKER

Introduced in 1992, this model was available in either a lightweight version or a Magnum version. The Light Stalker was available in 12 gauge with either 26″ or 28″ barrel with choke tubes. The Magnum Stalker is offered in 12 gauge (3″ chamber) with 28″ or 30″ barrel and choke tubes. The Light Stalker weighs 8 lbs. 4 oz. and the Magnum Stalker weighs 8 lbs. 11 oz.

LIGHT STALKER

NIB	EXC.	V.G.	GOOD	FAIR	POOR
675	600	550	400	300	225

MAGNUM STALKER

NIB	EXC.	V.G.	GOOD	FAIR	POOR
725	650	600	375	275	250

AUTO-5 FINAL TRIBUTE LIMITED EDITION

Introduced in 1999, this commemorative A-5 was limited to 1,000 shotguns. It represents the final production of this model. Chambered for the 12 gauge shell and fitted with a 28″ vent rib barrel, this shotgun had a special engraved receiver.

NIB	EXC.	V.G.	GOOD	FAIR	POOR
1750	1400	-	-	-	-

Double Auto. Courtesy Rock Island Auction.

DOUBLE AUTO

This is a short recoil-operated, semi-automatic shotgun chambered for 12 gauge only. It was offered with a 26″, 28″, or 30″ barrel that was either plain or vent ribbed. It has various chokes. The receiver is steel, and the finish is blued or silver with a checkered walnut stock. The tubular magazine holds only two shots, hence its name. It was manufactured between 1954 and 1972.

NOTE: These are quite strange weapons, and while they are not highly collectible in the usual sense of the word, they are worth buying if they are in mint condition are in the box. I once traded one of these in unfired condition and the box, for a virtually new 20 gauge Superposed.) Vent rib add 25 percent.

NIB	EXC.	V.G.	GOOD	FAIR	POOR
850	525	425	350	275	225

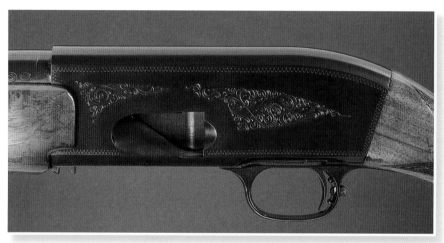

Left receiver detail. Courtesy Rock Island Auction.

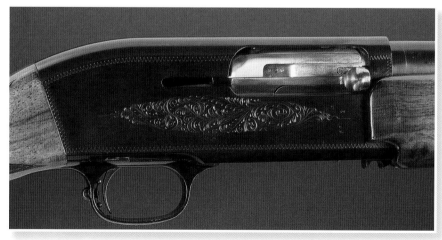

Right receiver detail. Courtesy Rock Island Auction.

TWELVETTE DOUBLE AUTO

This version is similar to the Double Automatic except that it has an aircraft aluminum alloy frame color-anodized in either blue, silver, green, brown, or black. Red-, gold-, or royal blue-colored receivers were the rarest colors and would command approximately a 50 percent premium. It was offered with either a plain or vent rib barrel. There were approximately 65,000 produced between 1954 and 1972. Vent rib add 25 percent.

NOTE: Buying one of these in red, gold, or royal blue, if they are in mint or in new condition, especially if they're in the box and have a ventilated rib, is almost always a good choice.)

NEW	EXC.	V.G.	GOOD	FAIR	POOR
1000	675	525	350	275	225

Scarce Double Auto slug gun with accessory standard barrel. Courtesy Rock Island Auction.

TWENTYWEIGHT DOUBLE AUTO

This version is similar in all respects to the Twelvette except that it is three-quarters of a pound lighter and was offered with a 26.5″ barrel. It was manufactured between 1952 and 1971.

NOTE: These little guns are very collectible and much sought-after by Browning collectors. This gun rates a Collectibility Factor of #1. Vent rib add 25 percent.

NIB	EXC.	V.G.	GOOD	FAIR	POOR
1100	750	575	375	300	250

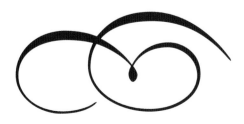

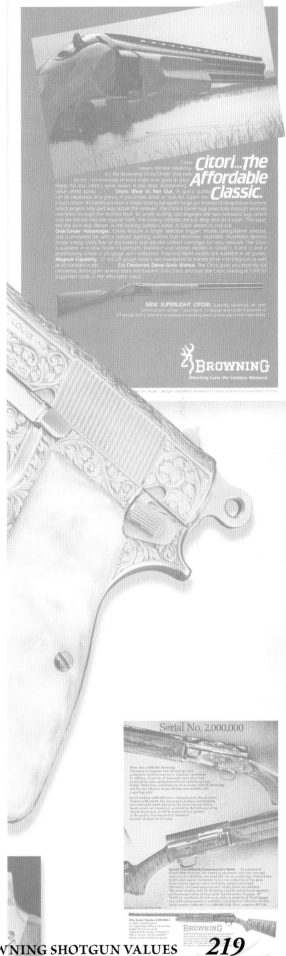

Citori...The Affordable Classic.

BROWNING
Browning Cures the Common Weekend.

Serial No. 2,000,000

BROWNING

Why you should buy your new gas auto from the people who invented the Automatic Shotgun.

The Browning 2000 is a lot more than just another gas auto. It's a combination of 75 years of knowledgeable automatic shotgun making experience.

The 2000's gas system not only softens recoil, it vents gases forward, away from your face. It's designed so you can disassemble it for complete cleaning in seconds. But most importantly, you can rely on the 2000's gas system to keep shooting when the action is hot and furious. And the weather's cold and rainy.

The unique design of the system also lets you shoot 3″ magnum shells by just adding a 3″ magnum barrel to your field gun. (Instead of buying a whole new gun.)

The Browning 2000's receiver is squared-off like John M. Browning's original Auto-5. This squared-off profile quickly catches your eye for fast, accurate pointing. And like the Auto-5, the hand-filling forearm and semi-pistol grip are expertly checkered for a good grip.

The tight grained French Walnut has a gloss finish that sluffs off dirt and rain. And all exterior metal sports fine Browning polishing and deep blueing.

Besides old time quality, the Browning 2000 gives you 20th century Speed Loading. Just push the first shell into the loading port, release it, and instantly it's whisked to the chamber ready for firing.

The exclusive loading system lets you quickly change the first shell in the magazine from a duck load to a goose load. Then by merely cycling the bolt, you're ready for that honker.

The Browning 2000 Gas Auto. 12 and 20 gauge hunting models from $354.95*. Skeet 12 and 20, $429.95*. Trap 12, $449.95*.

Compare the 2000 to other gas autos at your Browning Dealer's. You'll know why you should buy your new gas auto from the people who invented the automatic shotgun.   *suggested retail price

Copyright © Browning 1977

BROWNING
Inventors of America's Great Guns

FREE CATALOG: 120 full-color pages on all Browning Guns and Sports Equipment. Drop a postcard to: Browning, Dept. 131, Morgan, Utah 84050.

Period advertising for B-2000. Courtesy Browning. Pricing no longer valid.

2000 SERIES

B-2000

This is a gas-operated, semi-automatic shotgun chambered for 12 or 20 gauge and offered with a 26", 28", or 30", vent rib barrel with various chokes. The finish is blued with a checkered walnut stock. This shotgun was assembled in Portugal from parts that were manufactured by FN in Belgium. There were approximately 115,000 imported between 1974 and 1981.

NIB	EXC.	V.G.	GOOD	FAIR	POOR
625	550	475	300	225	175

B-2000 MAGNUM

This version features a barrel with 3" chambers and was offered standard with a recoil pad.

NIB	EXC.	V.G.	GOOD	FAIR	POOR
675	575	500	300	225	175

B-2000 BUCK SPECIAL

This version has a 24", cylinder-bored barrel with rifle sights.

NIB	EXC.	V.G.	GOOD	FAIR	POOR
575	475	425	275	225	175

B-2000 TRAP

This version has a 30", full-choke barrel with a floating rib and a Monte Carlo-type trap stock.

NIB	EXC.	V.G.	GOOD	FAIR	POOR
575	475	425	275	225	175

B-2000 SKEET

This version features a 26", skeet-bored barrel with a floating vent rib and a skeet-type stock.

EXC.	V.G.	GOOD	FAIR	POOR
500	450	375	275	200

NOTE: Add 20 percent for 20 gauge guns.

B-2000 left receiver detail. Courtesy Rock Island Auction.

Browning B-2000 with accessory slug barrel. Courtesy Rock Island Auction.

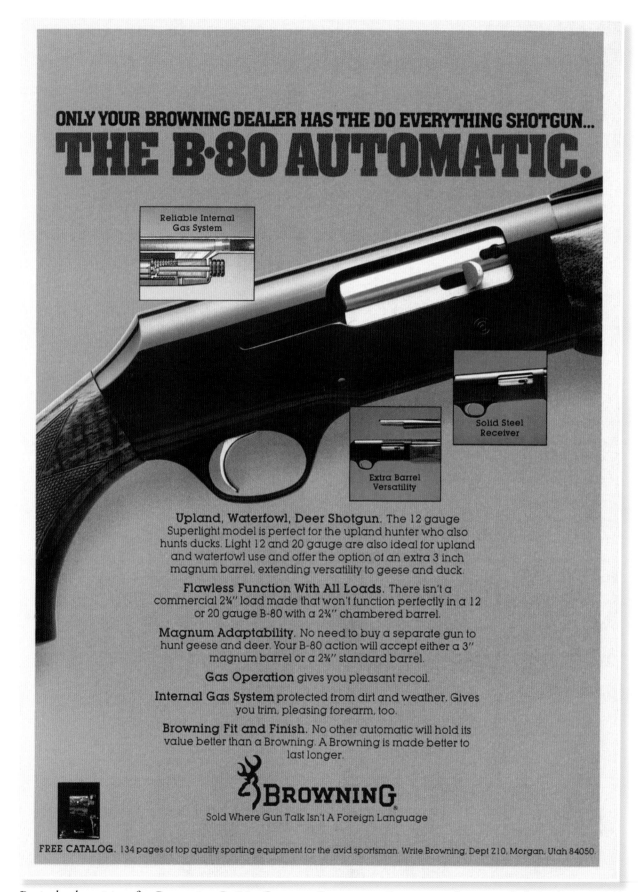

Period advertising for Browning B-80. Courtesy Browning. Pricing no longer valid.

Model Gold 10. Courtesy Browning.

Gold Evolve. Courtesy Browning.

MODEL B-80

This is a gas-operated, semi-automatic shotgun chambered in 12 or 20 gauge. It features 3″ magnum potential by simply exchanging the barrel. It features various-length barrels and was offered with screw-in Invector chokes as of 1985. The receiver is either steel or lightweight aluminum alloy. The finish is blued with a checkered walnut stock. This gun was assembled in Portugal from parts manufactured by Beretta in Italy. It was manufactured between 1981 and 1988.

NOTE: These weapons perform well, but are not yet undergoing accumulation, in my opinion. Add 20 percent for 20 gauge guns.

EXC.	V.G.	GOOD	FAIR	POOR
500	450	375	325	225

MODEL B-80 BUCK SPECIAL

This version features a 24″, cylinder-bored barrel with rifle sights. It was discontinued in 1984.

EXC.	V.G.	GOOD	FAIR	POOR
450	400	350	300	200

MODEL B-80 DU COMMEMORATIVE

This version was produced to be auctioned by American Ducks Unlimited chapters. In order to realize the collector potential, it must be NIB with all supplied materials. Values supplied are general.

NIB	EXC.	V.G.	GOOD	FAIR	POOR
950	750	550	425	325	275

GOLD SERIES

MODEL GOLD 10

Introduced in 1993 this is a gas-operated 5-shot semi-automatic shotgun chambered for the 10 gauge shell. Offered with 26″, 28″, or 30″ vent rib barrel. The standard model has a walnut stock, blued receiver and barrel while the Stalker Model is fitted with a graphite composite stock with non-glare finish on receiver and barrel. Both models are fitted with choke tubes. Weighs about 10 lbs. 10 oz.

NIB	EXC.	V.G.	GOOD	FAIR	POOR
950	700	550	450	300	150

GOLD EVOLVE

Introduced in 2004 this model is an updated version of the original Gold gun. It features newly designed receiver, magazine cap, ventilated rib design, checkering pattern and Hi-Viz sights. Offered in 12 gauge 3″ with choice of 26″, 28″, or 30″ barrel with choke tubes. Weight is about 7 lbs. for the 28″ model.

NIB	EXC.	V.G.	GOOD	FAIR	POOR
1196	875	700	-	-	-

Gold Light 10 Gauge Camo. Courtesy Browning.

Gold 10 Guage Combo. Courtesy Browning.

GOLD LIGHT 10 GAUGE CAMO

This 10 gauge model is offered with 26″ or 28″ barrels with Mossy Oak® or Shadow Grass camo. Lightweight alloy receiver reduces weight to 9 lb. 10 oz. Introduced in 2001.

NIB	EXC.	V.G.	GOOD	FAIR	POOR
1275	975	775	-	-	-

GOLD 10 GAUGE COMBO

This 10 gauge model has a choice of two vent rib barrels in lengths of 24″ and 26″, or 24″ and 28″. Walnut stock with black ventilated recoil pad. Weight with 28″ barrels is about 10 lbs. 10 ozs.

NIB	EXC.	V.G.	GOOD	FAIR	POOR
1050	800	675	-	-	-

GOLD STALKER

NIB	EXC.	V.G.	GOOD	FAIR	POOR
925	700	550	450	300	150

GOLD CLASSIC STALKER

Introduced in 1999 this model features a classic Browning squared receiver and fully adjustable stock. This model is chambered for 12 gauge shells with choice 26″ or 28″ vent rib barrels. Gun has 3″ chambers. Black synthetic stock. Weight is about 7 lbs. 3 ozs.

NIB	EXC.	V.G.	GOOD	FAIR	POOR
750	600	550	-	-	-

GOLD 3-1/2″ 12 GAUGE

Introduced in 1997 this model features a 3-1/2″ chamber. It can operate 2-3/4″ or 3″ shells as well. Choice of barrel lengths from 26″ to 30″. Invector-Plus chokes. Magazine capacity is four 2.75″ shells or three 3″ shells or three 3.5″ shells. The weight is approximately 7 lbs. 10 oz.

NIB	EXC.	V.G.	GOOD	FAIR	POOR
900	700	550	450	-	-

Gold Classic Stalker. Courtesy Browning.

Gold Stalker. Courtesy Browning.

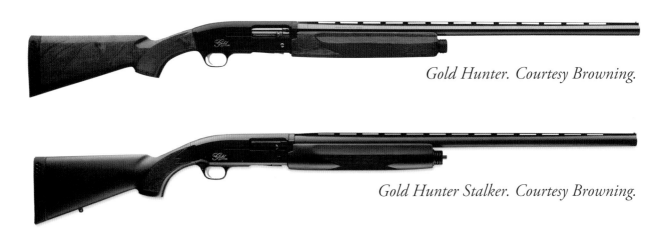

Gold Hunter. Courtesy Browning.

Gold Hunter Stalker. Courtesy Browning.

GOLD 12 GAUGE HUNTER

Introduced in 1994 this semi-automatic shotgun is built on the same gas operating system as the Gold 10. Offered with 26″, 28″, or 30″ barrel it has a magazine capacity of four 3″ shells. Walnut stock has full checkered pistol grip with black rubber recoil pad. Invector-Plus choke tubes supplied. Weighs about 7.5 lbs. Also available (as of 1998) in Stalker version with non-glare matte metal parts and stocks.

NIB	EXC.	V.G.	GOOD	FAIR	POOR
650	525	400	300	200	150

GOLD CLASSIC HUNTER

Introduced in 1999, this model features a squared receiver, fully adjustable stock, selected walnut stock, and deep blued barrels. Choice of 26″, 28″, or 30″ vent rib barrel. Offered with 3" chamber 12 gauge only.

NIB	EXC.	V.G.	GOOD	FAIR	POOR
750	600	500	400	275	225

Gold Classic Hunter. Courtesy Browning.

Gold Classic 20 Gauge. Courtesy Browning.

Gold Classic High Grade. Courtesy Browning.

Gold Deer Hunter. Courtesy Browning.

GOLD CLASSIC 20 GAUGE

Offered with choice of 26″ or 28″ vent rib barrels with select walnut stock. Adjustable comb. Squared receiver. Weight is about 6 lbs. 12 ozs. Introduced in 1999.

NIB	EXC.	V.G.	GOOD	FAIR	POOR
750	600	500	400	275	225

GOLD CLASSIC HIGH GRADE

Introduced in 1999, this model features a traditional square receiver with engraved silver gray finish. Offered in 12 gauge only with 3″ chambers and 28″ vent rib barrel. Select walnut stock. Weight is about 7 lbs. 6 ozs.

NIB	EXC.	V.G.	GOOD	FAIR	POOR
1400	1100	775	500	-	-

GOLD DEER HUNTER

Introduced in 1997, this model features a choice of a fully rifled barrel or a smooth bore barrel with Invector choke system. Both versions come with a cantilever scope mount. Stock and forearm are of select walnut. Receiver has non-glare black finish. Barrel is satin finish. Barrel length is 22″ on both barrels. Weight is about 7 lbs. 12 oz. Price listed are for smoothbore barrel.

NIB	EXC.	V.G.	GOOD	FAIR	POOR
775	600	500	400	200	150

NOTE: For fully rifled version add $40.

Gold Deer Hunter
with cantilever
mount and
scope. Courtesy
Browning.

Gold Deer
Stalker. Courtesy
Browning.

Gold Deer
- Mossy Oak®.
Courtesy
Browning.

Gold Waterfowl
- Mossy Oak®
Shadow Grass.
Courtesy
Browning.

Gold Waterfowl - Mossy Oak® Breakup. Courtesy Browning.

GOLD DEER HUNTER-20 GAUGE

Same as above but chambered for 20 gauge 3" shell. Furnished with fully rifled 22" barrel. Cantilever scope mount. Introduced in 2001.

NIB	EXC.	V.G.	GOOD	FAIR	POOR
975	800	625	-	-	-

GOLD DEER STALKER

This model, introduced in 1999, is the same as the model above but fitted with a black synthetic stock.

NIB	EXC.	V.G.	GOOD	FAIR	POOR
980	750	600	500	300	-

GOLD DEER-MOSSY OAK®

Introduced in 1999 with camo finish.

NIB	EXC.	V.G.	GOOD	FAIR	POOR
825	675	575	450	-	-

GOLD WATERFOWL-MOSSY OAK® SHADOW GRASS

Introduced in 1999 with camo finish.

NIB	EXC.	V.G.	GOOD	FAIR	POOR
850	700	600	500	-	-

GOLD WATERFOWL-MOSSY OAK® BREAKUP

Introduced in 2000 with camo finish.

NIB	EXC.	V.G.	GOOD	FAIR	POOR
850	700	575	450	-	-

GOLD TURKEY/WATERFOWL-MOSSY OAK®

Introduced in 1999 with camo finish.

NIB	EXC.	V.G.	GOOD	FAIR	POOR
850	700	575	450	-	-

Gold Turkey/Waterfowl - Mossy Oak®®. Courtesy Browning.

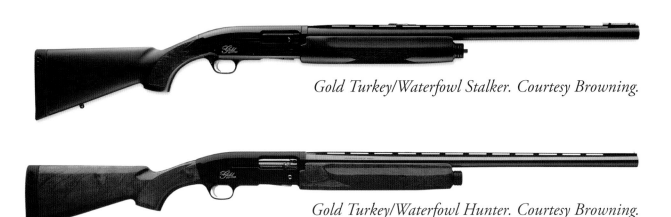

Gold Turkey/Waterfowl Stalker. Courtesy Browning.

Gold Turkey/Waterfowl Hunter. Courtesy Browning.

Gold 3.5 Ultimate Turkey Gun. Courtesy Browning.

GOLD TURKEY/WATER- FOWL STALKER

Introduced in 1999, this model features a black synthetic stock, 24″ barrel, Hi-Viz sight, and 3″ or 3.5″ chambers. Weight is approximately 7 lbs. 4 ozs.

NIB	EXC.	V.G.	GOOD	FAIR	POOR
800	650	575	450	-	-

GOLD TURKEY/WATER- FOWL HUNTER

This 12 gauge 3″ or 3.5″ chambered gun is offered with 24″ vent rib barrel. Select walnut stock with black ventilated recoil pad. Weight is about 7 lbs. Introduced in 1999.

NIB	EXC.	V.G.	GOOD	FAIR	POOR
775	625	550	450	-	-

GOLD NWTF SERIES

This model is finished in a Mossy Oak® Break- up pattern and bears the NWTF logo on the butt- stock. Fitted with a 24″ barrel, Hi-Viz front sight, X-full extended Turkey choke. Offered in the con- figurations listed.

GOLD LIGHT 10 GAUGE

NIB	EXC.	V.G.	GOOD	FAIR	POOR
1250	950	775	-	-	-

GOLD 12 GAUGE

3.5" Chamber, Shadow Grass

NIB	EXC.	V.G.	GOOD	FAIR	POOR
1175	900	800	700	-	-

3" CHAMBER

NIB	EXC.	V.G.	GOOD	FAIR	POOR
1000	775	650	575	-	-

3.5" CHAMBER ULTI- MATE TURKEY GUN

NIB	EXC.	V.G.	GOOD	FAIR	POOR
1280	1000	900	725	-	-

Gold 20 Gauge Hunter. Courtesy Browning.

Gold Sporting Clays. Courtesy Browning.

Gold Ladies/Youth Sporting Clays. Courtesy Browning.

GOLD 20 GAUGE HUNTER

Same as above but chambered for 20 gauge and offered in 26″ or 28″ barrel lengths. Weighs about 6.8 lbs.

NIB	EXC.	V.G.	GOOD	FAIR	POOR
650	525	400	300	200	150

GOLD SPORTING CLAYS

Introduced in 1996, this model features a ported barrel in 28″ or 30″ lengths. Recoil pad is standard. Weight is about 7.5 lbs.

NIB	EXC.	V.G.	GOOD	FAIR	POOR
700	575	475	375	200	150

GOLD LADIES/YOUTH SPORTING CLAYS

Offered in 12 gauge only with 2.75″ chambers this model features a 28″ vent rib barrel. Overall dimensions have been adjusted to fit women. Black solid recoil pad. Weight is about 7 lbs. 6 ozs. Introduced in 1999.

NIB	EXC.	V.G.	GOOD	FAIR	POOR
1100	850	625	450	300	-

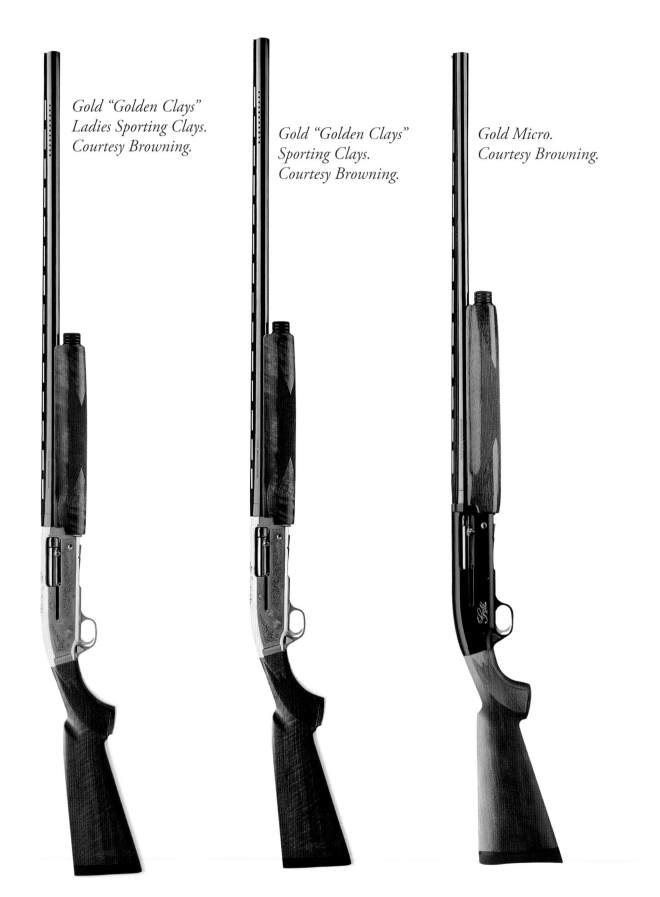

*Gold "Golden Clays"
Ladies Sporting Clays.
Courtesy Browning.*

*Gold "Golden Clays"
Sporting Clays.
Courtesy Browning.*

*Gold Micro.
Courtesy Browning.*

GOLD "GOLDEN CLAYS" LA-DIES SPORTING CLAYS

Introduced in 2005 this 12 gauge 2.75" chambered gun is fitted with a 28" vent rib ported barrel with four choke tubes. Silver receiver is engraved with gold enhancements. Weight is about 7.75 lbs.

NIB	EXC.	V.G.	GOOD	FAIR	POOR
1810	1300	1050	800	-	-

GOLD "GOLDEN CLAYS" SPORTING CLAYS

As above but with standard stock dimensions and choice of 28" or 30" barrels. Introduced in 2005.

NIB	EXC.	V.G.	GOOD	FAIR	POOR
1810	1300	1050	800	-	-

GOLD MICRO

Introduced in 2001 this model features a 20 gauge gun with 26" barrel, smaller pistol grip, shorter length of pull, and back-bored barrel with choke tubes. Weight is about 6 lb. 10 oz.

NIB	EXC.	V.G.	GOOD	FAIR	POOR
890	650	575	475	-	-

GOLD UPLAND

Offered in 12 or 20 gauge. The 12 gauge offered with 24" barrel and the 20 gauge with 26" barrel. Straight grip stock with 3" chamber. Weight is 7 lbs. for 12 gauge and 6.75 lbs. for 20 gauge. Introduced in 2001.

NIB	EXC.	V.G.	GOOD	FAIR	POOR
900	700	600	475	-	-

GOLD SUPERLITE HUNTER

Introduced in 2006, this gun uses an aluminum alloy receiver and alloy magazine tube to reduce weight to about 7 lbs. in 12 gauge. Gloss finish walnut stock. Available with 3" or 3.5" chamber and 26" or 28" barrel. Magazine cut-off feature on 3.5" model. A 6.5 lb. 20 gauge with 3" chamber and 26" or 28" barrel is also offered. Three choke tubes. Add 15 percent for 3.5" chamber.

NIB	EXC.	V.G.	GOOD	FAIR	POOR
900	-	-	-	-	-

Gold Upland.
Courtesy Browning.

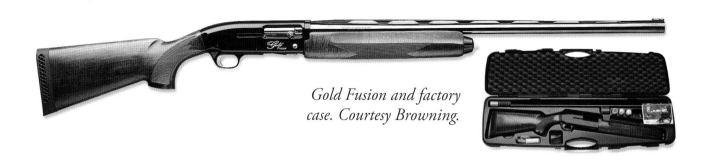

Gold Fusion and factory case. Courtesy Browning.

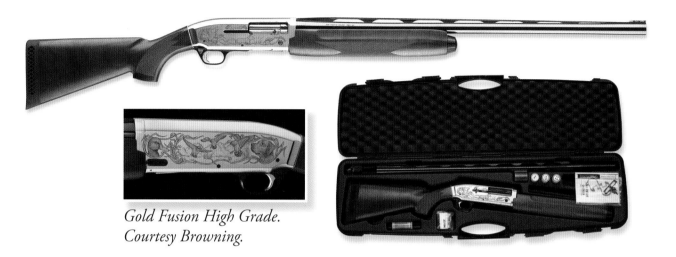

Gold Fusion High Grade. Courtesy Browning.

GOLD SUPERLITE FULL LINE DEALER HUNTER

Similar to Gold Superlite Hunter but with semi-humpback style receiver and satin finish walnut stock and 3″ chamber only. Magazine cut-off on 12 gauge models. Adjustable shim system and three choke tubes.

NIB	EXC.	V.G.	GOOD	FAIR	POOR
925	775	-	-	-	-

GOLD SUPERLITE MICRO

Similar to Gold Superlite Hunter but with compact dimensions for smaller shooters. Offered only in 20 gauge with 26″ barrel. Weighs about 6.25 pounds. Three choke tubes.

NIB	EXC.	V.G.	GOOD	FAIR	POOR
925	-	-	-	-	-

GOLD FUSION

This model features a new style vent rib, adjustable comb pro-comp sight, and five choke tubes. Offered in 12 gauge with 3″ chambers with 26″ or 28″ barrels. Introduced in 2001. In 2002 this model was offered in 20 gauge as well as 12 with choice of 26″ or 28″ vent rib barrel. Weight for 12 gauge is about 7 lbs. anbd for 20 gauge about 6.5 lbs.

NIB	EXC.	V.G.	GOOD	FAIR	POOR
1130	850	725	650	-	-

GOLD FUSION HIGH GRADE

Similar to the Gold Fusion with the addition of a high grade Turkish walnut stock, silver nitride receiver with game scene in gold. Five choke tubes and a hard case are standard. Introduced in 2005.

NIB	EXC.	V.G.	GOOD	FAIR	POOR
2095	1600	-	-	-	-

GOLDEN CLAYS

Introduced in 1999, this model features chambered for the 12 gauge shell with 2.75″ chambers. Choice of 28″ or 30″ vent rib ported barrels. Engraved silver gray receiver. Select walnut stock. Weight is about 7 lbs. 3 ozs.

NIB	EXC.	V.G.	GOOD	FAIR	POOR
1250	1000	825	675	-	-

500 SERIES

A-500G

This is a self-adjusting, gas-operated, semi-automatic shotgun chambered for 12 gauge only. It is offered with 26″, 28″, or 30″ barrels with a vent rib and screw-in Invector choke tubes. It has 3″ chambers and can fire any load interchangeably. The finish is blued with a checkered walnut stock and recoil pad. It features light engraving. It was introduced in 1987.

NIB	EXC.	V.G.	GOOD	FAIR	POOR
560	490	425	350	275	225

A-500G SPORTING CLAYS

This gas-operated version is designed for sporting clays and features a choice of 28″ or 30″ vent rib barrel with semi-gloss finish with gold lettering "Sporting Clays." Ventilated recoil pad standard. Weighs about 8 lbs.

NIB	EXC.	V.G.	GOOD	FAIR	POOR
520	425	350	300	200	150

A-500R HUNTING MODEL

Similar in appearance to the A-500G with the exception that this model operates on a short recoil design. The buttstock features a full pistol grip. Available with 26″, 28″, or 30″ vent rib barrels. Choke tubes standard. Weighs about 7 lbs. 13 oz.

NIB	EXC.	V.G.	GOOD	FAIR	POOR
475	385	300	250	200	150

A-500R BUCK SPECIAL

Same as Hunting Model with the addition of adjustable rear sight and contoured front ramp sight with gold bead. Choke tubes standard, as is 24″ barrel. Weighs 7 lbs. 11 oz.

NIB	EXC.	V.G.	GOOD	FAIR	POOR
500	425	350	300	225	150

A-500G Sporting Clays. Courtesy Rock Island Auction.

*Silver Hunter.
Courtesy
Browning.*

SILVER SERIES

This value-priced series of gas-operated auto-loaders was introduced in 2006. All models feature a semi-humpback design and aluminum alloy receiver. Weights vary from 7.25 to 7.5 lbs. depending on barrel length and stock material. Three choke tubes provided with all models.

SILVER HUNTER

This version features a satin finish walnut stock and forend. It is available with a 3″ chamber in 26″, 28″ and 30″ barrel lengths or with a 3.5″ chamber in 26″ or 28″ barrel length. Add 15 percent for 3.5″ chamber.

NIB	EXC.	V.G.	GOOD	FAIR	POOR
825	-	-	-	-	-

SILVER STALKER

Similar to Silver Hunter but with matte black composite stock and forend. Sling swivel studs. 3.5" chamber only.

NIB	EXC.	V.G.	GOOD	FAIR	POOR
825	-	-	-	-	-

SILVER-MOSSY OAK®

Similar to Silver Stalker but in choice of Mossy Oak® New Break-Up with 26″ barrel or Mossy Oak® New Shadow Grass with 26″ or 28″ barrel.

NIB	EXC.	V.G.	GOOD	FAIR	POOR
925	-	-	-	-	-

*Silver Mossy
Oak. Courtesy
Browning.*

BPS (BROWNING PUMP SHOTGUN) SERIES

This is a slide-action shotgun chambered for 10, 12, or 20 gauge. It is offered with various length vent rib barrels with screw-in Invector chokes. It features 3″ magnum chambers and a bottom-ejection system that effectively makes it ambidextrous. It has double slide bars and a 5-shot tubular magazine. It is constructed of all steel. It was introduced by B.C. Miroku in 1977.

BPS FIELD GRADE

NIB	EXC.	V.G.	GOOD	FAIR	POOR
425	325	295	225	210	-

BPS MAGNUM MODEL

10 or 12 gauge, 3.5″ chambers.

NIB	EXC.	V.G.	GOOD	FAIR	POOR
510	400	350	300	250	150

BPS 20-Ga. Field Grade. Courtesy Browning.

BPS 10 Gauge Magnum, matte finish. Courtesy Browning.

BPS 12-Ga. Field Grade. Courtesy Browning.

*BPS 10-Gauge
Mossy Oak Shadow
Grass Camo.
Courtesy Browning.*

*10-Gauge
BPS Mossy
Oak Breakup.
Courtesy
Browning.*

*BPS 12-Gauge
Waterfowl Camo.
Courtesy Browning.*

BPS 12 GAUGE WATER-FOWL CAMO (1999)

NIB	EXC.	V.G.	GOOD	FAIR	POOR
525	425	350	300	-	-

WATERFOWL MOSSY OAK® BREAK-UP

NIB	EXC.	V.G.	GOOD	FAIR	POOR
575	475	375	325	-	-

BPS 10 GAUGE MOSSY OAK® SHADOW GRASS CAMO (1999)

NIB	EXC.	V.G.	GOOD	FAIR	POOR
575	475	375	325	-	-

BPS NWTF SERIES

This model is finished in a Mossy Oak® Break-up pattern and bears the NWTF logo on the butt-stock. Fitted with a 24″ barrel, Hi-Viz front sight, Extra Full extended turkey choke. Introduced in 2001. Offered in the configurations listed.

BPS 10 GAUGE

NIB	EXC.	V.G.	GOOD	FAIR	POOR
625	475	400	325	-	-

BPS 12 GAUGE

3.5″ chamber.

NIB	EXC.	V.G.	GOOD	FAIR	POOR
625	475	400	325	-	-

3" CHAMBER

NIB	EXC.	V.G.	GOOD	FAIR	POOR
550	450	375	325	-	-

BPS UPLAND SPECIAL

12-ga. with 22″ barrel, straight (English) stock.

NIB	EXC.	V.G.	GOOD	FAIR	POOR
575	425	400	350	250	200

BPS UPLAND SPECIAL 20 GAUGE

This model is chambered for the 20 gauge shell and fitted with a 22″ vent rib barrel. The walnut stock is a straight grip. Weight is about 6.5 lbs.

NIB	EXC.	V.G.	GOOD	FAIR	POOR
475	375	300	275	-	-

BPS Upland Special 12 Gauge. Courtesy Browning.

BPS Upland Special 20 Gauge. Courtesy Browning.

BPS Stalker. Courtesy Browning.

BPS Stalker. Courtesy Browning.

BPS STALKER

Matte finish, black stock.

NIB	EXC.	V.G.	GOOD	FAIR	POOR
435	390	325	275	200	150

BPS STALKER-COMBO

A combination of a 28″ vent rib barrel and a choice of 22″ fully rifle barrel or 20.5″ Invector barrel with Extra Full turkey choke. Introduced in 2000.

NIB	EXC.	V.G.	GOOD	FAIR	POOR
650	525	475	-	-	-

BPS 10 GAUGE TURKEY

Fitted with a 24″ vent rib barrel and black synthetic stock with black solid recoil pad, this model was introduced in 1999. Weight is about 9 lbs. 2 ozs.

NIB	EXC.	V.G.	GOOD	FAIR	POOR
525	425	375	325	-	-

BPS MICRO 20 GAUGE

This model features a 22″ vent rib barrel with shorter pistol grip stock and lighter weight. Weight is about 6.75 lbs. Introduced in 2001.

NIB	EXC.	V.G.	GOOD	FAIR	POOR
450	350	300	-	-	-

BPS SMALL GAUGE

Introduced in 2000 this model is chambered for the 28 gauge and the .410 bore. The 28 gauge is offered with a choice of 26″ or 28″ vent rib barrel with Invector chokes. The .410 is available with 26″ vent rib barrel with Invector chokes. Both the 28 gauge and .410 bore weigh about 6.75 lbs.

NIB	EXC.	V.G.	GOOD	FAIR	POOR
525	450	325	275	-	-

BPS PIGEON GRADE

Furnished in 12 gauge only with high grade walnut stock and gold trimmed receiver.

NIB	EXC.	V.G.	GOOD	FAIR	POOR
500	400	300	225	175	125

BPS Micro 20 Gauge. Courtesy Browning.

BPS Small Gauge (28). Courtesy Browning.

BPS Game Gun. Courtesy Browning.

BPS Buck Special. Courtesy Browning.

BPS Rifled Deer with Mossy Oak Breakup camo. Courtesy Browning.

GAME GUN

Offered in 12 gauge only this model is available in either a Turkey Special or a Deer Special. Both have 20.5″ plain barrel and drilled and tapped receivers. The stock is walnut. The turkey gun is fitted with an Extra Full choke. The deer gun has a special rifled choke tube for slugs. Both weigh about 7 lbs. 7 oz.

NIB	EXC.	V.G.	GOOD	FAIR	POOR
250	200	175	125	100	50

BUCK SPECIAL

24″ barrel with sights.

NIB	EXC.	V.G.	GOOD	FAIR	POOR
450	400	350	300	225	175

TRAP MODEL

EXC.	V.G.	GOOD	FAIR	POOR
375	325	275	200	150

YOUTH MODEL

Short stock, 22″ barrel.

NIB	EXC.	V.G.	GOOD	FAIR	POOR
435	390	325	275	200	150

WATERFOWL DELUXE

This version is chambered for 12 gauge with a 3″ chamber and features an etched receiver with a gold-plated trigger. Otherwise, it is similar to the standard BPS.

EXC.	V.G.	GOOD	FAIR	POOR
600	525	425	325	250

DUCKS UNLIMITED VERSIONS

These were limited-edition guns produced to be auctioned by Ducks Unlimited. They were furnished with a case and must be NIB with furnished materials to realize their collector potential.

NOTE: These types of weapons will always be accumulated by certain types of firearm collectors. At this point in time I would give them a Collectibility Factor of #3.

NIB	EXC.	V.G.	GOOD	FAIR	POOR

BPS Trap. Courtesy Browning.

BPS HIGH CAPACITY

Introduced 2007. Features a black composite stock and 20" Improved Cylinder barrel. 3" chamber, 7-shot capacity.

NIB	EXC.	V.G.	GOOD	FAIR	POOR
375	315	-	-	-	-

MODEL 12

NOTE: All of these reproduction weapons are undergoing accumulation and are somewhat collectible. At this time. I would give all of these types of weapons a Collectibility Factor of #3.)

GRADE I

This is a slide-action shotgun chambered for 20 and 28 gauge with a 26", modified choke, vent rib barrel. It is a reproduction of the Winchester Model 12 shotgun. It has a 5-round, tubular magazine with a floating, high-post rib. It has a takedown feature and is blued with a walnut stock. Introduced in 1991, total production was limited to 7,000 guns.

NIB	EXC.	V.G.	GOOD	FAIR	POOR
825	625	425	300	250	200

GRADE IV

This is an extensively engraved version of the Grade I Model 12. It features a select walnut stock with deluxe checkering and a high-gloss finish. There are gold inlays. It was introduced in 1991, and production was limited to 5,000 guns. Discontinued 1992.

NOTE: As far as Model 12 reproductions go, this is the most collectible model of the bunch.)

NIB	EXC.	V.G.	GOOD	FAIR	POOR
1200	950	700	450	300	200

BPS High Capacity. Courtesy Browning.

Model 12 12-ga., Grade I. Courtesy Rock Island Auction.

LIMITED EDITION MODEL 42

A new version of the .410 bore pump shotgun that was last produced by Winchester in 1963. Available in two grades both fitted with 26″ vent rib barrels. The Grade I features a plain blued receiver with walnut stock. The Grade V features a blued receiver with scroll engraving and gold inlays. Both models are choked Full and weigh 6 lbs. 4 oz.

GRADE I

NIB	EXC.	V.G.	GOOD	FAIR	POOR
900	600	500	400	300	200

GRADE V

NIB	EXC.	V.G.	GOOD	FAIR	POOR
1150	900	700	500	350	200

A-BOLT SHOTGUN

Introduced in 1995 this bolt-action shotgun was offered in 12 gauge with 3″ chamber. Rifled barrel version has a 22″ barrel, while the Invector version has a 23″ barrel with a 5″ rifle tube installed. Has a 2-shot detachable magazine. Average weight is about 7 lbs.

HUNTER VERSION

NIB	EXC.	V.G.	GOOD	FAIR	POOR
625	550	450	300	200	100

STALKER VERSION

NIB	EXC.	V.G.	GOOD	FAIR	POOR
500	400	300	250	200	100

NOTE: For Invector rifled choke tube model deduct $50.

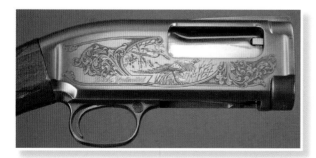

Model 12 Ducks Unlimited, right receiver detail. Courtesy Rock Island Auction.

Grade V Model 12. Courtesy Rock Island Auction.

BROWNING
HANDGUN VALUES

EARLY SEMI-AUTOMATIC PISTOLS

*I*n the period between 1900 and the development of the Model 1935 Hi-Power Pistol, Browning had a number of semi-automatic pistols manufactured by Fabrique Nationale of Herstal, Belgium. They were the Models 1900, 1903, 1905, 1910, 1922, the Baby, and the 1935 Model Hi-Power. These firearms will be listed in more detail with their respective values in the Fabrique Nationale section of this text.

All early model 1935 Hi-Power Pistols I rate at a Collectibility Factor of #1. At the same time, all of these pistols, if they are in high condition, are very desirable. I believe that these pistols, if they are in high condition, are not only very collectible but also highly desirable. These are a category of collectible weapons that have allowed me from time to time to pry loose from other weapon collectors things that I want, because they want what I have. Early Browning pistols are excellent trading capital.)

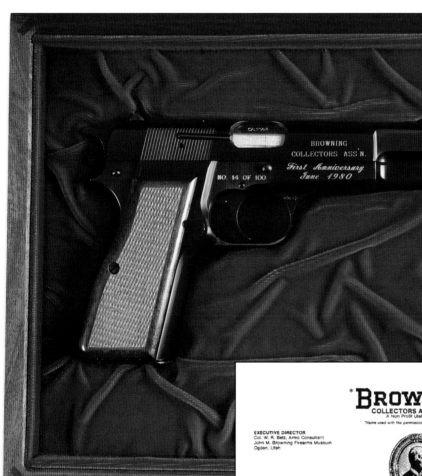

Browning Collectors
Association First
Anniversary High
Power. Courtesy Rock
Island Auction.

Certificate of Authenticity
for BCA First Anniversary
High Power. Courtesy
Rock Island Auction.

Engraved, gold-washed High Power. Courtesy Rock Island Auction.

HI-POWER MODERN PRODUCTION

This version of the FN Model 1935 is quite similar in appearance to the original described in the FN section. It is chambered for the 9mm Parabellum cartridge and has a 4.75" barrel. Models built before the passage of the "Assault Weapons" crime bill (1994 - 2004) have a double column, 13-round, detachable box magazine and is blued with checkered walnut grips. It has fixed sights and has been produced in its present configuration since 1954. Add a 10 percent premium for adjustable sights. A matte-nickel version, offered between 1980 and 1984, was also available and would be worth approximately 15 percent additional. This model is also available in .40 S&W.

To these modern production Hi-Power Pistols I assign a Collectibility Factor of #2, unless otherwise noted. Some are more collectible than others, and all should only be purchased in high condition. I believe the collectibility of these weapons will only increase with time. Recently, at a gun auction, I watched some of these more modern production guns bringing absolutely top dollar, and, because I know the persons who purchased them, I believe them to be undergoing the process of early acquisition.

HI-POWER WITH SPUR HAMMER AND ADJUSTABLE SIGHTS

SPUR HAMMER VERSION

NIB	EXC.	V.G.	GOOD	FAIR	POOR
800	600	450	300	200	150

Note: Add 33% for Grade II.

ROUND HAMMER VERSION

NIB	EXC.	V.G.	GOOD	FAIR	POOR
750	500	400	250	200	150

NOTE: Add $60 for adjustable sights.

2003-vintage High Power Grade II. Courtesy Browning.

Post-war High Power with (worn) original box, West German or Austrian police contract. Courtesy Rock Island Auction.

HI-POWER .30 LUGER

This version is similar to the standard Hi-Power except that it is chambered for the .30 Luger cartridge. There were approximately 1,500 imported between 1986 and 1989. The slide is marked "FN." The Browning-marked versions are quite rare and worth approximately 30 percent additional.

In high condition, this is a particularly desirable, modern production Hi-Power. It is an extremely low-risk acquisition, for purposes of trade or sale.

Browning High Power in .30 Luger.

EXC.	V.G.	GOOD	FAIR	POOR
800	650	450	300	200

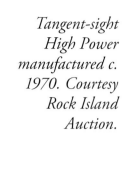

Tangent-sight High Power manufactured c. 1970. Courtesy Rock Island Auction.

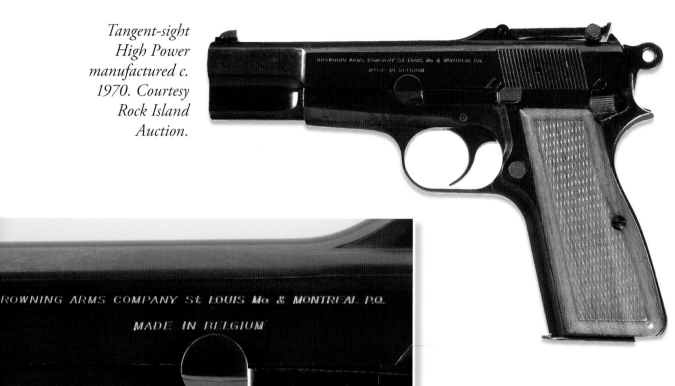

Slide markings on Tangent-Sight Belgian High Power. Courtesy Rock Island Auction.

TANGENT SIGHT MODEL

This version is similar to the standard Hi-Power with the addition of an adjustable rear sight calibrated to 500 meters. There were approximately 7,000 imported between 1965 and 1978.

EXC.	V.G.	GOOD	FAIR	POOR
950	800	650	450	200

NOTE: If the grip frame is slotted to accept a detachable shoulder stock, add approximately 20 percent to the value; but be wary of fakes. Add an additional 10 percent for "T" series serial numbers.

RENAISSANCE HI-POWER

This is a heavily engraved version of the above with a matte-silver finish. It features synthetic-pearl grips and a gold-plated trigger. Import on this model ended in 1979.

These particular variations of the more modern Renaissance Hi Power Pistols merit a Collectibility Factor of #1. They are beautifully done, and they were manufactured long enough ago that they have become, in and of themselves, highly collectible. However, I believe they should only be acquired if in unfired condition.

SPUR HAMMER MODEL

NIB	EXC.	V.G.	GOOD	FAIR	POOR
3000	2000	1200	925	325	175

NOTE: A premium of 50% should be added for new in the box guns; a premium of $700 should be added for the blue European case; a premium of $500 should be added for Coin finish, but only in new condition

Renaissance High Power with ring hammer. Courtesy Bruce Buckner, Jr.

RING HAMMER MODEL

NIB	EXC.	V.G.	GOOD	FAIR	POOR
4000	2500	1300	975	600	300

ADJUSTABLE SIGHT SPUR HAMMER MODEL

NIB	EXC.	V.G.	GOOD	FAIR	POOR
3200	2350	1275	700	575	300

RENAISSANCE .25 CALIBER

NIB	EXC.	V.G.	GOOD	FAIR	POOR
1850	1250	700	500	400	250

RENAISSANCE .380 CALIBER

Mother of pearl grips. These are the rarest of the Renaissance models.

NIB	EXC.	V.G.	GOOD	FAIR	POOR
2000	1300	1000	750	475	300

RENAISSANCE .380 CALIBER (MODEL 1971)

With wood grips and adjustable sights.

NIB	EXC.	V.G.	GOOD	FAIR	POOR
1500	1000	750	525	375	200

Browning Renaissance Set. Courtesy Bruce A. Buckner, Jr.

CASED RENAISSANCE SET

This features one example of a fully engraved and silver-finished .25 ACP "Baby," one .380 ACP pistol, and one Hi-Power. The set is furnished in a fitted walnut case or black leatherette and was imported between 1955 and 1969.

These cased sets are the most desirable of all the Renaissance pistols, and are, as indicated, highly collectible.

NIB	EXC.	V.G.	GOOD	FAIR	POOR
7250	6500	2700	1800	1100	900

NOTE: For early coin finish sets add 30 percent. Add 35 percent for early walnut case and high polish finish.

LOUIS XVI MODEL

This is a heavily engraved Hi-Power pistol that features a leaf-and-scroll pattern. It is satin-finished and features checkered walnut grips. It is furnished in a fitted walnut case. To realize its true potential, this pistol must be NIB. It was imported between 1980 and 1984.

This model of Hi-Power pistol is probably the most desirable and collectible all of the later production Hi-Power pistols. As mentioned herein, it should only be purchased in unfired condition.)

DIAMOND GRIP MODEL

NIB	EXC.	V.G.	GOOD	FAIR	POOR
3000	1850	800	675	400	300

*Browning 1878-1978 Centennial
High Power, one of 3500 produced.
Courtesy Rock Island Auction.*

MEDALLION GRIP MODEL

NIB	EXC.	V.G.	GOOD	FAIR	POOR
2750	1700	800	350	225	150

HI-POWER CENTENNIAL MODEL

This version is similar to the standard fixed-sight Hi-Power but is chrome-plated with the inscription, "Browning Centennial/1878-1978" engraved on the slide. It is furnished with a fitted case. There were 3,500 manufactured in 1978. As with all commemorative pistols, in order to realize its collector potential, this model should be NIB with all supplied material. Prices are for pistols built in Belgium.

It is my opinion that these weapons are undergoing accumulation.

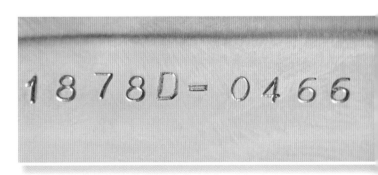

*Typical serial numbering on 1 of
3500 Centennial High Power.
Courtesy Rock Island Auction.*

NIB	EXC.	V.G.	GOOD	FAIR	POOR
1000	775	625	450	300	200

High Power Capitan.
Courtesy Browning.

High Power Practical.
Courtesy Rock
Island Auction.

HI-POWER CAPITAN

This is a new version of the Hi-Power model fitted with tangent sights. Introduced in 1993. Furnished with walnut grips. Weighs about 32 oz. Assembled in Portugal.

NIB	EXC.	V.G.	GOOD	FAIR	POOR
850	475	350	300	250	200

HI-POWER PRACTICAL

First introduced in 1993 this version is furnished with a blued slide and chrome frame. Has Pachmayr wraparound rubber grips, round-style serrated hammer, and removable front sight. Available with adjustable sights. Weighs 36 oz. Assembled in Portugal.

NIB	EXC.	V.G.	GOOD	FAIR	POOR
945	625	500	300	200	175

HI-POWER SILVER CHROME MODEL

Furnished in hard chrome and fitted with wraparound Pachmayr rubber grips. Weighs 36 oz. Assembled in Portugal. Add 10 percent for models with all Belgian markings. This pistol was introduced in 1981 and dropped from the Browning product line in 1984. It was reintroduced in 1991.

NIB	EXC.	V.G.	GOOD	FAIR	POOR
950	625	325	275	225	200

High Power Silver Chrome. Courtesy Browning.

HI-POWER .40 S&W

Introduced in 1994, this new version of the Hi-Power is furnished with adjustable sights, molded grips, 5″ barrel and a 10-round magazine. Weighs about 35 oz.

Standard High Power in .40 S&W, 2008 production. Courtesy Browning.

NIB	EXC.	V.G.	GOOD	FAIR	POOR
800	600	450	300	200	150

HI-POWER MARK III

The pistol, introduced in 1991, has a matte blued finish, low-profile fixed sights, and two-piece molded grips with thumb rest. Weighs 32 oz.

NIB	EXC.	V.G.	GOOD	FAIR	POOR
780	600	500	300	200	175

High Power Mark III. Courtesy Browning.

PRO-9. Courtesy
Browning.

Browning Model
1955. Courtesy Bruce
A. Buckner, Jr.

PRO-9/PRO-40

This 9mm or .40 S&W double-action pistol is fitted with a 4″ barrel. Stainless steel slide. Grips are composite with interchangeable backstrap inserts. Magazine capacity is 16 rounds for 9mm and 14 rounds for the .40 S&W. Weight is about 30 oz.

NIB	EXC.	V.G.	GOOD	FAIR	POOR
625	500	375	-	-	-

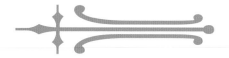

MODEL 1955

A commercial version of the Model 1922 chambered in .380 ACP with 3.5″ barrel. Manufactured from 1954 to 1969. Importation ceased because of the Gun Control Act of 1968. It was replaced in the Browning line by the Model 10/71 which, because of its adjustable sights and target grips, could be legally imported.

NOTE: Add 400 percent for the engraved Renaissance Model.

NIB	EXC.	V.G.	GOOD	FAIR	POOR
500	375	250	200	175	50

Nickel-plated BDA .380. Courtesy Rock Island Auction.

MODEL 10/71

A modified version of the Model 1955. .380 caliber with 4.5″ barrel, grip safety, grip with thumbrest, and target sights. Manufactured 1970-1974, and still manufactured by Fabrique Nationale as the model 125.

EXC.	V.G.	GOOD	FAIR	POOR
500	400	275	175	125

BDA-380

This is a double-action, semi-automatic pistol chambered for the .380 ACP cartridge. It features a 3.75″ barrel with a 14-round, double-stack, detachable magazine. The finish is either blued or nickel-plated with smooth walnut grips. This pistol was manufactured in Italy by Beretta and introduced in 1977.

The early variations of this model are starting to become more interesting to Browning collectors. At this point, I believe they deserved a Collectibility Factor of #3.)

NIB	EXC.	V.G.	GOOD	FAIR	POOR
500	375	325	275	200	150

NOTE: Add 10 percent for nickel finish.

MODEL BDA

This is a double-action, semi-automatic pistol manufactured between 1977 and 1980 for Browning by SIG-Sauer of Germany. It is identical to the SIG-Sauer Model 220. It is chambered for 9mm Parabellum, .38 Super, and the .45 ACP cartridges. The .38 Super is worth approximately 30 percent additional.

EXC.	V.G.	GOOD	FAIR	POOR
525	425	375	300	235

BDM PISTOL

This is a double-action, semi-automatic pistol chambered for the 9mm cartridge. The pistol is fitted with a selector switch that allows the shooter to choose between single-action model or double-action model. It features a 4.75″ barrel with adjustable rear sight. The magazine capacity is 15 rounds. Weighs 31 oz. First introduced in 1991.

NIB	EXC.	V.G.	GOOD	FAIR	POOR
560	450	350	250	200	150

MODEL BDM SILVER CHROME

This variation of the BDM was introduced in 1997 and features a silver chrome finish on the slide and frame. The balance of the pistol is in a contrasting matte blue finish.

NIB	EXC.	V.G.	GOOD	FAIR	POOR
560	450	350	250	200	150

*Browning Challenger,
4.5" barrel. Courtesy
Rock Island Auction.*

MODEL BDM PRACTICAL

This model, also introduced in 1997, is the same as above but with the silver chrome on the frame only.

NIB	EXC.	V.G.	GOOD	FAIR	POOR
560	450	350	250	200	150

MODEL BPM-D

Introduced in 1997 this new version of the BDM (Browning Pistol Model Decocker) features a double-action pistol with the first shot fired double-action and subsequent shots fired single-action. There is no manual safety. A decock lever also releases the slide.

NIB	EXC.	V.G.	GOOD	FAIR	POOR
525	400	300	250	200	150

MODEL BRM-DAO

This 9mm pistol is a redesigned version of the Model BDM but the initials stand for "Browning Revolver Model Double-Action-Only." This pistol also has a finger support trigger guard for two-handed control. All other features are the same as the BPM-D pistol. Weight is approximately 31 oz.

NIB	EXC.	V.G.	GOOD	FAIR	POOR
525	400	300	250	200	150

NOMAD

This is a blowback-operated, semi-automatic pistol chambered for the .22 LR cartridge. It was offered with a 4.5" or 6.75" barrel. It has a 10-round, detachable magazine with adjustable sights and all-steel construction. The finish is blued with black plastic grips. It was manufactured between 1962 and 1974 by FN.

NIB	EXC.	V.G.	GOOD	FAIR	POOR
350	250	200	150	75	50

CHALLENGER

This is a more deluxe target pistol chambered for the .22 LR cartridge. It was offered with a 4.5" or 6.75" barrel and has a 10-round magazine. It is constructed entirely of steel and has adjustable sights. The finish is blued with a gold-plated trigger and checkered, wraparound, walnut grips. It was manufactured between 1962 and 1974 by FN.

NIB	EXC.	V.G.	GOOD	FAIR	POOR
500	375	300	250	200	140

*Challenger II.
Courtesy Rock
Island Auction.*

RENAISSANCE CHALLENGER

This version is fully engraved with a satin-nickel finish and furnished with a fleece-lined pouch.

This is another one of the Renaissance model Browning that I believe are particularly collectible and desirable. However, this model should only be purchased if in new unfired condition.

NIB	EXC.	V.G.	GOOD	FAIR	POOR
2750	1500	1000	750	500	350

GOLD LINE CHALLENGER

This version is blued and has a gold-inlaid line around the outer edges of the pistol. It was cased in a fleece-lined pouch. Built in Belgium.

In my opinion, this is one of the most beautiful .22-caliber Browning weapons, in my opinion. It is also highly desirable and collectible, but should only be purchased if in new unfired condition.)

NIB	EXC.	V.G.	GOOD	FAIR	POOR
2800	1600	1000	750	500	350

CHALLENGER II

This is a blowback-operated, semi-automatic pistol chambered for the .22 LR cartridge. It has a 6.75″ barrel with an alloy frame. The finish is blued with phenolic impregnated hardwood grips. This pistol was manufactured between 1976 and 1982 in Salt Lake City, Utah.

EXC.	V.G.	GOOD	FAIR	POOR
350	225	175	140	100

CHALLENGER III

This version features a 5.5″ bull barrel with adjustable sights. It was manufactured between 1982 and 1984 in Salt Lake City, Utah. A 6.75″, tapered-barrel version was also available and known as the Sporter.

EXC.	V.G.	GOOD	FAIR	POOR
300	200	150	125	90

BROWNING COLLECTOR'S ASSOCIATION EDITION CHALLENGER

Fully engraved, 100 manufactured. This model was fitted with a two-piece grip.

These are very beautiful weapons, and are not only highly desirable but also highly collectible. These weapons should be acquired whenever feasible and rate, in my opinion, a Collectibility Factor of #1.

NIB	EXC.	V.G.	GOOD	FAIR	POOR
2750	2250	–	–	–	–

Medalist in fitted factory case. Courtesy Rock Island Auction.

MEDALIST

This is a high-grade, semi-automatic target pistol chambered for the .22 LR cartridge. It has a 6.75″, vent rib barrel with adjustable target sights. It was supplied with three barrel weights and a dry-fire-practice mechanism. The finish is blued with target type, thumbrest, walnut grips. It was manufactured between 1962 and 1974 by FN. There were four additional high-grade versions of this pistol that differed in the degree of ornamentation.

All of these Medalist semi automatic target pistols, in my opinion, rate a collectibility factor of #1. However, in my opinion, they should only be purchased in new unfired condition.

NIB	EXC.	V.G.	GOOD	FAIR	POOR
1300	850	575	475	375	250

NOTE: Subtract at least 25 percent if without case and accessories.

INTERNATIONAL MEDALIST

About 700 were sold in the U.S. from 1977 to 1980. Barrels were 5-7/8″ long. Built in Belgium.

NIB	EXC.	V.G.	GOOD	FAIR	POOR
950	800	600	450	300	150

SECOND MODEL INTERNATIONAL MEDALIST

Same as above but with flat-sided barrel, dull finish, and adjustable palm rest. Built in Belgium.

NIB	EXC.	V.G.	GOOD	FAIR	POOR
875	725	450	300	200	150

GOLD LINE MEDALIST

Introduced in 1962 and discontinued in 1974 with only an estimated 400 guns produced.

These are particularly beautiful weapons. I watched, fairly recently, at auction, one of these pistols bring 1.5 times the pricing number supplied in this book. They should certainly be accumulated, and are highly desirable and highly collectible – but it is my opinion, they should only be purchased in new unfired condition.

NIB	EXC.	V.G.	GOOD	FAIR	POOR
3200	2000	1250	1000	750	500

RENAISSANCE MEDALIST

This model was built entirely in Belgium from 1970 to 1974. Built with a one-piece grip.

NIB	EXC.	V.G.	GOOD	FAIR	POOR
3750	2000	1500	1200	900	700

Buck Mark Standard.
Courtesy Browning.

BUCK MARK SERIES

BUCK MARK

This is a blowback-operated, semi-automatic pistol chambered for the .22 LR cartridge. It has a 5.5″ bull barrel with adjustable sights. It has an 11-round, detachable magazine and is matte blued with skip-line checkered synthetic grips. It was introduced in 1985. Produced in the U.S.

NIB	EXC.	V.G.	GOOD	FAIR	POOR
320	250	175	135	110	85

NOTE: Add $25 for stainless steel version introduced in 2005.

Right and left schematic
views of typical Buck Mark.
Courtesy Browning.

The Mark of Quality.
Courtesy Browning.

*Buck Mark Plus.
Courtesy Browning.*

*Detail, Buck Mark adjustable
rear sight. Courtesy Browning.*

BUCK MARK PLUS

This version is similar to the standard, with plain wood grips. It was introduced in 1987. Produced in the U.S.

NIB	EXC.	V.G.	GOOD	FAIR	POOR
390	300	200	150	100	75

BUCK MARK PLUS NICKEL

Introduced in 1991. Add $35 to above prices.

*Buck Mark Plus Nickel.
Courtesy Browning.*

Buck Mark .22 Micro
Standard Nickel.
Courtesy Browning.

BUCK MARK VARMINT

This version has a 9.75″ bull barrel with a full-length ramp to allow scope mounting. It has no sights. It was introduced in 1987 and produced in the U.S.

NIB	EXC.	V.G.	GOOD	FAIR	POOR
375	285	250	200	175	125

BUCK MARK SILHOUETTE

This version features a 9.75″ bull barrel with adjustable sights. Introduced in 1987.

NIB	EXC.	V.G.	GOOD	FAIR	POOR
425	325	285	220	185	140

BUCK MARK 22 MICRO

This version of the Buck Mark 22 is fitted with a 4″ bull barrel. Available in blue, matte blue, or nickel finish. Also available in Micro Plus variation with walnut grips. Weighs 32 oz. Introduced in 1992.

NIB	EXC.	V.G.	GOOD	FAIR	POOR
320	250	175	135	110	85

NOTE: Add $25 for stainless steel version introduced in 2005.

MICRO PLUS

NIB	EXC.	V.G.	GOOD	FAIR	POOR
325	225	175	150	125	90

MICRO PLUS NICKEL

Introduced in 1996. Add $75 to above price.

Buck Mark 5.5"
Blued Target.
Courtesy Browning.

Sight picture, Buck
Mark Blued Target.
Courtesy Browning.

BUCK MARK 5.5

This .22 caliber pistol has a 5.5″ heavy bull barrel fitted with target sights. It is offered in the following separate models:

5.5 BLUED TARGET

This version has a blued finish, contoured walnut grips, target sights. Weighs 35.5 oz. Introduced in 1990.

NIB	EXC.	V.G.	GOOD	FAIR	POOR
450	350	250	150	100	100

5.5 BLUED TARGET (2005 VERSION)

Introduced in 2005 this model features a new target-style Cocabolo grips, a full length scope mount, and hooded target sights. Weight is 35 oz.

NIB	EXC.	V.G.	GOOD	FAIR	POOR
510	400	300	200	150	100

5.5 GOLD TARGET

Same as above but has a gold anodized frame and top rib. Slide is blue. Walnut grips. Introduced in 1991.

At this time, these Buck Mark 5.5″ models are not particularly collectible; however, I believe this will prove to be the first model to undergo accumulation.

NIB	EXC.	V.G.	GOOD	FAIR	POOR
500	400	300	200	150	125

Buck Mark 5.5 Gold
Target. Courtesy
Browning.

Buck Mark 5.5 Field.
Courtesy Browning.

Buck Mark Bullseye
Target. Courtesy
Browning.

5.5 FIELD

Same action and barrel as the Target Model but with adjustable field sights. Sights are hoodless. Slide and barrel is blued while the rib and frame are anodized blue. Grips are walnut. Introduced in 1991.

NIB	EXC.	V.G.	GOOD	FAIR	POOR
400	325	225	150	100	100

5.5 FIELD (2005)

This model features new target style grips and full-length scope rail. Introduced in 2005. Weight is about 35 oz.

NIB	EXC.	V.G.	GOOD	FAIR	POOR
510	400	-	-	-	-

BUCK MARK FIELD PLUS

This .22 caliber pistol has a 5.5″ barrel with Truglo/Marbles front sight. Grips are laminated rosewood. Barrel are polished blue. Weight is about 24 oz.

NIB	EXC.	V.G.	GOOD	FAIR	POOR
390	300	225	-	-	-

BUCK MARK BULLSEYE TARGET

Introduced in 1996 this pistol is designed for metallic silhouette competition. The fluted barrel is 7-1/4″ long. Adjustable trigger pull, adjustable rear sight. Weight is about 36 oz. Choice of laminated wood grips or rubber grips.

NIB	EXC.	V.G.	GOOD	FAIR	POOR
465	375	225	175	-	-

NOTE: For Rosewood target grips add $90.

BUCK MARK UNLIMITED MATCH

This pistol is fitted with a 14″ barrel with top rib. The front sight hood is slightly rearward of the muzzle for a maximum sight radius of 15″. All other features are the same as the Silhouette model. Weighs 64 oz.

NIB	EXC.	V.G.	GOOD	FAIR	POOR
425	325	275	225	-	-

Buck Mark frames undergoing CNC machining. Courtesy Browning.

*Buck Mark Challenge.
Courtesy Browning.*

*Security cable lock furnished
with many Buck Mark pistols.
Courtesy Browning.*

BUCK MARK CHALLENGE

Introduced in 1999 this model features a lightweight 5.5″ barrel with adjustable rear sight. Smaller grip diameter. Matte blue finish and 10-round magazine capacity. Weight is about 25 oz.

NIB	EXC.	V.G.	GOOD	FAIR	POOR
350	250	200	175	-	-

BUCK MARK CAMPER

This model is fitted with a heavy 5.5″ barrel and has a matte blue finish. Ten-round magazine capacity. Weight is about 34 oz. Introduced in 1999.

NIB	EXC.	V.G.	GOOD	FAIR	POOR
290	200	150	125	-	-

NOTE: Add $25 for stainless steel version introduced in 2005.

*Buck Mark Camper.
Courtesy Browning.*

Buck Mark 25th Anniversary Commemorative. Courtesy Browning.

Buck Mark Bullseye Target. Courtesy Browning.

BUCK MARK HUNTER

This .22 pistol features a 7.25" heavy round barrel with Tru-glo/Marbles front sights, adjustable rear sight and integrated scope base. Grips are Cocabolo target-style. Weight is about 38 oz. Introduced in 2005.

NIB	EXC.	V.G.	GOOD	FAIR	POOR
360	275	225	175	-	-

BUCK MARK LIMITED EDITION 25TH ANNIVERSARY

This model is limited to 1,000 pistols and features a 6.75" barrel with matte blued finish and scrimshaw etched ivory grips. Pistol rug furnished as standard equipment. Introduced in 2001.

NIB	EXC.	V.G.	GOOD	FAIR	POOR
475	350	300	-	-	-

BUCK MARK BULLSEYE TARGET

Blowback, single action .22 LR semi-auto. Matte blued, heavy 7.25" round and fluted bull barrel. Laminated rosewood grip, adjustable sights.

NIB	EXC.	V.G.	GOOD	FAIR	POOR
525	450	-	-	-	-

BUCK MARK BULLSEYE TARGET STAINLESS

Similar to above but in stainless steel.

BUCK MARK BULLSEYE TARGET URX

Blowback, single-action semi-auto in .22 LR. Matte blued, heavy 7.25" round and fluted bull barrel. Grooved, rubberized grip, 39 oz., adjustable sights. Introduced 2006.

NIB	EXC.	V.G.	GOOD	FAIR	POOR
450	-	-	-	-	-

BUCK MARK CONTOUR 5.5 URX

Blowback, single-action .22 LR semi-auto. Matte blued, contoured 5.5" barrel. Full-length scope base, 36 oz., adjustable sights. (Multiple barrel lengths and options.) Introduced 2006.

NIB	EXC.	V.G.	GOOD	FAIR	POOR
400	-	-	-	-	-

Buck Mark Bullseye Target Stainless. Courtesy Browning.

*Buck Mark Contour
Lite 5.5 URX*

*Buck Mark Contour
Lite 7.5 URX.
Courtesy Browning.*

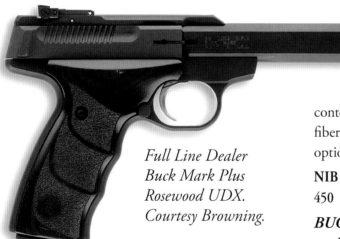

*Full Line Dealer
Buck Mark Plus
Rosewood UDX.
Courtesy Browning.*

BUCK MARK CONTOUR LITE
5.5 URX & 7.5 URX

A .22 LR blowback, single-action semi-auto.
Matte blued, contoured 5.5″ or 7.5 ″barrel. Full-
length scope base, 28 oz. Adjustable sights. (Multiple barrel lengths and options.) Introduced 2006.

NIB	EXC.	V.G.	GOOD	FAIR	POOR
450	-	-	-	-	-

BUCK MARK FULL LINE DEAL-
ER PLUS ROSEWOOD UDX

A .22 LR blowback single-action semi-auto.
"FLD" sculpted grip with rosewood panels. Blued,
contoured 5.5″ barrel, 34 oz., adjustable rear sight,
fiber optic front sight. (Multiple barrel lengths and
options.) Introduced 2006.

NIB	EXC.	V.G.	GOOD	FAIR	POOR
450	-	-	-	-	-

BUCK MARK LITE SPLASH 5.5 URX

Blowback single-action semi-auto. Matte blued
finish, gold splash anodizing. Chambered for .22
LR; 5.5″ barrel. Rubberized ambidextrous grip. Adjustable sights; fiber optic front sight. 28 oz. (Also
available with 7-1/2″ barrel.) Introduced 2006.

NIB	EXC.	V.G.	GOOD	FAIR	POOR
430	-	-	-	-	-

*Buck Mark
Splash 5.5 URX*

BUCKMARK MICRO STANDARD STAINLESS URX

With a 4″ stainless barrel, this .22 LR weighs 32 oz. Ambidextrous rubberized grip and adjustable sights. (Also available in alloy steel.) Introduced 2006.

NIB	EXC.	V.G.	GOOD	FAIR	POOR
375	345	-	-	-	-

BUCK MARK MICRO BULL

4″ stainless bull barrel; .22 LR; weight 33 oz. Plastic grip panels and adjustable sights. Introduced 2006.

NIB	EXC.	V.G.	GOOD	FAIR	POOR
260	225	-	-	-	-

Loading the thumb-friendly Buck Mark magazine.

BUCK MARK PLUS STAINLESS BLACK LAMINATED UDX

Similar to Buck Mark Standard Stainless UDX but with ambidextrous grips. Introduced 2007.

NIB	EXC	V.G.	GOOD	FAIR	POOR
460	-	-	-	-	-

BUCK MARK PLUS UDX

Similar to Buck Mark FLD Plus but with ambidextrous walnut grips. Introduced 2007.

Buck Mark Plus UDX. Courtesy Browning.

NIB	EXC	V.G.	GOOD	FAIR	POOR
425	-	-	-	-	-

FULL LINE DEALER BUCK MARK PLUS ROSEWOOD UDX

Similar to Buck Mark Plus UDX but with ambidextrous rosewood grips. Available only to full-line and Medallion-level Browning dealers. Introduced 2007.

NIB	EXC	V.G.	GOOD	FAIR	POOR
425	-	-	-	-	-

BUCK MARK PLUS STAINLESS UDX

.22 LR semi-auto with finger-grooved wood grips. 5.5″ barrel, 34 oz. Adjustable sights, fiber optic front sight. (Also available blued alloy steel.) Introduced 2006.

NIB	EXC.	V.G.	GOOD	FAIR	POOR
440	-	-	-	-	-

BUCK MARK STANDARD STAINLESS URX

.22 LR semi-auto. 5.5″ stainless bull barrel; 34 oz. Ambidextrous rubberized grip and adjustable sights. (Also available in alloy steel.) Introduced 2006.

NIB	EXC.	V.G.	GOOD	FAIR	POOR
380	-	-	-	-	-

SECTION V

FABRIQUE NATIONALE VALUES

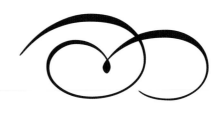

*F*irst, please read my additional comments contained in the introductory chapter on FN and Browning. It's important for Browning or FN collectors to understand the relationship between the two companies and between John Browning and FN.

In 1889 Fabrique Nationale (or FN) was founded by a group of Belgian investors for the purpose of manufacturing Mauser rifles for the Belgian army. This was to be accomplished under license from Mauser, with the technical assistance of Ludwig Loewe of Berlin. A few years later, in the late 1890s, John Browning arrived in Europe seeking a manufacturer for his semi-automatic shotgun (to be known as the Auto-5) after Winchester refused to give him a royalty on its sales.

John Browning's negotiations with FN led to a long association that worked out extremely well for both parties. John Browning later became associated with Colt, who bought the rights to manufacture Browning-designed hnadguns in the Western hemisphere. As far as pistols were concerned, FN retained exclusive manufacturing and marketing rights in the Eastern hemisphere.

In this section, we list arms that bear the FN banner. The FN-manufactured firearms produced under the Browning banner are listed in the Browning section of this book.

HANDGUNS

MODEL 1899

This was the first model designed by John Browning that Fabrique Nationale produced. The prototype of this weapon was delivered to Fabrique Nationale 18 months before manufacturer was to begin. Only 3900 of these models were produced. They are extremely rare, especially in United States. They are very similar to the model 1900, which was an improved model.

NOTE: These pistols are very seldom are seen in United States, and even less often in excellent condition. They should, however, be accumulated whenever possible for they are very desirable and very collectible. The Collectibility Factor of this pistol is a very strong #1.) Add 60 percent for factory nickel finish. Add $600 for a factory presentation case with all accessories.

EXC.	V.G.	GOOD	FAIR	POOR
850	675	410	300	150

MODEL 1900

A blowback-operated semi-automatic pistol chambered for the 7.65mm (aka .32 ACP) cartridge. This was the first firearm ever chambered for the Browning-designed .32 Auto. It has a 4″ barrel and fixed sights and is blued with molded plastic grips. This model is notorious as the pistol

The gun that started the War to End All Wars: the FN Model 1900. Courtesy R. J. Holloway, UK.

FN Model 1900 with original holster. Courtesy Simpson.

that was used to assassinate Archduke Ferdinand, the pivotal event that touched off WWI. It was manufactured between 1899 and 1910. This model is referred to as the "Old Model."

NOTE: This is the improved model of the Model 1899. It was very desirable in its day as it was quite small and ideal for carrying concealed. This model was really quite cleverly designed, well-made, and quite attractive. The Collectibility Factor of this weapon is #1. Add $600 for a factory presentation case with all accessories Add $800 for the Russian contract model. Add up to $500 for special contracts or retailer stampings.

EXC.	V.G.	GOOD	FAIR	POOR
750	575	250	150	100

MODEL 1903

A considerable improvement over the Model 1900. It is also a blowback-operated semi-automatic; but the recoil spring is located under the barrel, and the firing pin travels through the slide after being struck by a hidden hammer. The barrel is held in place by five locking lugs that fit into five grooves in the frame. This pistol is chambered for the 9mm Browning long cartridge and has a 5″ barrel. The finish is blued with molded plastic grips, and the detachable magazine holds seven rounds. There is a detachable shoulder stock/holster along with a 10-round magazine that was available for this model. These accessories are extremely rare and if present would make the package worth approximately five times that of the pistol alone. There were approximately 58,000 manufactured between 1903 and 1939.

NOTE: This weapon was brought to Belgium by John Browning on his first visit to the factory. Upon receipt, the weapon was refined by Fabrique Nationale prior to manufacture. This weapon is most notable because of the number of imitations it inspired. It is very collectible and rates a Collectibility Factor of #1. Double the price if slotted for shoulder stock – but be aware that there are many fakes out there. A minimum of $150 should be added for special contracts or retailer's stampings.

EXC.	V.G.	GOOD	FAIR	POOR
750	525	375	275	175

MODEL 1905

Vest pocket model. 6.35mm (.25 ACP) caliber, 2″ barrel. Approximately one million manufactured between 1906 to approximately 1950.

FIRST VARIATION

EXC.	V.G.	GOOD	FAIR	POOR
550	450	325	200	100

NOTE: Add a premium for a 50 percent factory nickel finish; add a premium of $500 for an original factory presentation case; add a premium of $100 for special contract or retailer stampings.

2ND VARIATION, OVER SERIAL NUMBER 100000

NOTE: Collectibility Factor #1.

EXC.	V.G.	GOOD	FAIR	POOR
450	275	200	175	100

MODEL 1907 (MANUFACTURED BY HUSQVARNA)

Identical to the Model 1903 and supplied to the Swedish military. It was originally chambered in 9mm Browning Long, a cartridge not often seen in the United States. Many of these weapons were imported into the United States and converted to .380 ACP caliber.

EXC.	V.G.	GOOD	FAIR	POOR
550	450	300	200	100

NOTE: Add a premium of 50 percent for early factory finish; subtract as much as 30 percent for weapons converted to .380.

MODEL 1910 "NEW MODEL"

Chambered for 7.65mm and 9mm Short (aka .380 ACP). It has a 3.5″ barrel, is blued, and has molded plastic grips. The principal difference between this model and its predecessors is that the recoil spring on the Model 1910 is wrapped around the barrel. This gives the slide a more graceful tubular appearance instead of the old slab-sided look. This model has the triple safety features of the 1906 Model 2nd variation and is blued with molded plastic grips. This model was adopted by police forces around the world. It was manufactured between 1912 and 1954.

Model 1910, Japanese Contract. Courtesy Rock Island Auction.

Nazi-marked FN 1910. Courtesy Rock Island Auction.

Standard FN Model 1922. Courtesy Rock Island Auction.

NOTE: This model was meant to replace the Model 1900. As it worked out, this was the last handgun that was wholly designed by John Browning for Fabrique Nationale. Collectibility Factor #1.

EXC.	V.G.	GOOD	FAIR	POOR
450	300	250	175	125

MODEL 1922

Similar to the Model 1910 but with a longer barrel (4.5″), longer grip frame, and greater magazine capacity (eight rounds rather than seven). Chambered in .32 ACP and .380 ACP. Developed specifically for the country later known as Yugoslavia and subsequently adopted by sevral other European nations.

NOTE: I give this pistol a Collectibility Factor #1.

EXC.	V.G.	GOOD	FAIR	POOR
425	350	175	125	100

Two "Babies," blued and nickel.
Courtesy Bruce A. Buckner, Jr.

"BABY" MODEL

A smaller and lighter version of the Model 1906. It is chambered for the 6.35mm (.25 ACP) cartridge and has a 2″ barrel. There is no grip safety or slide lock on this model, and it appears to be more square in shape than the Model 1906. This model was offered in blue, with molded plastic grips. Early models have the word "Baby" molded into the grips; post-1945 versions do not. There is also a nickel-plated version with pearl grips. There were over 500,000 of these manufactured between 1931 and 1983.

NOTE: This is a very attractive pistol and was popular wherever it was sold. It was designed to compete against the Walther Model 9. It was even smaller than Walther's pistol – as well as being extremely well-made. I give it a Collectibility Factor of #1. Add a premium of $450 for factory presentation case; add a

"Baby" .25, blued finish. Courtesy Rock Island Auction.

premium of $125 for original plastic box or cardboard box with accessories; subtract $100 if marked BAC; subtract $50 if lightweight model first introduced in 1954; add a premium of 350 percent if the weapon is the Renaissance Model, which is engraved with satin gray finish.

EXC.	V.G.	GOOD	FAIR	POOR
525	375	300	225	150

MODEL 1935, AKA HIGH POWER, HP, P-35, GP

The last design from John Browning and was developed between 1925 and 1935. This pistol is known as the Model 1935, the P-35, High-Power or HP, and also as the GP (which stood for "Grand Puissance") and was referred to by all those names at one time or another. The basic design of the pistol was Browning's, but FN designer Dieudonne Saive refined it into the pistol we know today.

The HP is essentially an improved version of the Colt 1911 design. The swinging link was replaced with a fixed cam, which was less prone to wear. It is chambered for the 9mm Parabellum and has a 13-round detachable magazine. The only drawback to the design is that the trigger pull is not as fine as that of the 1911, as there is a transfer bar instead of a stirrup arrangement. This is necessary due to the increased magazine capacity resulting in a thicker grip. The barrel is 4.75″ in length. It has an external hammer with a manual and a magazine safety and was available with various finishes and sight options. Occasionally furnished with a shoulder stock. The Model 1935 was used by many countries as their service pistol as such there are many variations. We list these versions and their approximate values.

NOTE: In the author's opinion, this is one of the most collectible semi-automatic pistols in the world. There are some American collectors, but too few. This presents an opportunity to collect these weapons, and certainly do some degree, they are underpriced and a very good value. They should be accumulated, especially in high condition. Collectibility Factor #1.)

PRE-WAR COMMERCIAL MODEL

Found with either a fixed sight or a sliding tangent rear sight and is slotted for a detachable shoulder stock. It was manufactured from 1935 until 1940.

FIXED SIGHT VERSION

EXC.	V.G.	GOOD	FAIR	POOR
1200	850	500	375	275

TANGENT SIGHT VERSION

EXC.	V.G.	GOOD	FAIR	POOR
2200	850	675	550	400

NOTE: For wooden holster stock add 50 percent. Add a premium of $800 for an original prewar commercial stock with attached holster; commercial models are unmarked.

PRE-WAR MILITARY CONTRACT

The Model 1935 was adopted by many countries as a service pistol, and they are listed below.

BELGIUM

EXC.	V.G.	GOOD	FAIR	POOR
2500	1850	1200	600	375

DENMARK

EXC.	V.G.	GOOD	FAIR	POOR
2500	1200	950	650	400

GREAT BRITAIN

EXC.	V.G.	GOOD	FAIR	POOR
1950	1200	850	550	325

ESTONIA (VERY RARE)

EXC.	V.G.	GOOD	FAIR	POOR
3500	2200	1100	600	375

HOLLAND

EXC.	V.G.	GOOD	FAIR	POOR
3300	2100	1000	650	400

LATVIA

EXC.	V.G.	GOOD	FAIR	POOR
3500	2050	1050	775	500

LITHUANIA

EXC.	V.G.	GOOD	FAIR	POOR
3500	2000	1100	650	400

ROMANIA

EXC.	V.G.	GOOD	FAIR	POOR
3400	2200	1050	775	500

WWII-era High Power with shoulder stock. Courtesy Rock Island Auction.

Nazi-marked High Power. Courtesy Rock Island Auction.

GERMAN MILITARY PISTOLE MODELL 640(B)

In 1940 Germany occupied Belgium and took over the FN plant. The production of the Model 1935 continued, with Germany taking the output. The FN plant was assigned the production code "ch," and many thousands were produced. The finish on these Nazi guns runs from as fine as the Prewar Commercial series to downright crude, and it is possible to see how the war was progressing for Germany by the finish on their weapons. One must be cautious with some of these guns as there have been fakes noted with their backstraps cut for shoulder stocks, producing what would appear to be a more expensive variation. Individual appraisal should be secured if any doubt exists.

FIXED SIGHT MODEL

EXC.	V.G.	GOOD	FAIR	POOR
950	650	400	300	250

Nazi marking on High Power. Courtesy Rock Island Auction.

TANGENT SIGHT MODEL

50,000 manufactured.

EXC.	V.G.	GOOD	FAIR	POOR
3500	2250	1200	550	400

CAPTURED PRE-WAR COM-MERCIAL MODEL

These pistols were taken over when the plant was occupied. They are slotted for stocks and have tangent sights. There were few produced between serial number 48,000 and 52,000. All noted have the WA613 Nazi proof mark. Beware of fakes!

EXC.	V.G.	GOOD	FAIR	POOR
2500	1400	1150	750	500

POST-WAR MILITARY CONTRACT

Manufactured from 1946, and they embody some design changes-such as improved heat treating and barrel locking. Pistols produced after 1950 do not have barrels that can interchange with the earlier model pistols. The earliest models have an "A" prefix on the serial number and do not have the magazine safety. These pistols were produced for many countries, and there were many thousands manufactured.

FIXED SIGHT

EXC.	V.G.	GOOD	FAIR	POOR
750	500	375	300	250

TANGENT SIGHT

EXC.	V.G.	GOOD	FAIR	POOR
1200	850	575	400	300

SLOTTED AND TANGENT SIGHT

EXC.	V.G.	GOOD	FAIR	POOR
1400	1050	750	500	400

POST-WAR COMMERCIAL MODEL

Introduced in 1950 and in 1954. Those imported into the U.S.A. are marked Browning Arms Co. These pistols have the commercial polished finish.

FIXED SIGHT

EXC.	V.G.	GOOD	FAIR	POOR
700	525	350	300	250

TANGENT SIGHT

EXC.	V.G.	GOOD	FAIR	POOR
950	650	500	400	350

SLOTTED AND TANGENT SIGHT

EXC.	V.G.	GOOD	FAIR	POOR
1500	1100	800	550	450

GOLD LINE MODEL HIGH POWER

This is a very rare model and, it is my opinion that this weapon should be purchased for any reasonable price, but only if original and in new condition, and originality should be checked closely.

EXC.	V.G.	GOOD	FAIR	POOR
3500	3000	2000	800	500

NOTE: A premium of $2000 should be added if new in the box.

MODEL 125

An FN-marked version of the Browning Model 10/71.

EXC.	V.G.	GOOD	FAIR	POOR
500	400	275	175	125

*Model 1949 SAFN with bayonet.
Courtesy Rock Island Auction.*

*FN Sniper Rifle. Courtesy
Rock Island Auction.*

RIFLES

MODEL 1889

The Mauser rifle that Fabrique Nationale was incorporated to manufacture. It is chambered for 7.65mm and has a 30.5″ barrel. The magazine holds 5 rounds. The unique feature that sets the Belgian rifle apart from the Mausers made by other countries is the thin steel tube that encases the barrel. This was the first Mauser to use a charger loaded detachable box magazine. The sights are of the military type. The finish is blued, with a walnut stock. This rifle was also made by the American firm of Hopkins and Allen (rare).

EXC.	V.G.	GOOD	FAIR	POOR
550	400	350	200	150

MODEL 1949 OR SAFN 49

A gas-operated semi-automatic rifle chambered for 7x57, 7.92mm, and .30-06. It has a 23" barrel and military-type sights. The fixed magazine holds 10 rounds. The finish is blued, and the stock is walnut. This is a well-made gun that was actually designed before WWII. When the Germans were in the process of taking over Belgium, a group of FN engineers fled to England and took the plans for this rifle with them, preventing the German military from acquiring a very fine weapon. This model was introduced in 1949, after hostilities had ceased. This model was sold on contract to Egypt, chambered for 7.92mm; to Venezuela, chambered for 7x57; and to Argentina, Colombia, Indonesia, Belgium, and Luxembourg chambered for the .30-06. Argentina models were chambered for the 7.65x53mm as well as the Argentina navy which had its rifles chambered for the 7.62 NATO cartridge. The FN 1949 bears serial numbers on the receiver, top cover, bolt and bolt carrier. Deduct 25 percent for any MM parts.

NIB	EXC.	V.G.	GOOD	FAIR	POOR
900	500	300	225		150

NOTE: Add a premium of $300 for the Egyptian model; add a premium of $400 for the Luxemburg model; add a premium of $700 for the Columbia model; subtract 35 percent for rebuild or nonmatching rifles, or anything with a reproduction stock.

MODEL 30-11 SNIPER RIFLE

Chambered for the 7.62 NATO cartridge. It has a 20″ heavy barrel and Anschutz sights. There is a flash suppressor mounted on the muzzle. It is built on a highly precision-made Mauser bolt action fed by a nine-round, detachable box magazine. The walnut stock is rather unique in that the butt is made up of two parts, with the rear half being replaceable to suit the needs of different-sized shooters. It is issued with a shooting sling, bipod, and a foam-lined carrying case. This is a rare firearm on the commercial market as it was designed and sold to the military and police markets.

EXC.	V.G.	GOOD	FAIR	POOR
5000	4500	3500	2750	2000

FN-FAL

A gas-operated, semi-automatic version of the famous FN battle rifle. This weapon has been adopted by more free world countries than any other rifle. It is chambered for the 7.62 NATO or .308 and has a 21″ barrel with an integral flash suppressor. The sights are adjustable with an aperture rear, and the detachable box magazine holds 20 rounds. The stock and forearm are made of wood or a black synthetic. This model has been discontinued by the company and is no longer manufactured.

The models listed below are for the metric pattern Type 2 and Type 3 receivers, those marked "FN MATCH." The models below are for semi-automatic rifles only. FN-FAL rifles in the "inch" pattern are found in the British Commonwealth countries of Australia, India, Canada, and of course, Great Britain. These rifles are covered separately under their own country headings.

50.00–21″ RIFLE MODEL

NIB	EXC.	V.G.	GOOD	FAIR	POOR
3500	3000	2500	2000	N/A	N/A

50.63–18″ PARATROOPER MODEL

NIB	EXC.	V.G.	GOOD	FAIR	POOR
4000	3500	3000	2750	N/A	N/A

50.64–21″ PARATROOPER MODEL

NIB	EXC.	V.G.	GOOD	FAIR	POOR
4000	3500	3000	2750	N/A	N/A

50.41–SYNTHETIC BUTT H-BAR

NIB	EXC.	V.G.	GOOD	FAIR	POOR
3250	2800	2500	2000	N/A	N/A

50.42–WOOD BUTT H-BAR

NIB	EXC.	V.G.	GOOD	FAIR	POOR
4000	3500	3000	2750	N/A	N/A

NOTE: There are a number of U.S. companies that built FN-FAL receivers and use military surplus parts. These rifles have only limited collector value as of yet.

*FN FAL.
Courtesy Rock
Island Auction.*

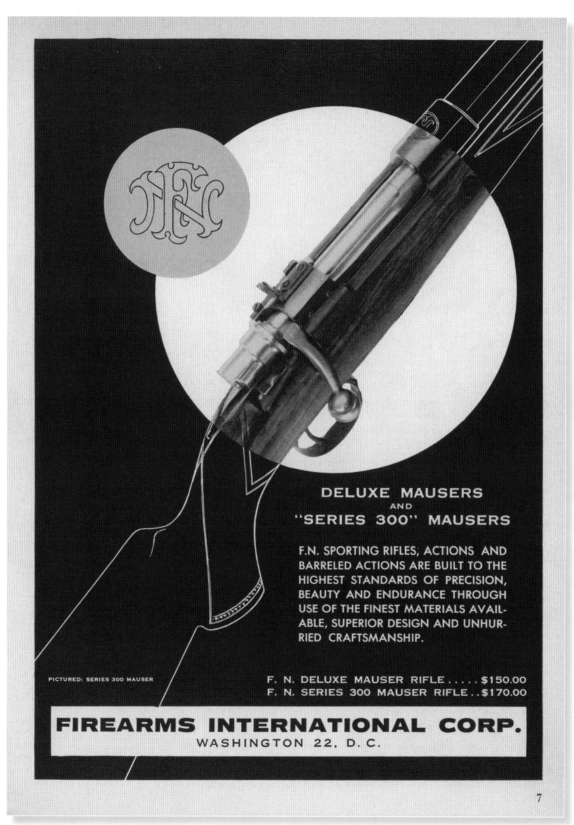

Period advertising for FN Deluxe Mauser.

MUSKETEER SPORTING RIFLES

A bolt-action rifle built on the Mauser-action chambered for various popular cartridges. It has a 24" barrel and is blued, with a checkered walnut stock. It was manufactured between 1947 and 1963. Also marketed under the original FN Series 300 brand name.

EXC.	V.G.	GOOD	FAIR	POOR
450	350	300	250	200

DELUXE SPORTER

A higher-grade version of the Musketeer with the same general specifications. It was also manufactured between 1947 and 1963.

EXC.	V.G.	GOOD	FAIR	POOR
550	450	400	275	200

FN SUPREME

Chambered for the popular standard calibers and has a 24" barrel with an aperture sight and a checkered walnut stock. It was manufactured between 1957 and 1975.

NEW	EXC.	V.G.	GOOD	FAIR	POOR
900	700	650	500	400	400

SUPREME MAGNUM MODEL

Similar to the standard Supreme except that it is chambered for .264 Win. Mag., 7mm Rem. Mag., and .300 Win. Mag. It is furnished with a recoil pad and was manufactured between the same years as the standard model.

NEW	EXC.	V.G.	GOOD	FAIR	POOR
1000	800	650	500	400	400

FN SNIPER RIFLE

In .308 Winchester caliber, equipped with a 20 inch heavy barrel, 4X scope, in hard case, with bipod; only 51 complete factory sets were imported into the United States, with additional surplus rifles being imported on a private basis

NEW	EXC.	V.G.	GOOD	FAIR	POOR
6000	4800	3500	–	–	–

ABOUT THE AUTHOR

*B*orn and raised in the rifleman's paradise of Montana, Joseph Cornell is a member of the International Appraiser's Guild, the International Society of Appraisers and the American Society of Appraisers. A lifelong admirer of Browning firearms, he lives in Denver, Colorado.

RIA
ROCK ISLAND AUCTION COMPANY

The World Leader for Quality Collectable and Antique Firearms

Current Proven Results in Browning Firearms:

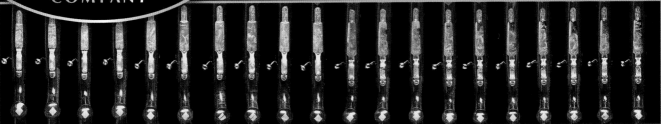

Magnificent 20 Set of Browning Olympian Grade Rifles
SOLD $494,500

Exhibition Engraved & Gold Inlaid Dual Signed Belgium Browning Superposed Shotgun
SOLD $28,750

Engraved Dual Signed Belgium Browning Olympian Grade Rifle
SOLD $11,500

Engraved Browning Gold Classic High-Power Pistol
SOLD $3,738

Engraved, Gold Inlayed Browning Model A-5 Gold Classic Shotgun
SOLD $5,750

Browning Medalist Semi-Automatic Pistol
SOLD $3,450

SEEKING CONSIGNMENTS

Seeking quality firearms valued from $1,000 to $1 million (or more). We have the venue to suit your needs.
WE UNDERSTAND ALL LEVELS OF COLLECTING

SIMPLE AND STRAIGHT FORWARD CONTRACTS WITH RIAC
Our contracts are a flat percentage with all charges included. Beware of auction houses with sliding scale contracts which are confusing and could cost you money. Question the auction house that charges you insurance based on the selling price. At RIAC there are no hidden charges. We keep it honest, straight forward, and up-front with a simple percentage.

NEED YOUR ITEMS PICKED-UP?
If your items are in need of pick-up, rest assured that we can handle the packing and transit to our facility and we have in-transit and on-site insurance coverage and are D.O.T. certified. Once your items are at our facility they are stored in padded racks and drawers and under a high security state-of-the-art alarm system and bank type vault.

WE ARE A FULL SERVICE AUCTION HOUSE
We cater to all levels of collecting. We offer two types of auction venues to ensure the perfect spot for your collectables in order to obtain the best price for you - our Premiere sale or our Regional sale. We can manage 100% of your collection with the strength of the RIAC name.

97% SELL-THROUGH RATE
The firearms that come to the auction block at RIAC SELL. We have maintained a record of selling 97% of the items offered for sale over the past 5 years.

WORLD CLASS MARKETING & ADVERTISING
We advertise with **full page ads** in the Wall Street Journal, USA Today, Chicago Tribune, the Baltimore Sun, Orlando Sentinel, and others as well as dozens of industry publications. We

excite the firearms collecting market with broad direct mail campaigns, we attend gun shows across the country, we market through our state-of-the art internet site, as well as extensive telemarketing. We stay in touch with our customers via email, fax, phone and much more. Nobody does it better!

WE HAVE THE FINEST FIREARMS AUCTION FACILITY IN THE WORLD
23,000 SQ FT dedicated specifically to the auctioning of fine antique and collectable firearms and related items.

WE HAVE AN AWARD WINNING FINEST PRINTED & ONLINE CATALOGS IN THE INDUSTRY
As technology improves, so does RIAC. Multiple photographs and in-depth correct descriptions allow potential buyers to bid with confidence from around all the world.

To sell at auction please call Patrick Hogan or Judy Voss: (800) 238-8022 or email us at: inforockislandauction.com

4507 49th Avenue, Moline, IL 61265
Phone: 309-797-1500 or 800-238-8022 Fax: 309-797-1655
Email: info@rockislandauction.com

WWW.ROCKISLANDAUCTION.COM
17.5% Buyer's Premium - Discount offered to 15% for pre-approved check or cash.
Fully Licensed Class III Auctioneer. Auctioneer's License #044000109

INDEX

STOCK YOUR
GUN LIBRARY WITH
STANDARD CATALOGS

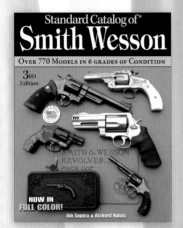

Standard Catalog of®
Smith & Wesson
3rd Edition
by Jim Supica and Richard Nahas
Identify and appreciate any
Smith & Wesson firearm more
with the easy-to-locate listings,
rarely seen production data and
historical details and more than
350 color photos featured in this
definitive guide!
Hardcover • 8-¼ x 10-7/8 • 384 pages
350+ color photos
Item# FSW03 • $39.99

Standard Catalog of®
Remington Firearms
by Dan Shideler
Review historical background,
production data and 2,000+
real-world values and more
than 700 expertly photographed
Remington firearms in this
beautiful gun book.
Hardcover • 8-1/4 x 10-7/8 • 288 pages
700+ color photos
Item# Z1828 • $29.99

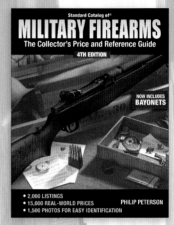

Standard Catalog of®
Military Firearms
*The Collector's Price and
Reference Guide*
4th Edition
by Phillip Peterson
Satisfy your need to know more
about military firearms history
and arms know-how with this one
volume of 130+ years of military
weaponry – which contains 300
more listings than the previous
edition.
Softcover • 8-1/4 x 10-7/8 • 520 pages
1,400 color photos
Item# Z0741 • $29.99

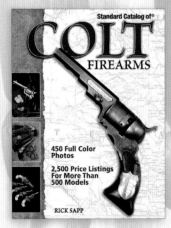

Standard Catalog of®
Colt Firearms
by Rick Sapp
Make the most of a robust
Colt collector firearms
market with the historical
and production details you
gain in this one-of-a-kind
and beautiful gun guide.
Hardcover • 8-1/4 x 10-7/8
288 pages
500 color photos
Item# Z0931 • $29.99

Standard Catalog of®
Winchester Firearms
by Joseph Cornell
Immerse yourself in
expertly analyzed prices,
500 superb color photos,
and technical details
for Winchester rifles and
shotguns, manufactured
between 1866 and the
present.
Hardcover • 8-1/4 x 10-7/8
288 pages
500 color photos
Item# Z0932 • $29.99

Order directly from the publisher at **www.gundigestbooks.com**

Krause Publications, Offer **GNB9**
P.O. Box 5009
Iola, WI 54945-5009
www.gundigestbooks.com

Call **800-258-0929** M-F 8 a.m. - 6 p.m. to order direct from the publisher, or from
booksellers nationwide or firearms dealers and outdoors outfitters

Please reference offer **GNB9** with all direct-to-publisher orders

Get the latest gun news at www.gundigestmagazine.com